The Marble Game
(Therapeutic Metaphors for Life)

Gaelen Billingsley LMFT

Illustrations by Dana Sweany-Schumacher
Graphics by Logan Billingsley

SILO PUBLISHING

First Edition
Port Orchard, Washington

Silo Publishing
3965 Bethel Road SE Suite 1 #224
Port Orchard, Wa 98366

Copyright 2016 by Gaelen Billingsley LMFT
Printed in The United States of America

ISBN-13: 978-0692575246

Library of Congress Control Number: 2015920041
Create Space Independent Publishing Platform, North Charleston, SC

I want to thank my teachers:

- Camelia Rose Bloom – for "I am committed to working on it!"
- Carol Gaskin – for permission to care deeply for my clients and for Rumi, and Hafiz
- Daniel Seigel – for proving that parenting beautifully can heal our own attachment wounds
- David Schnarch – for the bowling ball
- Diane Schacter - for "Great influence can be found in the small details."
- Dennis Walsh – for peace with diversity through compassionate flexibility
- Donald Williamson – for the transformative magic of surprise,
       and with his colleague
- Tim Weber - for integrity as the path to both freedom and spirit
- Eckart Tolle – for the staggering power of "Full presence in this present moment."
- Fritz Reitz – for saving me from drowning in a sea of commas
- Garett Sweany – for "It is never too late to build a new identity."
- Karen Sweany – for "If you don't like it, it is up to you to change it."
- Lao Tsu – for balancing paradox
- Pam Beyette – for "Love is a verb."
- Phyllis Romano – for permission to speak the naked truth
- Sue Johnson – for peace with needs, my own and everyone else's
- William Billingsley – for creating the space for me to be simultaneously wrong and ok
- Every precious soul who has graced my practice – for learning partnership
- And my greatest teachers Logan and Io Billingsley - for having demanded my best self with your perfect, innocent mindfulness, and also for why all of this is important enough to spend years working on, instead of just buzzing around in the garden.

Table of Contents

Disclaimer

This book is designed to empower people to create the lives they want. It is not designed to replace a course of psychotherapy, or consultation with medical providers when that action is called for.

Introduction

Dear You,

Welcome to my book, my work, and my best attempt to operationalize myself in written form so I can reach more people than the few clients who fit physically into my private practice.

I am in the business of helping people see themselves and the world around them more clearly so they can be strategic and intentional about becoming the people they aspire to be, and creating the lives they aspire to have. I am a bit nervous about writing this book. We never found out what happened in the end to the kid who called out, "The emperor has no clothes!" But it seems very likely he lost his head! People don't often like it when the daylight of reality shines down upon their dearest fantasies, or when their most favored anti-anxiety strategies are placed squarely on the table in front of them to be evaluated. Within the confines of my office I am there to help people through the uncomfortable experience. I am not there with YOU now, however.

I am writing this book because I have a tendency to come to care deeply about the people I work with, and I am reasonably certain that if you walked through my door and sat on my couch long enough, I would learn to care for you too. But I can't work with everyone. If you feel shaken by the words you read, I hope you will seek counseling from a systems-trained therapist. I like to tell my clients that if the insight brought on by self-help books were enough to make change happen I would be out of a job! Or at least, I would be in the business of writing self-help books instead of doing therapy!

This is not a textbook. It is a text based mostly from the synthesis of anecdotal evidence I have gathered over twelve years of doing therapy. As you read further, I will offer a few metaphorical models that help illustrate the basic tenets of human behavior so almost anyone can understand what one is seeing in the self and others. Once you have an understanding of what is happening inside you, and what is behind your interactions with other people, you will begin to wake up to the world at a whole different level. I will then go on to outline how you can go about making intentional changes happen in your life with a new capacity for authorship*.

On a side note, all of the clients referred to in this book are scrambled compilations of any number of friends, acquaintances, clients, family members, text book cases, and the DSM (The Diagnostic Statistical Manual of Mental Disorders) diagnoses. So while it might be disingenuous to print the usual tag-line, "all similarities to persons living or dead is purely coincidental," no confidentiality agreements have been breached in the writing of this book.

I am a Licensed Marriage and Family Therapist. People come to me looking for answers to their personal problems, and almost everyone who first contacts me is carrying the impression that their questions are uniquely complicated and horrible. Most clients walk through my door for

Word definition - "Authorship": You as the author of your own life, and life story, rather than you at the mercy of the people's definitions and stories about you, or the belief structures of the greater world around you.

the first time thinking, "Few have suffered anything quite like what is happening **inside** of me, as a result of the problems happening **to** me." However, the truth is that 99% of new clients come through my door looking for answers to the same few common human questions:

1) Who am I and why do I feel so crazy*?

2) Who is that other person I thought I knew, and why is s/he driving me so crazy?

3) Why do I keep doing the crazy stuff I do, even though I want to change!?

4) In the face of all of my flaws how do I become the person I want to be?

5) How do I get that other person over there to be and do what I want?

6) Why does Life/God/the universe either a) seem so crazy that the way the world works makes no sense, or b) hate me personally so much that I am punished again and again no matter how hard I try?

7) Why bother to ever do anything? What is the point?

Laying out this list of people's most common existential questions is intended to have the effect of demonstrating that the problems of post-modern humans are not as complicated as we fear. But, what may be even more surprising is that the answers to those questions are also usually not as complicated as we fear.

I want you to get free of all the unconscious baggage that weighs you down, and keeps you from being your finest self – from living your most excellent life. I want you to get an adventurous sense that there might be a lot to know about you that you don't already know. And even though it could seem scary and dangerous to learn about yourself, until you see yourself clearly, you will never be free to be the author of your self, your life, and your own destiny.

So here we go!

* *Word definition - "Crazy": Giving the appearance of making no sense. Some of my colleagues are going to take issue with my use of the word "crazy" in this book, because "crazy" has become a pejorative judgment-word used to oppress the mentally ill. I use "crazy" because my clients use it. They use it again and again. They fear it. It has power over them. It has been used against them. They use it against other people. "Crazy" is the cardinal sin of the mechanized industrial world. I am out to reclaim and normalize it. People make sense. If you get to know anyone well enough, if you get inside their unique cocktail of brain structure, and genes, and life experience and chemistry, people always make sense. But we are all "crazy," in that we all look to others as if we are not making sense, at least some of the time.*

Chapter 1: The Marble Game

Section 1: The Game

Welcome to the epic existential struggle of humanity. <Just close your eyes and imagine the swelling of Fanfare For the Common Man here…> You are about to be awakened to the titanic free-for-all that is **The Marble Game**. You are about to discover that you have been a player all your life, even though it is likely that you didn't even know it.

Inside the psyche of every person on the planet, I would like you to imagine a large ceramic bowl.

You can imagine yours looking whatever way you would want it to look because this bowl belongs to you. It is the bowl of your sense-of-self, and it contains your identity.

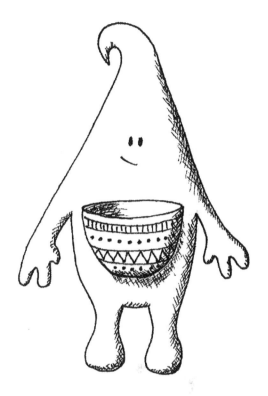

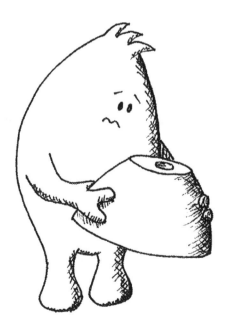

Everyone has a hole in the bottom of his or her bowl. Everyone.

If you came from a family of caregivers that consistently sent you the message that "you don't have to do any certain thing or be any certain way to be worthy of our love," then you have a teeny little hole in the bottom of your identity-bowl. But if you came from a family of caregivers that sent you the message that "to be worthy of our love and approval, you have to do what we tell you to do, and more importantly BE who we say you are," then you have a great big hole in the bottom of your bowl.

Some people have such a huge hole in the bottom that anything that gets put into the bowl stays in only as long as it takes to fall from the rim, right out the bottom.

OK. The purpose of life, after securing food and shelter, is to keep your bowl full of marbles.

So what is a marble?

A marble is a piece of validation from another person that confirms one's positive value, worthiness, or preferred identity. For example, with many people if you were to say to them, "Great hair cut!" or "You are the best friend I have ever had," they get a shiny marble to put in their bowl. **A marble can also represent a piece of validation regarding one's paradigms*.** "Money is the source of all evil," or "Life isn't fair," are examples of marbles a person can receive that validate a paradigm about reality or "the way the world works".

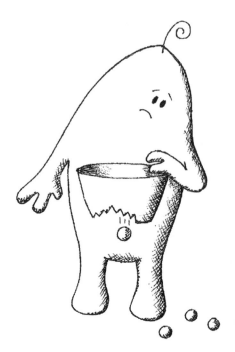

Everyone needs to have an identity-bowl that is full to feel calm and secure in the world. So it follows that if you come from a childhood experience that left you with a large hole in the bottom of your bowl, you will have a more difficult time feeling generally ok in the world than a person with an average or small hole, because marbles are falling out the bottom of your bowl as fast as you can put them in. The lower the level of marbles in your bowl, the more uncomfortable you will feel: worried, depressed, worthless, angry, or critical. And if the bowl of your identity is empty, you will tend to feel desperate, like you are steeped in not-enoughness, or like you don't matter at all. Some people even report feeling as if they barely exist; like they are walking ghosts in a world they can barely touch.

This phenomenon is cross-cultural. After securing basic food and shelter needs, people everywhere, down through history, have developed innumerable strategies to collect and win marbles from each other, in the attempt to keep their identity-bowls full. I call humanity's single-minded pursuit of validation, **The Marble Game**.

*Word Definition – "Paradigm": An unquestioned philosophy or belief that helps an individual form a conceptual framework regarding how life or the world 'works', and the roles individuals should play within the belief structure.

Section 2: Marble Gathering Strategies

As I said, the human race has developed innumerable strategies for collecting marbles. I could write a fat trilogy on marble-gathering strategies alone, but for the purposes of this book, I am just going to cover the top-ten I see in my practice here:

1) Giving a Marble to Get One Back
2) Morphing
3) Pursuing
4) Nagging and Complaining
5) Withholding
6) Caretaking and Fixing
7) Judging and Criticizing
8) Guilting
9) Suffering
10) Intimidation and Volatility

I will return to these top-ten marble-gathering strategies again and again, over the course of this book.

Strategy 1) Giving a Marble To Get One Back

The first validation-strategy we learn as babies is "give out a marble to get one back". If baby-me smiles at my care-giver – sending out the parent-validating message "I am glad to see you!", Mom or Dad will tend to smile back. Thus, the first seeds of the idea that validation is transactional are laid. It has been found that babies who are not met with consistent validating interactions with their caregivers grow upset and finally despondent. (1) Young children, unlike adults, have little capacity to validate themselves up to age three. In fact, infants don't even seem to grasp that they are separate beings from their primary caregivers. A baby's sense of self is derived entirely from the connection that child has to the caregiver. Babies must have consistent external validation or they grow into adults with lifelong psychological problems (2), an issue I will address later in this chapter.

However these formative forays into the marble game turn into elementary school transactions, the **trading of compliments,** that sounds something like: "Your dress is pretty!" "Yeah? Well I like yours too!" And, by adulthood, trading compliments often turns into a subtle system of unconscious accounting regarding who we are in debt to, and by how many marbles, and who is in debt to us.

The drive to pay back the marbles that have been given to us can seem so exhausting, that many people are driven frantic with it. Zoe was an 8th grader who feared praise as much as rejection. She was constantly feeling that she couldn't keep up with the marbles her peers were doling out, and so she was failing as a friend. Surely, if she couldn't step it up, they would eventually stop giving her the variety of marble-validation she most desired: keeping her as a friend.

Zoe also lived in constant anxiety because her boyfriend didn't always text her back when she sent him a message. She felt that if he didn't immediately return her 'sweet-text' marbles with his own 'sweet-text' responses, it meant she wasn't worthy and he didn't care about her. On his side, he was playing Zoe's role in the pattern she had with her girlfriends. There was no way he felt he could live up to Zoe's expectation with regard to numbers of marbles he could produce or speed of their delivery. Her constant solicitation for marbles from him, and the pressure he was under to produce them, was ultimately what he pointed to when Zoe's boyfriend ended the relationship. The words he used? "You are too high-maintenance!" "High maintenance" is often a familiar term to people who use the "give a marble to get one back" strategy.

Gift-giving is the most sophisticated form of the 'give a marble to get one back' strategy, because it has the potential for being a strategy that keeps on giving! Skillful "gift-giving" can bring the giver a cascade of marbles in return. In fact, though I am most certainly putting at risk a portion of the marbles I could receive from you, the readers, by saying so, I am nonetheless going to say that 'authentic gift-giving'* is rare in our culture. Most gift-giving is a marble-solicitation strategy.

Yolanda's grandmother was very reliable when it came to sending Birthday, Christmas, Valentines, Easter and Mother's Day gifts, providing her granddaughter with a steady supply of "I am thinking of you even though you are far away" marbles. But, if Yolanda ever forgot to send a thank you note, there was hell to pay. See, there was an unspoken transactional expectation at play in their relationship: I, Grandma, send you this gift, and in return you send me a marble telling me I spent too much, or I know you so well, or I am the best grandmother you know. Then, I take the thank you note around to my friends so they can read it and give me marbles like, "Your granddaughter has such nice manners." Or "You are so deservedly appreciated by her."

A lot of parents pay for their kids to go to college, but, in many cases, what that means is the parents get to dictate where the kid goes to school (receiving the "My daughter is at MIT." marble), what they study (receiving the "My son is an engineer." marble), and maybe even who they marry ("Lovely girl joins the family." marble) and where they live ("Close by me" or "Uptown offspring" marbles).

One of the most disturbing uses of gift-giving I have seen, as a strategy for **getting validation for one's world view**, is illustrated by the behavior of 16 year-old Yvonne's step-father who gave her sexy lingerie for her birthday. The "thank-you" marble from Yvonne, which she felt obliged out of politeness to give, validated his world-view that sexualizing an adolescent step-daughter was ok.

Strategy 2) Morphing

Zach was a human chameleon, a really sparkly number. He would fiercely study each new situation or person life sent his way, then figure out what each most wanted him to be: Useful? Clever? Sexy? Flattering? Zach was a savant when it came to intuiting the kind of validation that other people most wanted, and giving out the marbles that each was most hungry for. He

---

* Definition: "Authentic gift-giving" – The giving of a gift with no expectation of return, or attachment to how or even if the gift is used. Example: You give me a new car, and I give it to a friend who needs it more than I do, or you give me $20 and I use it to start a fire. If that is ok with you, then it was actually a gift. If you have an expectation around what the receiver does with a gift, then it is appropriate to make the expectation transparent so the receiver is fully informed before deciding whether or not to accept the gift!

wore a different face at work, than he wore to the clubs, than he wore for each of his three girlfriends (only two of whom knew about the other). He wore a different face with me too, I guess, because for a while there I thought he was the best, most intuitive, hard working client I had ever had! He wore the persona of 'super-therapy client' for his own benefit, so I would be pleased with him. But Zach was really there in my office because his anxious racing thoughts about being found out regarding some rather outrageous lies he had told in order to get his current job had started to give him panic attacks. He was also afraid that sooner or later girlfriend #1, who was the one he liked the most, was going to run into him when he was out with flirtation #2, or flirtation #3. Zach was running smack into the biggest problem with morphing.

Pretending to be everything that everyone wants is a great strategy for getting marbles, but eventually it starts to catch up to you. It had caught up before with Zach, as this was a life-long pattern with him. He had been fired from his last job for sleeping with a college intern for whom he had been wearing the persona of her preferred romantic-fantasy counterpart: the misunderstood and misplaced artist.

Almost everyone does some morphing at one time or another when it comes to the pursuit of romantic, sexual, or life partners. Dating is the very process of studying and interviewing another person in the interest of finding out about what that person most wants in a partner. (That way, if you really like them, you can try to embody his or her dearest fantasy.) The trouble with this very normal strategy is even that kind of morphing tends to catch up with you eventually, which is part of the reason "S/he is not the person I married!" is one of the most common phrases I hear in my office.

Getting found out is not even the worst cost of morphing. If you are playing a different role in every scene of your life, no one ever gets to know who you really are. And if no one ever gets to know the real you, no one can ever really love you. Zach was one of the loneliest people I have ever met, even though he was out all the time, and never spent a night alone in his bed.

Strategy 3) Pursuing

A lot of people run after marbles. Xavier believed that if he pursued his father hard enough, with enough evidence for how hard he was working, how much money he was making, and how fast his business was growing, his father would finally hand over the "you are worthy of being my son." marble. Xavier showed up for family dinners every Sunday and would regale his father with stories to prove how exceptional he was, and promises that Dad and Mom would never need to worry about being cared for in their old age. Year after year, Dad would sit there expressionless, and Dad never did give Xavier that marble. So Xavier spent much of his time trying to squeeze "you are awesome!" marbles out of everyone else in his life.

William was obsessed with a girl he had met in an American Sign Language class. She had agreed to go on one date with him, which only confirmed for him that she **was** the most wonderful girl in the world, and that they were meant to be together. After the date, she did not concur, and one date had been plenty of opportunity to determine it for her. But William was sure that if he could only put his feelings into words that were skillful enough, often enough, the object of his desire would open her arms with an "I want you too" marble. He wrote her pages-long emails day after day, and left notes on her car and sent flowers to her work. She asked him to stop many times, but he could not seem to stop himself. Every time he thought of a new way to express himself, or something he had forgotten to say that he was sure would move her, he would think, "I finally have the magic words!! She can't object to hearing **this**!" The object of William's obsession eventually slapped him with an order of protection for **stalking**. Stalking is the 'pursuing' marble-gathering strategy taken to the nth degree.

Strategy 4) Nagging and complaining

If you examine nagging and complaining closely, you will notice that they are close cousins of pursuing. Pursuers who are not successful with their strategy often resort to nagging and complaining in their determined effort to force marbles out of their close friends and family. If the people around you won't produce marbles at all, or won't produce marbles fast enough, or won't produce the kind you think they should be producing, the hope is that louder and more strident pursuing will get them to do what they are supposed to be doing!! (i.e. meet your marble needs).

There are two primary troubles with nagging and complaining. 1) They work even less well than pursuing. Humans hate to be nagged, and fight to resist the Nagger! 2) The second reason is that complainers and naggers are so unpleasant to be around that the family members, friends, and co-workers on the other side of the nagging-dynamic start tuning out most everything the complainer says, maybe even avoiding contact completely. That is, nagging and complaining tend to create exactly what the nagger wants least, the feeling that s/he doesn't matter to anyone. Nagging is a self-reinforcing self-torture; the more I nag, the more people avoid me and my demands, and the less I feel as if I matter... so the more I feel compelled to nag.

Strategy 5) Withholding

Ironically, the opposite of pursuing, "withholding," is also a common marble-solicitation strategy. 'Withholding' is the practice of shutting down, or retreating, in hopes that other people will chase after you. Being pursued provides the withholder with a constant stream of "I want you!" marbles from whomever the withholder has successfully hooked with the strategy.

Vesta's husband always expected her to approach him when they needed to talk about anything. Even if he had something he needed to talk about, she was supposed to intuit it, and approach him to bring it up. Otherwise he became increasingly taciturn and withdrawn. When Vesta pursued him with "What's the matter?" it validated to her husband that he was important to her. He was also the lower-desire partner when it came to affection and sex, uniformly leaving it to her to approach him for physical contact. The more she pursued him, the more wanted and valued he felt.

Vesta told me the story of how this pattern had been passed down in her family system. "My grandfather wouldn't even budge to get a spoon for himself. He would just sit there until someone realized he needed one - - like it was some power game. Grandmother played the game, but really she ran the family. She practically tied his shoes for him! He was helpless without her."

Strategy 6) Caretaking/Fixing

Vesta also confided that, "In our family we women are taught to validate the male ego, but actually we run the show!" Vesta was pointing out her own primary marble-gathering strategy, one that commonly plays out opposite someone else's 'withholding' strategy. Withholders choose 'caretaking' partners as often as they choose pursuing partners. In fact, 'caretaking' (making yourself needed), the next marble-gathering strategy in the list, often goes hand in hand with 'pursuing'.

Making yourself "needed" is a very old and very common marble-gathering strategy perfected by a group that had little power in society throughout most of human history: women. While women may not have a monopoly on caretaking, they have certainly taken it to a high and sophisticated form - perhaps out of necessity. For the same reason it appeals to members of any oppressed group, some of the people with the largest holes in the bottom of their bowls develop a care-taking marble-gathering strategy because the only resources that caretaking requires are hard work and the inability to say "no". The primary aim is to become so indispensable to potential marble-dispensing people in your life that those people can't live without you.

Nothing fills the bowl of a caretaker like, "I don't know what I would do without you", or just plain "thank you" marbles. After watching her mother care-take her father all her life, Ursula took over the role after her mother died, stepping forward to perform all the functions for her father that his lost wife had performed. In addition to working sixty-hour weeks at her healthcare job, Ursula did all the shopping and housekeeping and cooking for her sixty-five year old, perfectly healthy, father. He never asked her. No one did. Her work was entirely preemptive. Her dad was grateful, however, and not only did she get marbles from him, but other family members, and friends, and neighbors validated her on a regular basis for her attentiveness. "You work so hard!" "You do too much!" "Thanks for taking such great care of Dad!"

When I asked Ursula about how she kept it up (bestowing on her a "you have super-human capabilities" marble), she said, "I get my marbles from always keeping other people from needing anything. When I go without, working selflessly for everyone else, I feel superior." Though she was struggling with anxiety, feelings of worthlessness and weight-related health issues, Ursula felt so good about her hard work and selfless giving, that she felt it entitled her to a steady stream of appreciation, marbles she needed to stem the tide of the fear that she was not actually worthy of love. When the people around her fell short of her expectations on marble-delivery, however, Ursula had a tendency to feel tired and resentful – which, in turn, would cause her to redouble her dedication to the caretaking strategy. If those frantic efforts at helping went unnoticed, Ursula had a tendency to slip into the next strategy in her effort to get the people around her to help fill her bowl.

Strategy 7) Judging and Criticizing

Judging, and its close cousin, criticizing, are powerful strategies that work in three different ways:

1) Judgers engage in a constant pursuit of ranking themselves against other people, in the interest of finding others wanting by comparison. As long as Therese didn't gain as much weight as her younger sister, she stole a marble from her sister every time they met. Her sister didn't even know she was giving them out. Therese might be fat in her own eyes, but if she wasn't as fat as Tabitha, it felt so soothing! I credit the marble-gathering strategy of 'judging' for the success of 'reality television' in our culture. As one of my clients said, "No matter how bad I feel about myself, no matter how crazy or unlovable I feel, I am not as bad as those whack-jobs on the television!"

2) The second way judgers gather marbles is by attacking other people who are not able to effectively defend themselves against the strategy. If the target of the judger has no adequate defense to counter the assault, the judger triumphs, extorting "you are right" marbles, or "you are superior" marbles from the victim of the attack, whether the target says anything out loud or not. Sarah's husband had spent years complaining that if she really loved him, she would know what he needed when he needed it. He wouldn't have to tell her what he was thinking, if she really loved him, because she would just know. Sarah finally realized that she had spent a 15 year relationship trying to prove to him that she loved him. She had allowed herself to become his constant marble dispenser, and that his "You don't really love me" strategy had been used on her as tool for extorting more marbles for the whole marriage.

3) One of the favorite pursuits of individuals who cultivate the judging strategy is finding allies who share their judging stance. Picture adolescent girls in the lunch room at school, huddled together in a pod, **gossiping** about the object of their derision. They are trading "I validate your view of reality." marbles, and "We are all superior to that pathetic sod." marbles, all around. **Creating alliances,** and **critical gossiping,** are strategies that tend to produce lots of return on the initial judging investment.

The Judger's Trick: If you have people in your life who use a judging strategy for getting marbles, you will often note that their expectations keep shifting. 15 year-old Rebecca worked very hard to meet her stepmother's expectations around what she wore, schoolwork and housework. But Rebecca's stepmother's sense-of-self was so fragile that she needed to complain and criticize other people as a strategy to feel better about herself. There was no chance that she was ever going to allow Rebecca to be 'good enough' in her eyes. And no matter how thoroughly she addressed the expectations placed on her, Rebecca would still get punished for not meeting them fast enough, or perfectly enough, or with a good enough attitude.

Strategy 8) Guilting

"Guilting?", you say. "Guilt' is a noun!" Not any more, I say. The term "guilting" has joined the common vernacular of my clients. And people who have it done to them, or do it to others themselves, bring the word to my office all the time.

Remember Vesta, whose husband's strategy was to hook her into pursuing him by withdrawing? When Vesta finally let her husband know that she was done with the hopeless task of trying to make him feel as if he was worthy by chasing him, his initial response was "You are so selfish! I knew you didn't care about me!"

"You are so selfish!" is the most common complaint people use to get another person back into marble production. "You are so selfish" has become a powerful cultural weapon, used to engender guilt, the painful internalized twin-sister of judgment, in another person. "You didn't send a 'thank you' note!? You are so selfish!" "You didn't go to engineering school!? You are so selfish!" "You won't come home for Christmas!? You are so selfish!" "You didn't notice I folded the laundry? You are so selfish!"

The line between judging and guilting is fuzzy; more like a field with a lot of overlap. I would say judging is an overt attempt to control someone else's behavior, and guilting is a more covert way to get the other person to shape **their own** behavior into the ways you want, without them noticing that you are pressuring them, and without you needing to remind them so often. Guilt has staying power!

Quinn told me about the time his mother cried over his grades when he was in the 6th grade. "If you really loved me you would do better! I must have been a bad mother! How can you do this to me!?" That scene stayed with him all the way through school, giving him test-anxiety all his school life. When he came to see me, he was in law school and kept having panic attacks every time finals week rolled around. "I can't stop feeling as if I don't get straight "A's" I am failing my mom! I keep thinking that I might kill her!"

Paula, another client, had a father who kept threatening to have a heart attack when he did not get responses from his kids that felt adequate, to his solicitation for marbles. The bind was, he wouldn't actually define what an adequate response was, so everyone just had to keep trying! "If you really loved me I would not have to tell you what I need - you would just know! And if I did tell you what I needed, you would just do it out of loyalty - not from authentic love!" The marbles he was looking for? It was something like a constant supply of: "Please Daddy! Please don't go! We need you!!" and "It is so important to me that you are happy, I'll do and be whatever you want from now on. Just tell me what that is!"

Paula's father was actually exhibiting several marble-gathering strategies at once. Along with guilting, you may recognize a bit of withdrawing. He also fell into the pattern of the next strategy.

Strategy 9) Suffering

Those who feel the most helpless in the pursuit of marbles, tend to resort to permanently taking on the role of "suffering victim" in relation to the world and within the context of their relationships. If you have the sense that you are so worthless as to not be worthy of personal validation for anything about your identity, then "It's not your fault." or "Let me take care of you." may be the only marbles that you can recognize. As you might imagine, 'sufferers' often end up in close relationships with caretakers.

Olivia came from a family with a strong caretaking mother. Her mother needed to be needed so much that the only way to get marbles from her was to be the most messed-up one in the family. Olivia vied with her sisters for the position of sickest, most helpless, and most unstable member of the family. It didn't seem to matter how messed up she was though, she could never seem to be the one who was suffering worst, or longest, to feel as if she mattered to her mother. So Olivia was constantly looking around to friends and a string of boyfriends to validate her worth through both caretaking and suffering strategies. Of course the subtext of an "It isn't your fault" marble is a "There is nothing wrong with **you**." marble. And the subtext of "I will take care of you." is a "You are worth taking care of." marble.

Olivia's view of herself was so constricted both by the need to be the victim, and the constant sense of losing the marble game, that she had gotten to the point where if she wasn't suffering, she could not even feel ok about accepting a marble for her bowl. It was almost as if suffering was all she was good for, the sum total of her identity. Luckily she was not like the small percentage of victims who are so desperate that they will actually secretly harm themselves in order to get health-care providers to take care of them. Those particular sufferers get a DSM* diagnoses of "Munchausen Disorder". (3)

Strategy 10) Intimidation/Volatility

Of the strategies-of-last-resort, developed by those who did not hit upon a more benign marble-gathering system, the most disturbing is **intimidation**. The basic idea behind intimidation is that if the intimidator can't get marbles any other way, s/he will squeeze them out of people using fear! The more helpless an individual feels in the context of the marble game, and the less that person feel s/he matters, the more likely s/he is to resort to extorting validation through intimidation. Large subgroups of people who are oppressed by economics or lack of education are vulnerable to falling into the intimidation-strategy also, because members of oppressed groups have fewer options for validation-of-identity available to them than dominant cultural groups.

Nigel was a member of such an oppressed group. "Respect" was something that Nigel demanded from everyone in his world. It was something that his older brother had demanded from him all his life. What he meant when he said "respect", though, was actually "fear," fear of his volatility, fear of his potential for violence. For individuals who have a fragile sense of self, engendering fear may be the only way to have the subjective experience that they matter in the world. "Maybe I can't find a job. And maybe I suck at school. And maybe my dad left and my mom is never home, (subtext: 'maybe I seem utterly insignificant') but I can sure make a significant impact on **you** if I want to!"

Volatility and intimidation are strategies of the most fragile, the most brittle identities. Sitting across from Nigel, or many clients with what is referred to as an "anger management" issue, I often feel as if I were to reach across and flick a fingernail against his skin, he would shatter like glass. I think Nigel often felt that way too, though of course he never would have admitted it.

Intimidation is not always overt. Sometimes the intimidation strategy wears the mask of the suffering strategy. Ellie's mother threatened to cancel her trip to come from Minnesota to Seattle for her daughter's Christmas wedding, because Ellie planned to leave right after the ceremony for her Hawaii honeymoon, only two days before Christmas. One of the themes in her mother's preferred identity, was that she was the most important person in Ellie's life, and Ellie's decision to spend the holiday without her, and alone with her new husband, was terrifically threatening to her sense-of-self. So Ellie's mom resorted to something I call 'threats in lamb's clothing'. To my sadness, Ellie caved, and ended up losing four days off of her ten-day Hawaiian honeymoon in order to validate her mother. <sigh>

* Definition: "DSM" – The Diagnostic Statistical Manual of Mental Disorders (3)

"Controlling" Behavior and The Marble Game

*The entire Marble Game is about virtually everyone on the planet attempting to **control** relational interactions, hierarchical structures, and life logistics, for the purpose of maximizing the confirmation of a preferred identity, in order to prove to the self and others that "I matter!" By popular definition, "controlling" tends to be recognized as some unpleasant combination of caretaking, criticizing and intimidation, and I almost included "controlling" in my top 10 marble-solicitation strategies. But then I realized that **all** of the top 10 strategies are attempts to manipulate the behavior of others, and as such, meet the definition of "controlling". The most effective controlling-behavior-practitioners often combine marble-gathering strategies, or are able to rapidly shift between more than one to maximize effectiveness and quell resistance.*

Building marble-producing machines

A good percentage of parents groom their kids to be marble-producing machines. Please don't misunderstand me. This practice is not intentional! Parents have no idea they are doing it, and a certain amount of this grooming is ubiquitous, even desirable. I have yet to meet a parent/kid system without the dynamic of "If you make yourself pleasing to me, little primate, this relationship will go better for you." But, in some family systems, the marble-production-programming reaches startling levels. The type of programming depends on the kind of marble-validation the parent most wants: "I can't live without your guidance!", "You, parent, are the source of my success!", "I believe everything you believe!", "You're the best!", etc.

I already told the story of Olivia, who took on the role of suffering-victim along with her sisters in order to validate her mother's need for "I need you." marbles. Remember Quinn's panic attacks, triggered by fear that he would let his mother down with any slip in his school performance? Both Olivia and Quinn had received repeated indoctrination as children from their parents for maximum marble production.

Nan was a 5-foot tall, pale, slight girl who came in to my practice wearing clothes that looked like they had been purchased for a person who outweighed her by at least fifty pounds. I am not exaggerating when I say that she had to cinch her belt up, bunching her jeans all about her waist, to keep her pants from falling off. Initially I thought she must have recently lost a bunch of weight, which can be a sign of anxiety and/or depression, or sometimes drug use. But when I asked her my intake question about recent weight gain or loss, she denied any changes. She also denied any eating-disordered behavior. It wasn't until several sessions into our work together that I finally discovered that Nan thought she was fat. Her mother (who was not overweight either) had been in an epic battle with her weight all of Nan's life, and Nan had somehow been programmed never to 'be any thinner' than her mother. If her mother struggled with her weight, Nan needed to struggle even more, and because her mom wore a size 12, Nan unconsciously 'needed' to wear a size 14. This 100-pound girl in my office actually believed she fit into a size 14. It wasn't until several months into our work together that Nan came into session and asked me, "Do you think my clothes are too big for me?" Her pants had fallen down around her knees when she had been trotting across the street in order not to miss the light, when. It had taken a wake-up call of that magnitude to begin to wake Nan to her internalized, parental-marble-producing programming.

Marike came to me in her mid-twenties stalled in her course of the medical school application process, after a quarter century of constantly trying please her father and everyone else. Her parents wanted a doctor in the family. Even before walking through my door, Marike had realized on her own that the game of validation-exchange was rigged. She hated getting marbles from her father because she had come to recognize them for what they were, bald demands for more marbles from her. In Marike's words: "I hate it when he praises me! He only praises me when I do what he tells me to do. And if I want to stay on his good side, it's like I have to live up to this expectation he sets for me to be what he wants me to be!"

In addition, Marike had started to notice that the only time her father seemed really happy with her was when Marike was unhappy. After discussing this perplexing dynamic, the double-bind she was in was clear, and Marike completed the homework exercise of making a list of all the reasons why her father could not allow her to be happy. It went something like this:

- When I am happy, he has less control over me. He loses leverage.
- I depend on him less, so he feels like he has less value.
- He loses a prime avenue for caretaking and fixing me if I am happy.
- It invalidates his negative world-view if I find a way to be happy in my life.
- If I became happy my own way instead of through the path he lays out – it is a slap in his face, like he did his life wrong.
- If he ever were to let me know he was happy with me, he would lose because I might stop working so hard to make him happy with me.

After several months of therapeutic work, Marike came to realize that she had been raised on a steady stream of "I know what is best for you. You owe it to me to do what I want, so you don't upset me. You can't trust yourself. You can only trust me, because I know what is best for you." These are the messages of controlling individuals who are attempting to program others to produce marbles for them.

Adults too can be groomed to make marble-production, on behalf of another person, the focus of their lives. Some of the most sociopathic* strategies I have seen in my work were at play in adult relationships. Laura was in a domestic violence relationship that was free of **physical** violence, so she did not recognize it as abusive at first. She didn't see it, though she was expected to let him know where she was every minute of every day, and she had discovered that he had installed Spyware on her computer and a hidden GPS tracking device in her car. He controlled all of the money, what she did with her free time, and even what she wore. Laura's husband had slowly gained control over her by dispensing three marble-messages: 1) I only want what is best for you. (Subtext: "You matter to me.") ; 2) You can't trust yourself. You can only trust me, because I know what is best for you. (Subtext: "You might be undeserving of marbles, but I will show you the path to worthiness."; 3) I feel hurt when you don't appreciate my love by doing what I want, and you owe it to me not to hurt me. (Subtext: "If I am ever unhappy with you, it means you are looking after me badly and don't deserve any marbles.") Domestic violence situations are always steeped in marble-solicitation strategies gone horribly wrong.

With children, the stakes are even higher because they must rely on their caregivers for the very stuff of life. If children can't comply with parental pressure to produce marbles, at their most insidious, marble-production grooming-behaviors can carry threat to safety or security. Remember the movie <u>Mommy Dearest</u>? The message is "If you stop playing the role I have given you to shore up my identity, I have the power to starve you or kick you to the curb (either emotionally or physically)." Children have no way out of the game but drugs or death, and some of them do choose that.

Playing for Marbles is Not Evil!

At this point, I think it is important to stress that playing the Marble Game does not mean you are a bad person. One's participation in the game is largely, if not entirely, unconscious in just about everyone. And getting marbles from other people feels great! Your marble-solicitation

__Definition__ – "__sociopathic__": demonstrating a pattern of behavior that displays a pervasive of unawareness of, disregard for, and violation of the rights of others that begins in childhood or early adolescence and continues into adulthood.

strategies are not about your **character**. Furthermore, if your bowl is empty, or close to it, you will not be able to keep yourself from soliciting marbles to help yourself feel better. I will go so far as to say that walking around with an empty bowl causes you to feel as if you could die from the pain of it, or as if you matter so little that it would not make a difference if you were dead. In a state of that kind of scarcity, the drive to find a way to matter to someone is irresistible.

If you have seen yourself in an unflattering light when looking through the lens of the Marble Game, I just want you to remember that any guilt or self-judgment you are feeling right now are simply a manifestation of the strategies you were taught, or have developed in your life, for getting more marbles. It does not make sense to feel bad about something you didn't know you were doing and that you have not been able to help. Furthermore, at a certain developmental stage, humans need outside validation of their worth desperately. As I intimated at the beginning of the chapter, no-strings-attached validation that a baby receives from the caregiver is instrumental in keeping the hole that a child will develop in his or her identity-bowl small.

Section 3: Attachment and The Hole in Your Bowl

Earlier in the chapter I asserted that if you came from a family system that consistently sent you the message when you were little that you don't have to do any certain thing or be any certain way to be worthy of our love and approval, you have a little-bitty hole in the bottom of your bowl. But if you came from a family system that sent you the message "to be worthy of our approval, you have to do what we tell you to do and be who we say you are" you will have a big whole in the bowl of your identity. Now I will take it further. What if the expectations for your behavior or identity kept changing all the time, or no one would tell you what they were? Or what if no matter how hard you tried to figure out and comply with your caregiver's demands they were so emotionally disorganized that you were punished no matter what you did? People who come from childhoods like that tend to end up with a bowl that is more like a ceramic donut. What I am talking about now is how important consistent outside caregiver-validation is, in the context of infant attachment, and long-term participation in the marble game.

I want to make a distinction here. When I say "validation" in the context of secure parent/child attachment, I do not mean: "praise." "Praise" is something else entirely, a simple variety of marble. Praise comes in response to behavior by the child that the caregiver finds desirable, and has the effect of reinforcing that behavior because the child wants to receive the praise again. Thus praise lays the preliminary foundation for how we exchange marbles with our families, what kinds of marbles those are, and how we play the game for the rest of our lives. Remember what Marike said about her father's praise? "I hate it when he praises me! He only praises me when I do what he tells me to do."

Creating a secure infant attachment and resulting resilient psyche is not about praise. At the infant and young child level, the essential external validation-experience that is required to wire a young person with a fairly solid psyche is the experience of seeing regular, predictable, unconditional positive responsiveness on the face of the caregiver, in the present moment. In plain English what that means is seeing a beloved familiar face that communicates, "I am taking you in, right this very minute, and I am glad you are here" (subtext: "You matter to me"). When we get a regular, predictable influx of outside "You matter to me" validation, in the critical window of childhood, instilling in our identities the primal stamp of "I matter", then the drive to prove it to ourselves, or get other people to convince us of it for the rest of our lives is just not as strong.

We adults, while we believe we long for marbles of praise-flavored validation, what we actually unconsciously long for is the same kind of in-the-moment unconditional positive regard, that helps babies grow up with a solid sense-of-self: "I am so glad you are here in this moment. You matter to me!" Further, "You don't have to do any certain thing or be any certain way to be worthy of my love. You are intrinsically precious to me."

The "You matter to me." caregiver-validation moment cannot be faked. Babies and children can not be fooled with words alone, or by distracted kisses given by a parent who is lost in his or her own mind. Loving words and kisses are meaningless without the full, present, focused awareness of the caregiver. The "You are the only thing that matters right now." moment is a moment of exchange in which we become awake to each other. Babies can do it from birth. It is hard wired. But adults can cultivate it too! My partner calls it "quality time". It is the experience of gazing into another person's eyes as we both come alive to the awareness that we are both fully present to the experience of connection, and liking it. We smile with happiness.

Are you squirming at the thought of it? If you are, I'll bet money that you had the natural longing squeezed out of you as a child by the repeated experience of looking into the face of a caregiver who gazed back with judgment, indifference, or anxiety. You read, "I am not glad you are here." or "You do not matter." or "Your attempts to get close to me are making me nervous." or even, "DON'T Stop looking! Never stop looking into my eyes even if you need a break! Keep validating ME!" The experience was so painful that you learned not to look – that gazing into someone's eyes is a bad idea.

Infant Attachment Impacts Game Strategy

There are lots of books written about attachment, and how one's style of attachment to the original caregiver will tend to impact mental-health over the course of one's life. So I will only give only a brief overview here, through the lens of the Marble Game. (For more information on infant attachment see Daniel Seigel's Parenting From the Inside Out (4), and for adult attachment, Hold Me Tight (5) by Sue Johnson.)

Secure-Attachment

I described the etiology of secure attachment at the end of the last section. Baby communicates a need, and caregivers consistently and appropriately respond to the baby's requests for both care and connectedness. This kind of attachment will predispose a person to a lifetime of keeping a bowl full of marbles more easily. Marbles are easier to get if you have a small hole in your bowl, and they stay in there longer when you get them.

Anxious/Ambivalent-Attachment

Anxiously attached babies have caregivers who are erratic or inconsistent in answering the babies' requests for care and validation or caregivers who need constant reassurance from the baby that they, the adults, matter to the baby. Anxious-attachment can also arise out of a family system with paths to validation that are changing all the time, or expectations that are full of double-binds*. Babies with this kind of attachment tend to grow into adults who suffer from anxiety, and tend to choose the more active strategies for marble-solicitation with a sometimes frantic single-mindedness. With needs that were met at least some of the time in childhood, there grew a sense that "if only I can figure out what worked that one time: ask in the right way again, or ask often enough, that I'll get the response I need." Anxiously-attached people tend to be the work-horses of the game: Giving out marbles, Morphing, Gift Giving, Pursuing, and Caretaking.

Avoidant-Attachment

Babies whose bids for care and connectedness were largely ignored, will tend to grow into adults with depressive tendencies, people who have developed a world-view that 'I am pretty irrelevant' to God, the universe and people in general. They also tend to adopt the more passive strategies for marble-soliciting because they absorbed as babies that they had little efficacy in the world. That is, "It doesn't make sense to spend my energy actively trying very hard with other people because that strategy never gets me very far." Withholding, Judging, Guilting, and Suffering are common choices for the individual who was avoidantly attached. They also tend to lean more towards 'conservation' as a way to keep marbles in their bowls, rather than active pursuit of validation. I will outline "conservation" as a strategy for winning the game in the next section.

Disorganized Attachment

Babies who are punished for drawing attention to themselves and asking for care and validation develop the most disassociative, volatile and sometimes dangerous strategies for getting marbles for their bowls. Numbing out, intimidation, and violence towards the self, others, or the structures of society are the common strategies of an individual who experienced such childhood trauma.

Section 4: Marble Conservation

Conserving Marbles by Avoiding Judgment

In addition to soliciting them from other people, the other way of trying to cultivate a full bowl is to defend and conserve the ones you have, and many people play the game as if each marble is an actual piece of gold, as if validation is a scarce and valuable commodity. "Ack! If I want to give you a marble, I have to take one away from my own bowl to do it!" How that plays out in the psyche of a real person looks something like: 1) "If I tell him that I appreciate his contribution to the team, then my own contribution will appear smaller. He might then even he think I am admitting to being less valuable than he is." Or 2) "If I ask her on a date, I make myself a supplicant at the mercy of her potentially identity-destroying rejection."

* *Definition: "Double Bind" - a situation in which a person is confronted with two irreconcilable demands or a choice between two undesirable courses of action.*

Does telling someone else that you notice and appreciate his contribution mean there actually **is** less appreciation available for you? If there is **real** scarcity in the pool of appreciation? If so, how do we find out how big the supply of appreciation is so we can know when it is safe to share some?

Does asking someone out on a date actually put your value as a person at risk? If she says "no" does that mean you have lost a bit of your worth? If so who judges so? Is God hanging over your head, or a panel of invisible judges, recording how wanted or respected you are by other people, in order to keep your worthiness score up to date? Whatever the true answers to those questions, many people live as if identity really works that way. As a result, the conserving of marbles becomes paramount to them.

The primary path chosen by the bulk of marble-conservationists is avoiding the judgment of other people. If you are a conservationist, judgment from other people can feel as if it has the power to pop the marbles in your bowl as if they are soap bubbles, or worse, that judgers have the power to snatch marbles right out of your bowl to fill their own, as their comparing stance lauds themselves and finds you wanting. There are almost as many strategies for defending the bowl as there are for soliciting validation, but they tend to fall into 10 general categories:

1) **Don't Stick My Neck Out**
2) **Jumping the Gun**
3) **Never Let Them See the Real Me**
4) **Walking the Right(eous) Path**
5) **Taking on Godlike Responsibilities**
6) **Organizing: Sort/Categorize/Parse**
7) **Just Keep Moving**
8) **Attack as Defense**
9) **Intimidation**
10) **Residing Safe in the Bosom of Self-Loathing**

1) Don't Stick My Neck Out

"Whatever", "I don't know", and "I don't really care." are the calls of **the pacifist**, an individual who is unwilling to stick out even a tiny bit of self and risk judgment! Kevin was utterly passive in the context of his relationship with Kim. He never had any opinion about where he wanted to go for dinner. (She might shoot down his choice.) He never initiated a hug, let alone sex. (She might shoot him down.) He had no opinion about how they should invest their money. (He might get blamed for being wrong if they made a bad investment.) And ultimately, by the time they were in my office (Kim shouting "Doesn't anything matter to you at all!? Don't **I** matter to you!?"), Kevin was unable to step up and say he wanted her to stay. It was too risky. She might discover his terrible fear, that he wanted her more than she wanted him, and that he was unworthy of her. Kevin thought Kim had the power to dump his whole bowl of marbles if she knew about his vulnerability. So Kevin remained in his passive role to the very end, saying to his weeping wife, "It is up to you to choose if YOU want to stay married. You shouldn't be swayed by me."

You can also imagine that if Kim had chosen to stay with Kevin, without even a speck of encouragement from him, he would have received a fat marble of validation from her for his identity-bowl. The marble solicitation strategy **"Witholding"** is very often partnered with the conservation strategy, **Don't Stick My Neck Out.**

2) Jumping the Gun

Some people who were raised in environments that were emotionally or physically dangerous have a tendency to leap to reactivity, or action way before they have gathered enough information to leap effectively. In their formative years, Jumpers learned that you better figure out what is happening and quick, or you are going to get judged, guilted or worse. Jumpers have a hard time reprogramming themselves because their knee-jerk reactions are so fast. They tend to have leaped to conclusions, and are jumping forward as if their defensive stories are 100% true, before they or anyone else realizes what is happening.

If you are a jumper, it is challenging to get you to slow down, collect more information, and check out your read, before you misjudge a situation and act against your own best interest. Checking out one's story can feel scary or even humiliating to a person who is used to jumping the gun. S/he might not even have any idea what questions to ask, so may come off sounding accusatory to the people around him, garnering a reaction that would discourage future fact-checking attempts.

3) Never Let Them See the Real Me

Remember the marble gathering strategy, "morphing"? "Never letting people see the real me" is **"morphing"** used as a defensive strategy. The idea is this: if I present judgers with a mask that averts judgment (pretending to be something they admire or ignore), or a mask that looks threatening or dangerous, they will leave me alone. The face or fake identity that the defense-morpher wears is dependent on the nature of the judging environment. Virtually everyone morphs to defend, at least at some point in life. What face did you wear? Mousey and non-threatening? Bouncy and stupid? "Nothing bothers me?" "Mess with me and I'll mess you up?" "I always follow the rules?" At least one face was likely the face of your parents' fantasy ideal-child.

I think the most common mask I see in my office is the same one I see around my son's high school, which is the same one I see on the streets of the city: "**I am so tough** <you had better not mess with me>." Or sometimes: "I'm so tough <it will be a waste of your time to mess with me>".

"I'm so tough," probably squeezes my heart more than any other mask a person can wear, particularly when I see it in children. The aim of the mask is to drive other people away so they won't threaten the individual, either physically, or threaten their bowl of marbles; but of course the mask has the collateral effect of driving away the chance of having another person gaze into the child's eyes to say, "Welcome, dear heart, I am glad that you are here." Appearing impermeable, or even dangerous IS a great strategy for keeping people from attempting to steal your marbles with their judging, but it can come at the cost of your very self. Zarrah was one of those people who would hand you a Kleenex for the spot on your dress if you had just had your head blown off by a drive-by. She was even more laissez-faire when it came to wounds to her self. The only member from a family of six to get out of North Africa alive, she claimed that she couldn't feel anything anymore, and only wanted people to leave her alone. That could not actually have been true though, or she would not have followed the direction of her minister and sought some help from me. People who really want to be left alone don't seek therapy, and there are an awful lot of lone wolves out there who do. You are very hard to reach though. Your strategy for looking like you don't care can be pretty off-putting.

There is a painful paradox to toughness. It is this: toughness as defense or protection is actually extremely brittle and fragile, while it is actually in the vulnerability of being real and transparent that true strength comes - - because one has nothing to hide.

4) Walking the "right(eous)" path, i.e. "Being Right"

Deciding you have found the "right" path, so you can quit taking in any new information about yourself or the nature of life, is a common defense strategy against outside judgments that might threaten your identity, or even more importantly, threaten your conviction that the way you see the world is the only way to see it. A righteous stance allows you to keep your attention firmly inward, focused on what you think you know, discounting anything you don't understand and anything that doesn't support what you think already know: You and your paradigms, untouchable, as if your identity gets married to rightness itself. Feeling so right even creates a partial force field above the bowl, so external judgment is deflected before it can land, at least while you are focusing your attention on your righteous stance. The trouble, of course, is that it is really difficult to keep fresh ideas out of a system, even a closed system like a cult, or North Korea. Eventually there is a good chance that some fresh perspective can get in and cause the whole strategy to collapse.

There is a collateral defense strategy that "righteous path" devotees often adopt to help reinforce the stance. 'Walking the right(eous) path' fits hand in glove with "creating alliances," a tactic I described when discussing the marble-gathering strategy: Judging. Remember how effective holding a shared view with a bunch of people, who want to band together to judge others, was for collecting marbles? If you profess that you are the holder of the "right path", then other fragile people who are desperate to have a something to belong to, so they can feel as if they matter, often flock to you. Now you have a pack, a gang, a flock, or a nation. Ha! Now you can guard each other's bowls. And now it is a lot easier to buffer yourself against information that might be counter to what you "know". Even if there are people on the outside of the circle judging you, you can face inward towards the center, and focus your attention on the marble validation of the members of your group, instead of the judgement coming from the outside. "You are right! You are right!" your friends say to you. "Don't pay any attention to those people outside the circle. They are idiots! Let's only listen to each other!"

Note: *Before we leave "righteousness", I would like to say something about people like you, that is, the people who are seekers and explorers interested in the human experience, and paths to happiness, and personal evolution. If we pursue our adventure unconsciously, we put ourselves at risk of becoming the kind of Marble Game player that I have just described above. There is no "right path." Many paths lead to insight. There is always more to wonder about, and more to ask about on the other side of every insight, as we continue to broaden our wonderful understanding about the mysterious nature of all things. Each level of truth has another deeper layer under it. We are just small beings and will likely never know what is "right" with a capital "R", but continuing to try to figure it out is the great adventure that evolves the self!*

5) Taking on Godlike Responsibilities

Some of us, at least at some point in ours lives attempt to control the whole chaotic universe outside the self as a way to avert judgment. This defense-strategy is usually married to the gathering-strategy "caretaking". The Caretaker's vulnerability to falling into this conservation-trap is so universal, it is almost ubiquitous. The drive to control the universe arises out of one of two fantasies: 1) "Ack! If I could just get all you people to do what <I think> you are supposed to be doing, everything would go perfectly, judgment would not come my way, and I could finally relax!" 2) "Your fear, anger or sadness is making me feel nervous and responsible! I must be failing at my caretaking job! Let me fix you so I don't have to feel anxious about, and responsible for, your suffering!"

Part of why the managing-the-universe-habit is so hard to kick, is that sometimes it works! For the same reason that individual lives need some amount of organizing to run smoothly, human systems need some level of organization and leadership to run smoothly. However, just as with any other necessary aspect of life, how much it too much? I will let you know. I am still working on this one in my own life. ☺

6) Organize: Sorting and Parsing

People who rely on organizing for marble-conservation have a tendency to break relationship obligations and logistics into smaller and smaller pieces over time, in the effort to systematize life and get a handle on each piece. This strategy is another slippery one, in that just like 'taking on Godlike responsibilities', a bit of organizing is an effective anti-anxiety strategy, but too much engages the law of diminishing returns! Our psyches tend to work under the mistaken impression that if a little of something is good, more must be better! However, while a bit of organization does allow you to spend a lot more of your life energy having fun rather than juggling logistics, "organizing" as a marble-conservation strategy can steal away your entire experience of life itself!

Allan was a client who felt so overwhelmed with the feeling that his to-do list was slipping out of his control, that he had an appointment calendar in which he had parsed each day into fifteen-minute increments. Because each day by itself felt so overwhelming, the hope was that if he got a handle on each small segment of the day, he could be more efficient.

Ok, first let's look at the to-do list. For many people, a to-do list is an extremely useful structural tool for organizing a day, a week, or even a month. But Allan's was a life to-do list! Allan himself had composed this to-do list, and on it he had gathered a collection of all the things he felt he needed to accomplish by the time he died, to feel as if his life had mattered. (He was determined to amass enough important and interesting accomplishments that he, himself, would end up having mattered.) Again, sometimes it is fun to write an adventure-list of all the interesting things you might like to do in your life, but Allan's list made him miserable because it was a list of all the things he HAD to do to avoid not mattering! Allan lived with the constant slipping feeling that he was falling behind schedule with the list; thus the calendar.

As I said, the calendar was divided into fifteen minute blocks, wherein absolutely everything he intended to do for the next several months was blocked in, in tiny increments, from work, to commuting, to home projects, to eating, to teeth brushing, to reading the paper, to playing with his son, to shopping, to everything. Absolutely everything was there. I am not going to spend a lot of time illustrating what is wrong with this strategy, because I think you may be able extrapolate his results, given the law of diminishing returns. Just imagine what happened inside of Allan when there was an accident on the freeway, or his wife got sick, or if his kid fell off the play structure and knocked out a tooth just about the time they were supposed to leave the park? Or any of an infinite number of potential world wrinkles messed up the schedule? Got the picture?

Take it one step farther. What do you suppose it was like to be Allan's wife, or child, or co-worker? Organizing was the strategy he adopted to keep from being judged as unworthy, but how effective do you suppose his best marble-conservation strategy was at avoiding the judgment of the people in his life? In Allen's rigid, well-meaning determination to both achieve all the goals on his list, and parse out time to meet the needs of anyone and everyone who said they required his attention, Allen ended up so paralyzed with stress, and spread so thin, and that he was unable to meet his agreements with anyone else, let alone himself.

7) Just Keep Moving

Irene was constantly moving. It was a pattern she had gotten into with her mother when she was a child. Every time they didn't have the money to cover the next month's rent, or every time her mom had a bad enough fight with her current boyfriend, Irene's Mom would ditch the place, take her and move – sometimes in the middle of the night. And while Irene eventually grew up and was able to put herself through college (moving 13 times in five years), and while as an adult she was able to create a secure enough life for herself that she didn't need to ditch her living situations for financial reasons, she kept moving all the time. If her boss gave her a piece of critical feedback about her work, she quit and got a new job. If a neighbor looked at her cross-eyed or complained about her dog, she moved. If she and her boyfriend had any tension in the relationship, she broke up with him and got a new boy. Irene was exhausted!

There are three primary motivations for "moving" as a marble-defense strategy: A) Staying out of Judgment's eye, B) Looking hardworking and productive, and C) Staying so busy there is no time to either self-reflect or notice any judgment that might be coming your way. Irene's story is an example of "staying out of Judgment's eye." In her mind, if she wasn't there any more, no one could judge her!

Remember Marike, who was caught in the happiness double bind with her father? Marike was a great example of the "looking productive" type. In her mind, she had to keep avoiding judgment by looking industrious, while at the same time making certain that she did not undermine her father's sense-of-value by succeeding at what she was doing. One of the hallmarks of Marike's depression was a sense of being bone-tired, like she just could not **force** herself to actually **do** anything productive. After a couple of sessions we ended up talking about her primary focus and unearthed where her exhaustion was coming from: Marike spent so much energy looking as if she was moving forward and being productive, to avoid parental judgment, and then defending herself against criticism regarding how she was proceeding, that she didn't have any energy left over to actually **be** productive. Marike had a strong felt sense that she was a hamster on a wheel, expending all of her life's energy to go nowhere.

Staying busy, the pursuit of distracting yourself by staying so busy that you have no time to judge yourself, let alone notice someone else judging you, is one of the most common marble-conservation strategies I see in my office. Busyness reaches the level of addiction in the lives of many of my clients. Busyness is a consummate distraction both from feelings of desperation in an individual who has the creeping feeling that despite her best efforts, she is losing the marble game, and the feelings of self-judgment that "if only I were a better person, that would not be the case."

8) Attack as Defense

When some individuals feel as if someone is threatening their bowls with judgment, they will metaphorically threaten to kick over the potential-judger's bowl to get that person to back off. Threatening that "**If you judge me, I'll judge you back and harder**!!" can be an effective way of getting a judger to back off, and think twice before judging you the future. I see defensive attack, in the face of judgment, or even perceived judgment, pop up in every relationship I have ever worked with in my office, and I see it in my own. Defending one's bowl, by threatening someone else's stash of marbles is a virtually ubiquitous human knee-jerk reaction. Do any of these examples sound familiar?

1. "You think I don't listen to YOU!? You never freaking listen!"
2. "You have the nerve to complain about my family, when YOUR family…!"
3. "You think I am slow at learning this, remember when I was trying to teach you about <whatever>?!"
4. "You don't fool me with all that stuff about changing, I will never forget that you cheated on (weren't there for) me!"
5. "You want to complain about the kitchen? Have you taken a look at your car?!"
6. "You want to get on my case for screwing up? Remember that time you <insert mistake you once made> !?"
7. "You want to bug me about working out? Well, I don't see it doing a damned thing for you!"
8. "You always…! You never…!"

Ouch. Defensiveness can be an effective judgment-averting strategy, but it also drives people apart, and often escalates the judging to another round that is even more threatening to one's stash of marbles.

9) Intimidation: Active and Passive

While "attack as defense" threatens the judger's bowl of marbles, **active intimidation** threatens someone's actual person either with physical retaliation, or some other future material cost to the judger. This is the phenomenon of "Just look at me wrong, and I'll bash your face in." or "Say something I don't want to hear, and I will do something to you that will make you so sorry." The active intimidation defense strategy tends to arise in individuals with a history of disorganized attachment, and is almost always paired with the marble gathering strategy of the same name: Intimidation and volatility.

Passive intimidation, also known as "stonewalling", is used as a tactic to punish or threaten the judger, making it less likely that they will finish a criticism, or that they will dare judge the intimidator again. "If you dare judge me, I will abandon you completely, either emotionally or physically in retaliation."

I already explored "intimidating" in the first chapter, as a marble-gathering strategy with the story of Nigel, the loneliest boy in the world. Used for gathering, or for defense, intimidation is a dual-purpose self-torture machine, with plenty of terrified users.

10) Safe in the Bosom of Self-Loathing

The marble-conserving, judgment-avoidance strategy that I have found to be therapeutically hardest to budge is also the one that is probably the most damaging to that individual's sense of identity: Rapidly owning blame before anyone else can pin a judgment on you.

"It's all my fault!" can be a preemptive diversion from outside criticism, if it comes out fast enough, and for some people this strategy becomes almost a reflex action. Then if that action alone is not enough to avert outside judgment, taking it to "if I feel bad enough about what I am blaming myself for, it would be mean of you to get mad at me," is the next level of defense. Continuing to criticize someone who has already rolled over to expose his or her belly exposes the criticizer to the risk of being judged themselves, as culturally, it is viewed as cruel to kick someone who is already down.

I have seen the "It's all my fault!" strategy come at two different levels. With the lighter version, the individual doesn't necessarily believe what he is saying. Often I'll see children or teens jump to say the right words, "It'sMyFaultI'mSorry!!", to assuage a caregiver's anger before any judging gaze can fully turn their way. In those cases the strategy may only go as deep in the psyche as any other useful life-coping skill. With the heavy version, however, the "It's all my fault" is internalized deeply - to the level of "I am a Walking Fault, so it is always going to be my fault."

"It is always my fault" is most often the last-ditch strategy of the person who comes from abuse history, raised in a household where avoiding violent judgment was a matter of survival, or with a history of brutal contempt by caregivers. In such cases, the skill of avoiding abuse can be the only thing a person learns to appreciate about the self.

Janice told me, "I like hating myself. It makes me unassailable! No one can hate me more than I hate myself, so no one can say anything to hurt me. There is nothing I haven't already heard." She also said, "Coming up with new reasons to hate myself is kind of satisfying. It feels like picking at a scab." In this, the harshest form of an "it is always my fault" identity, Janice could sometimes almost produce her own twisted and broken marble out of her own self-loathing, as she viewed herself at excelling below all others in the arena of lowliness, taking the crown of the greatest, most broken person in the world.

I refuse to play!

When I have spoken with them about the marble game, I have had a few clients who told me that they had figured out a long time ago that the game was impossible to win, so they just refused to play. One of those clients was Kevin (Kevin-who-would-not-stick-his-neck-out), by the way. And another was self-loathing-Janice. These and those like them learned early in life that trying actively to play the game hurt them more than pretending they didn't need it. What is ironic about that is that the bowls (identities) they created for themselves cried out for "WOW! That's impressive! You don't need this stinking Marble Game?!"- marbles, and "Wow! You don't need anything or anyone! You are a badass island in and of yourself!"- marbles.

Of course, they did actually have needs. If Janice had not needed anything or anyone, she would not have been in my office desperate to retain custody of her small son. If Kevin really had not needed anything or anyone, he would not have become suicidal when his wife left him. Both Janice and Kevin had a tendency to "numb out", sort of disassociating from our conversation when I pressed them on something. That was likely a strategy that had served them well in childhood when they were under fire. Likely "numbing-out" was a safe place to go to escape the pain of having an empty bowl as well.

I am going to assert that *if your bowl is close to empty*, you cannot stop from playing the Marble Game any more than you can keep from breathing. Don't believe me? Are you annoyed with what I am saying? If you are, then you have proved my premise. The only reason to have a feeling-based resistance to my hypothesis, is that you feel judged by me calling into question one of **your** preferred identities, or paradigms, regarding who **you** are or how the world works.

Is it possible that there are people with apparently empty bowls who don't play the game? Sure. I am not God, and I don't know everyone. Maybe they are happy enough that they never show up in my office. I did have a guy one time who did indeed give a remarkably believable impression that he truly did not need anything from anyone, though he had no meaningful relationships with people or pets. He also turned out to meet the diagnoses for Aspergers, so perhaps I was simply unable to read his need for connection. He was in my office for a couple of sessions simply because a co-worker had suggested it, in the interest of developing better working-relationships with his colleagues. They were calling him "robot boy" at work. Also, a friend of mine has a brother diagnosed with Schizoid Personality Disorder, one of the primary characteristics of that diagnoses being an aversion to human connection. Both of these diagnoses are not well understood, and require more research before I will be able to comment on if or how they fit within the Marble Game metaphor.

I also think that a person can suffer a depth of clinical depression so severe that s/he does indeed give up even trying to matter, and quits playing the game. S/he gives up on life too, in this instance. This is the type of depression where the sufferer takes to her bed, pulls the covers over her head and doesn't get out again. Or perhaps s/he plugs into the television, and permanently abdicates her own real-life in favor of a vicarious existence through the medium of the lives of characters in a virtual universe. Some types of mental illness have physical components that are not completely understood at this time.

Based on what I have seen in my practice, however, "I refuse to play" is generally a version of "Withdrawing," "Never Stick My Neck Out," or "Residing Safe in the Bosom of Self-Loathing." If you create the structures in your psyche that allow you to pretend you don't need to matter, what tends to happen is that you cut yourself off from the very things that make life worth living: connection, collaboration, and play, not to mention your basic primate evolutionary biology!

Section 5: Is Marble Conservation Necessary?

Jimmy's story

I want to call into question the very need for strategies that help you guard and hoard your marbles. An awful lot of people are spending an awful lot of energy on a practice that to my eyes looks as if it causes a good deal more harm than it prevents! At the beginning of the defense and conservation section, I asked the questions: Does asking someone out on a date actually put your value as a person at risk? If she says "no" does that mean you have lost a bit of your worth? Who says so? What if it was a marriage proposal? Does a marriage proposal put your very sense of self worth on the line?

Jimmy was in love with a girl (Ingrid) who was three years older that he was. Had he been 30, and she 33, this might have not made very much difference. But Jimmy was 21 and finishing up his junior year of college. Ingrid was 24, a young professional, veteran of the dot-com upheavals. They had begun as friends who met at the college gym, workout partners. But he was so cute, and they spent so much time together, that Ingrid's boyfriend got jealous and broke up with her. Soon they were dating, against what Ingrid thought was her better judgment. (She just "couldn't be taking a kid seriously, when she was such a grown up woman.") After a year of dating, Jimmy asked her to marry him in a fit of earnestness, and Ingrid thought it had gone too far. She couldn't marry this **kid**! This was just too much! So she broke up with him.

Was he broken? Was he personally invalidated? Had she upended his bowl of marbles? Nope.

What happened was this:

Jimmy said to Ingrid in a perfectly level and matter of fact tone of voice: "You are making a terrible mistake. I am the one for you. No one will ever love you as much as I do. And you are going to go out into the world now, and date a bunch a stupid guys who you are not going to like as much as me. They are not going to be as fun as me. And they are not going to understand you like I do. Meanwhile, what I am going to do is this: I am going to hang around periodically to remind you what you are missing, and so it stays fresh in your mind who you have to compare all your dates to. If I am wrong, so be it. I am going to be here until you marry someone else, or die of old age. But what I think is, eventually you are going to get bored and realize that you have made a mistake, and call me up so we can get back together."

That was exactly what happened. Jimmy's sense of self had not been invalidated. In fact, he kept every marble that Ingrid had ever given him right there in his bowl, even in the face of her rejection. He knew who he was. He was not a kid. He was a grown man, a hot commodity. Jimmy knew that he mattered so much that Ingrid was a fool to let him go. And he was right. She dated half a dozen guys over the next eleven months, missing Jimmy's presence in her life the entire time. He popped in now and again to take her to coffee or spot her on the weight machines, grinning with secret assuredness all the while, until Ingrid finally relented and asked to have him back. They were married a year later.

How did he do it? After she bestowed the dreaded "No. I do not want you." Why didn't he take his wounded carcass back to his cave to grieve? Or why didn't he lash out at Ingrid in an attempt to grab his marbles back? Jimmy behaved as if his bowl was brimming with marbles in the midst of the most externally invalidating moment of his life! <insert mysterious foreshadowing theme-music here> Could it be that he had discovered the secret to winning the game?

Section 6: Winning the Marble Game!

At some point in a course of therapy with me, just about everyone hears about The Marble Game. And after telling the story to a variable chorus of laughter, moans and wincing on the other side of the aisle, I always ask my clients towards the end, "What is the only way to win the game?"

I get various responses: "Hallelujah! You can win?" "You mean there's a way out?!" and "Don't play!" I must have a particularly intelligent crew though, because more than half of them eventually come up with some version of "Fill in the hole!" "**Brilliant!**" I shout, completely cognizant of the fact that "Brilliant!" marbles are some of the most valuable. ☺

How do you do that? How do you fill in the hole?

For the purposes of this allegorical model, the way that I say it is: "Grow your own bowling ball."

If you figure out how to grow your own bowling ball, the hole in the bottom of your bowl gets plugged with it, and now when someone hands you a marble, it stays in the bowl.

So how do you do that? What is a bowling ball made of in the real world, and how do you grow one? One of my therapy gurus Dr. David Schnarch would say, "learn to validate yourself", so you can stop depending on unreliable others to do it for you. (For more on self-validation, check out his revolutionary book, <u>Passionate Marriage</u> (6).) Another way of saying it in plain English is "figure out how to matter to yourself."

Check out this play on words: **Why you matter is the very matter from which your bowling ball is comprised!** <No wincing people!> But first you need a seed from which to germinate it.

The Seed

You can't begin to know that you matter and why, until you know what you actually are. If you don't know what you are, how could you know if you matter? So the seed you grow your bowling ball from is your knowledge about 1) who and what you really are, and 2) what you are here for in this lifetime, i.e. your calling. (I'll cover some practices for finding your seed in chapter 4.) We all ultimately come to all sorts of different answers to those two questions, but what everyone does next, with the information they discover, is the same.

Growing the seed into a ball

Living your life in alignment with what you really are is synonymous with the way I define "integrity"* in my practice. Living your life in alignment with what you really are, and why you are here in this existence, grows a bowling ball that is fat and healthy. The reason is very simple: The Marble Game is all about the frantic need of the self to find someone to prove to you that you matter. But putting yourself in the center of a path that is central to the very core of what you are, will mean in and of itself that you matter, **to you**. In contrast, when you are not true to the core of what you are, your bowling ball gets fragile and wobbly, sometimes allowing

---

My definition of "integrity" – Living one's life in accordance with one's own internal knowing; true to self and spirit and calling.

marbles to slip out the bottom of your bowl, sometimes disappearing altogether. Then, until you can figure out how to grow your bowling ball back, the internal drive to pursue external validation-marbles will begin again. Before you know it you'll be back in the game. You may already have noticed in your life that your need for external validation tends to skyrocket when you have made choices that violated your personal integrity.

Losing the ball

Temporarily losing your bowling ball isn't always a response to a breach of integrity, however. Sometimes regular life experiences can simply smack you so hard in the solar plexus of "I matter" that what looked like a perfectly healthy bowling ball crumbles before your eyes. I recently experienced just such a humility-engendering experience from a completely unexpected quarter. Normally, as you might imagine, given my work and intentional cultivation, I walk around the planet all relaxed and sassy, sporting a fat healthy bowling ball. But it only took a few weeks of my teen-age daughter going through a perfectly developmentally normal phase wherein I was invisible, and utterly irrelevant to her, to erode my bowling ball to the point that it popped like a soap bubble. Repeatedly receiving the message that I did not matter in the least to someone so beloved and close to my heart, had the power to make me burst into tears at the dinner table for the first time since I was a teenager myself.

Losing a job, losing your house, your partner having an affair, and any number of painfully invalidating, normal life experiences can have disastrous effects on your bowling ball. The good news is, once you have grown one, everything you need to grow it again is there, and people generally do. You still know what you are, and why you're here. All you have to do is live your life again in accordance with your integrity, even if it is difficult, and you'll have your ball back before you know it... unless you have one of life's periodic existential crises, that is, an experience which will require you to create new self-definition and reason for being. But, even in that case, if you grew it once, you can do it again. (I'll cover existential crises in chapter 5.)

Perhaps it is beginning to dawn on you that the only way to win the Marble Game is to realize that it is not a competition. It never was. On the scale of all existence, there has always been enough validation to go around, because everybody matters! ... unless you want to get into an existential conversation with me with the argument that no one matters. (I think there is a good intellectual argument that can be made about that, though anyone struggling to prove such a meaning-destroying world-view always looks to me as if s/he is playing a game of "chicken" with God, the Universe, or some other authority figure. In any case, the fear that actually nothing matters is my explanation for why there is a hole in the bottom of every bowl.) In the context of the worldview of those who play the marble game as if their lives depended on it, because of course they do, if one person matters, then every person matters. It is only the delusion that some people are not as important as other people that creates the illusion of scarcity that causes one to play the game like one has to beat everyone else to win!

A Ninety Pound Bowling Ball?!

As I have mentioned before, my crew of clients are the cleverest in the world <note the patter of marbles dropping like rain>, so periodically one of my geniuses will pop out with something like: "Hey, if I grow a big enough bowling ball, I won't ever need anything from anyone else ever again! I'll be like a superhero!" "Brilliant!" I cry.

I suppose it is theoretically possible to grow a bowling ball of such epic proportions that you could fill up your bowl entirely, and any marble that someone tried to give you for your bowl would bounce out on to the ground. But I have never met anyone so enlightened.

I actually have begun to suspect that the process of learning to keep your own bowl filled is a quest that is inherent to the human experience, and if you ever were to permanently and entirely fill it up, you might just transcend this mortal coil and float away! Life might become irrelevant to a person who utterly eclipsed all space for outside marbles with their bowling ball, because connection with other people might become inevitably ubiquitous.

Perhaps there have been beings on the planet who had bowls that full: Jesus, Mohamed, Siddhartha. Regarding the lives of each of those teachers, however, I note that their existence was all about giving authentic gifts outward to the people. They received little in return. Central to my understanding of the **human** experience, is that mutually beneficial relationships run on a pattern of energy being **exchanged**. If this were a book on spirituality, I might get into a conversation about the possibility that highly evolved psyches exchange energy with the divine. But while I am curious about that level of existence, I don't feel qualified yet to postulate hypotheses about it.

There is no shame in playing the game!

I would not want any reader to think, upon exploring the Marble Game metaphor, that the answer to peace and happiness in life is simply to will yourself to stop giving out marbles, or toss them away when people offer them to you. I have actually seen a few clients try that strategy, and it made them either angry and resentful of life itself, or plagued with alienation and meaninglessness. If you do not authentically figure out how to plug the hole in your bowl first, quitting the Marble Game cold turkey is the psychological equivalent of deciding not to eat anymore because there might be pesticide on all the food. Your psyche will feel as if you are starving to death of pointlessness, loneliness, and/or alienation.

Marbles are not bad for you, in and of themselves, anymore than a glass of wine with dinner is bad for you. (Most of you!) A glass of wine only becomes a problem if wine is the only thing that soothes the suffering inside of you, and your life becomes a single-minded quest to get the people around you to keep pouring wine in your glass (while they are simultaneously trying to get you to keep pouring wine in their glasses, while not using up too much of their own wine on you, to trick you into doing it!) Phew! (If wine or its equivalent, **is** a problem for you, hang in there until chapter 7. I will be addressing addictive behaviors then.)

Furthermore, exchanging marbles can feel great! I certainly would not want to live my life without them! We humans are small fuzzy creatures, biologically designed to want to matter to one another at a level so deep I think the need is rarely, if ever, re-programmable. Would you even want it reprogrammed? Not me.

Receiving Marbles from a Full Bowl

That said, I do want to mention that being given a marble from the bowl of someone who has plugged the hole with his or her own bowling ball can be a different experience from getting a marble from someone who unconsciously wants something back for it. Authentic gift marbles tend to feel more solid, and they have a sticky quality that allows them to roll to the bottom of the bowl more slowly. Another way of saying this is that people with full bowls feel more trustworthy than people with empty ones, because they have little reason to manipulate you. They are working no angles, no strategies to get more marbles back from you. Why do you think the marbles given by the great teachers of humanity were so powerfully healing and have had such staying power? You may say what you like about how humanity has been hurt by world religions (i.e. what humans ended up doing with the great teachings of the masters, in the interest of amassing great collections of marbles) but if you look at what the teachers actually said, they offered humanity some powerful healing marbles, for those who care to, to take into their bowls.

You may know people who are able to keep their bowls fairly full, at least some of the time. They tend to be people who feel good to be around. You may notice that when you are with them, you feel more relaxed and open. You may find you listen more closely when they speak to you, that the self-judging voice in your head pauses for a moment, and you want to trust what they are saying. They may even be able to help you find a seed to get your ball started growing, because they are able to see themselves and you so clearly, that they can reflect back to you things about your self that you may never have suspected, even though they are true to the core. There is no one in the world who can grow a bowling ball on behalf on someone else. However, individuals with full bowls can sometimes help people who never received the infant secure-attachment message that is fundamental to a healthy psyche to finally receive that message, thus assisting them as adults in the fundamental reprogramming of their own sense of mattering.

Before you think I am referring to a race of superheroes, and a club to which you could never belong, I want to give you some good news about yourself. You can do this too. It is even possible for someone whose bowl has habitually been empty to attain fullness in the present moment to connect with someone else in a healing way. That is part of the reason why fragile parents can sometimes raise psychologically healthy children. Babies can be so completely and wonderfully absorbing to their parents, that sometimes when gazing into a baby's eyes, parents forget absolutely everything they think they know about themselves, including the delusion that they don't matter, just to be in the present moment with the most wonderful creature in the world. It helps that babies are born with perfect mindfulness, because while the parent is looking down loving the baby, baby is looking back with the whole truth of babyhood: "Mom, Dad, there is nothing that matters to me as much as you." And for a moment, as long as the parents fall into the present moment and pay attention, fully formed bowling balls pop into their bowls. It is so patently obvious that they matter!

The work of Sue Johnson (5) has demonstrated that ordinary adults sometimes have the capacity to do this for each other too. I guess this is the paradox of the marble game. While you may not actually be able to heal someone with your love by growing a bowling ball for her, if s/he will cooperate with you, s/he may be able to get started on the process in the context of a relationship with you. I have also noticed that a loving partner can help you remember who you really are, making it easier to grow back a ball that has collapsed. Let me stress, I am not talking about the game of passing validation marbles back and forth. What I am talking about is consistent in-the-moment experiences of connection between two people who are gazing into each other's eyes with the simple message "you matter to me." The words themselves don't matter all that much. The power is in the moment of mutual appreciative connection.

Surrendering fully to the present moment temporarily drops you out of the Marble Game completely, and is one route people use both to search for their seed and to grow a bowling-ball-in-progress. Every moment you spend in the present moment instead of immersed in the game causes the game to lose a little bit of its hold on you. It looks as if that is why meditation and mindfulness practice are being found to be such powerful tools for rewiring brains that are prone to anxiety, depression, and anger. (7)

One more thing about the marbles that come out of a full bowl: When a person with an overflowing bowl gives another person a marble, there is a wonderful and startling magic that happens in the giving-person's hand. Though a marble was handed over, it somehow stays in the giving-hand too, splitting in two in a moment of transfiguration and alchemy. What I am saying is that it is as nourishing to give a marble from a bowl that is overflowing, as it is to receive a marble from such a bowl.

Perhaps that is the reason that the great teachers of humanity kept doing the work they were doing -- It fed them too...

Section 7: The Ones We Want

Why We Want the Ones We Want

By now you may have begun to watch yourself and other people play the game, and recognize your own preferred strategies, and the strategies of the people around you. Have you noticed that some marbles are more desirable than others, while there are others you would hardly bother to take the time to put in your bowl? And some marbles seem so rare and valuable that your craving for them takes on drug-addicted proportions.

The marbles we hunger for tend to be colored with a combination of what was most valued in the environment we were raised in (i.e. the behaviors that got the most praise), crossed with what we are most afraid we are not, and will never be. It is also common that if you come from a childhood environment that was heavily steeped in judgment, your most prized marbles are the ones that would have made you unassailable by judgment in your family system. So, among the following, what is your drug of choice?

1) "You are perfect!"

Also known as "you're the best" and "I've never met anyone like you", this variety of marble temporarily soothes a deep fear that one is flawed, broken, or a walking mistake just waiting to happen. And, because perfection, if you define "perfect" as "never making a mistake", is a standard no one can achieve, this variety of marble is particularly slippery and has a tendency to shoot out the bottom of a bowl like a rocket, almost as fast as it comes in! 'Perfect' is a preferred identity that is impossible to live up to.

2) You are going somewhere!

You are special! You have potential! Some of my most anxious clients live with the feeling that they are "the man behind the curtain"; a horrifying sense of inevitability that they will ultimately be exposed as ordinary, lazy, boring, or a disappointment. Hannah remembered that when she was a little girl, her mother would hold her on her lap and tell her over and over again; "When you grow up, you are going to be very rich and successful and have an important job. You are going to be beautiful and have lots of nice things." And that is exactly what happened. The problem was, Hannah always had the sense that she did not deserve the life she had made for herself, and that the rug could get ripped out from under her at any moment: Someone would decide she was doing a bad job, she would get old, her husband might leave her and take half her things. "You are special" was the marble she desperately wanted as proof that she mattered enough to stay safe from the exposure of the worthlessness she feared.

3) You are tough!

"Badass" "Nothing fazes you!" "You did that all by yourself!?" This variety is the one that temporarily soothes the fear that one is weak, vulnerable or open to attack. A preferred "tough" identity, and the validation to support it, often gets generated one of three ways: A) as a defense against real attacks in childhood, either physical or emotional; B) as a defense against the shame inflicted by caregivers, who could not tolerate expressions of vulnerable emotion in their kids, who would either praise a lack of emotional expression, or criticize and withdraw when vulnerability was expressed; C) as a defense against the culturally reinforced judgment that a kid with feelings is weak.

4) You're beautiful!

I have yet to hear a man come into my practice pining for physical-attractiveness marbles the way that many women do, though I do think there are of course men out there who are heavily identified with an identity around attractiveness. But a huge percentage of women of all ages, in my practice, still long to hear the magic words, "you're beautiful." And nothing seems to push women off their center faster than the intimation that they aren't. I think it is a testament to the truth of this that in our culture, maybe even in most cultures, beauty in a girl is still the thing that is most prized. Ugh. Spending your life's energy trying to maintain that particular identity is a losing game. No one can maintain it.

5) Poor you! "You are the good guy!" "It's not your fault!" Validation for a victim identity protects one who fears s/he is congenitally at fault from taking the blame for anything. Gretchen and I talked about what her mom got out of being a doormat for her father, a pattern she was repeating in her own relationship. This was the list of benefits that she came up with for "poor you" marbles: A) Long–suffering martyr whose efforts are never adequately appreciated (so her kids need to keep trying to validate her). B) Not responsible for her unhappy experience of her own life, or anything that goes wrong in it. C) Gets to be the "good-guy" counterpart to father's intimidating and controlling "bad-guy" role.

6) I choose you! - "Will you have coffee with me?" "Friend-request me on Facebook!" Oh this is a popular variety! After all "wanted" means you matter, right? At least to the person doing the wanting. Nothing feels quite so filling as the message that you're wanted, particularly to an individual who has never been quite sure of his or her own worth. Fredrick had been born to an unwed teen-age mom who had been forced to drop out of high-school because it was the early 60s, live with her grandparents, and work a service job part-time. Fredrick was convinced that he had ruined her life by being born. He had spent 50 years trying to make it up to her, in an effort to convince her that he had been worth the cost. In his private life, he had never had an intimate relationship longer than a couple of years. The way he put it was "The shine wears off so soon. As soon as he wants me in return, I can't remember why I liked him." Fred was hungry for the experience of feeling chosen because he felt so unworthy, especially if it was by a man who he had worked really hard to win, the harder the better. But as soon as the choosing was over, he would hunger for the experience again, almost immediately, because he couldn't hold on to the truth of his own worth. The marble fell right out the bottom of the bowl. He just needed to get chosen and again and again and again!

I think **the fattest, shiniest, marble of the Game**, and the most popular variety to the greatest number of players, falls into this general category. Try this one on for size: **"You are THE one I want."**

It is almost as if a lifetime of feeling as if you don't matter can be washed away, or an entire life of suffering redeemed, with one "Will you marry me?" (You are the one I want.) It happens that way in the movies, anyway. Not getting chosen in return can up-end a bowl of marbles permanently in the most fragile psyches, as if getting chosen was the last chance at happiness. 'You are the one I want' is powerful magic, and the fantasy surrounding getting chosen once is that if it lasts forever you will never be hungry for marbles again. We have a whole cultural mass-fantasy built around getting "saved" by love. Trouble is, even the powerful rush of getting 'chosen for life' slips out of the bowl eventually if you can't figure out how to keep it in there by choosing yourself. Then the sense of the beloved's betrayal is fierce. "She is not the woman I married!" "He doesn't meet my needs!" "She tricked me!" The cultural mythology is that "real" love is supposed to permanently fill your bowl for you; not until death do you get to stop industriously convincing me I matter.

Not choosing someone back, who has chosen you, can be utterly demoralizing to that person's sense-of-self, a wound that feels devastating. There is a common notion that the pain of not being chosen arises most commonly in the context of romantic relationships, but in my experience it happens in the context of family relationships just as often. In November and December, my practice is full of clients agonizing over how to manage the holidays yet again this year, because in some family systems not showing up for Thanksgiving is an unforgivable breech, a betrayal of the family unit itself. If my clients don't spend enough time with their families during the holidays, the social repercussions can be huge. Not continuing to give the family you came from the marbles that indicate that they come first, even after you have your own partner and children (plus your partner's family expectations) is unforgivable in some family systems.

7) "You are right!"

"Correct!" "Don't bet against Dad, he always wins!" "You're right" is the only marble that might be able to vie for the position of 'most popular marble' with "I choose you." It is almost as if, when we are found to have been right about something, then we are, for that moment, **the personal embodiment of right-ness!** Every mistake we have ever made becomes irrelevant for that instant. Being 'right' is the fierce and abiding hunger of those who were judged, shamed, or embarrassed for making mistakes as children, or perhaps even for just being beginners at something. When Daniel was six or seven, he and his older sister made a batch of muffins, but confused the salt tin with the sugar tin. They were awful! But to add trauma to embarrassment, their stepfather made them sit at the table and eat them one after another, in order to 'teach them to be more careful' until Daniel vomited. He had a string of stories like this one. The childhood lesson was very clear: Mistakes are very, very costly. As an adult, Daniel became the client who wanted to continue arguing with me about my own zip code, and wouldn't continue with the session until I went and got a piece of mail to show him that it had been successfully delivered to my address. People with a strong need for the "You are right" marble will tend to defend a position into idiocy rather than admit to fallibility, as if being caught in a mistake could cost their whole sense of self.

The desperate need to be right also has a tendency to bring with it a black/white world-view; i.e. there is an elusive "right path", and a fat field of "wrong path". And, if only I can figure out where the skinny line of the "right" path is, I can avoid making any mistakes, nothing bad will happen to me and I'll stay permanently validated! If I do stray off the 'right' path, and do make a mistake, then everything I champion about myself is at risk of being of being viewed as suspect.

Being "right" is equated with trustworthiness to such an extent in our culture that our leaders are labeled "flip-floppers" if they ever allow themselves to change a position based on new information. Many voters have the childlike demand that our leaders be prescient and omnipotent beings, who know how they will weigh in on a question even before they have the information to make an informed decision.

Basing an identity on being 'right,' destines the marble game player to a lifetime of looking like an idiot. You have only two choices in this arena: 1) Scramble around trying to backpedal, argue, intimidate or distract people, when you get caught being wrong or 2) Pretend you already know everything, cover your eyes and ears, and withdraw from the world so no contradictory information gets in. The only way out of the trap is to surrender to the truth that you are just a small mammal in a permanent state of learning, and changing your mind is appropriate, based on new information as it becomes available to you. Flexible is the preferred way to be!

Section 8: Kids and Pets

Pet Popularity

According to PetPlace.com, there are 163 million dogs and cats in America. That is more than twice the number of human children, which is less than 74 million. (8) Why do you suppose that is? While I think I could write a whole book about the subject (and there are probably people who actually have), one main reason has to be the consistent validating experience that pet-owners have in the context of their relationships with their pets. What does your dog do when you get home? With every fiber of their wiggly being, that creature says: "Welcome home!!! You are perfect! You are beautiful! I choose you! YOU ARE THE ONE I WANT!" What does it mean to you when your cat slips quietly up on your lap the minute you sit down, or singles you out in a room full of people? With a quieter voice, and with her unfakeable purr, she is saying the same thing.

Pets have no capacity for lying, and they do not play the Game. That makes them the most uniquely trustworthy marble-producers on the planet. All they ask from us is kindness, food, and exercise, and they will validate us regularly and without complaint all their lives long.

Is it possible to begin to repair the attachment injuries of childhood by having authentic, in-the-moment "you matter to me" exchanges with your pets? Can they help us heal broken hearts and fragile identities? My answer is: maybe! I certainly have had friends and clients say that they have been fundamentally helped with the sense that they matter through connection with a pet. And, there is good research on the long term mental health and even physical health benefits of pet ownership. I have one acquaintance who says that her first dog as an adult was the only mother she ever had, the first relationship in which she felt pure love, untainted by the marble game. She says it healed her, permanently.

In the World of a Child

Sometimes parents ask me, "Is it wrong to praise my child? Am I setting him up to be addicted to marbles!?" It is a question that is both fascinating and poignant to me, but I have to answer honestly that I don't really know the answer. I don't even know of a way to study the question, because I have never heard of a safe and loving family that did not try to shape child behavior with parental response. Even the most child-centered hippie parents who are determined not to 'quash child spirit', shape behavior with responses that are more and less positive, even when they don't know they are doing it. I am not sure humans can help that. Our kids read our faces, our energy. Should we help it if we could? I don't know. It sounds a little creepy, like we would all be robot parents.

So is praising a bad idea? Sometimes. There are books written championing that idea. (Check out Punished by Rewards (9), by Alfie Kohn) I have to admit I do wince on the playground when I overhear one of those enthusiastic well-meaning cheerleader parents exhorting "Good job! Good job!" every three seconds to a kid who is just doing regular kid stuff. (Good job for walking, Mom? Are you going to cheer my breathing too? My hair is growing even as we speak…) But I don't like the idea of having watched my daughter at the age of 6 twirling and twirling until her hair was wild and her cheeks were rosy, with me constrained from saying "You look like a fairy princess!" Or imagine my son bringing me a recording of one of his new compositions for the first time. Am I not supposed leak my pride and awe? One of the greatest joys of parenting is noticing how amazing our children are – how lucky we are to have them in our lives – and expressing that joy out loud.

In answer to the question, I would have you make a study of your own praising behavior. Are you praising as a way to get leverage with your kid in an effort to mold her into the daughter you want her to be? Are you mouthing positive affirmations in a sort of unconscious, pre-programmed and distracted way, to get your kid be satisfied, shove off, and stop bothering you? Are you over-compensating for your own emotionally impoverished upbringing, by making sure your kid knows that everything he does is the most wonderful, the most special, the best! Or do you cheerlead because you think that is what good parents are supposed to? Or because it seems to make your kid happy? If so, you might just see if over time you can train yourself to tone it down a little. Say, "I like how tidy our house looks when you put your shoes away," instead of "good job with the shoes!" And "no matter what you do, you will always be my special boy" instead of "you are so special!"

Just remember the elements that create a "you matter to me" moment. Perhaps when praise is delivered in the context of a moment of mutual present appreciative connection, it is nothing more or less than that. When my son looks up from his piano, or my daughter comes off the soccer field to find me standing there, my eyes shining with appreciation at his or her very existence, they each know what I am thinking even if I don't say it out loud. "Wow!!" So I just say it.

Chapter 1 Questions:

In the introduction of this book, I posed six questions that post-modern humans wrestle with on a regular basis. In this chapter I have offered you a lens through which to see yourself and other people, and begin to think about the answers to three of those questions:

1) Who am I and why am I so crazy?
2) Who is s/he and why is s/he driving me so crazy?
3) Why do I keep doing the crazy stuff I do… and then do it again and again!?

What do you know so far about your own answers? I am going to suggest you write your thoughts down, taking as much time and space as you need before going on to the next chapter. In fact, in my ideal universe you are dropping everything else right this minute, and heading out to get yourself a fat spiral notebook. There will be questions for you to answer at the end of every chapter, and writing down your thoughts will allow you not only to flesh them out, but track your rising self-understanding over time, as you make your way through the book.

If you find yourself struggling or confused with the previous questions, start by spending some time (hours, days, weeks, family holidays ☺) with the following questions instead. Don't forget that your marble-solicitation strategies are not about your character. You didn't even know until now that you were playing the game, and your strategies were programmed into you in childhood without your permission. If you don't like what you see in answer to these questions regarding how you play the game, studying your strategies with a patient, kind and discerning eye is the best way to begin to figure out another way of being. And remember that self-judgment is just another trick your psyche uses to try to make you perfect enough that you can collect more marbles!

1) What are your primary marble-solicitation and gathering strategies?
2) What are the primary strategies that other people use to try to get marbles out of you? (Your parents, your kids, your partner, your friends, your co-workers.)
3) What varieties of marbles do you long to receive, and from whom do you most want to receive the various different kinds?
4) What does your choice for the most addictive marbles mean about what you most fear about your self?
5) What varieties of marbles do the people in your life long to receive from you? When do you hand them over, and when do you withhold them, and why?
6) What are your preferred marble-conservation strategies? How are they working for you?

Again, I suggest you write your answers down. Writing has a way of flushing out insights that thinking alone does not unearth, because it engages different and more creative areas of the brain than thinking alone. It is also easy for your psyche to forget (or bury) truths that you discover, as you come awake to yourself, and go back to ancient, preprogrammed ways of being and seeing reality. Writing helps you wake up to yourself, and keep the ground you have gained! It is another path people use in the search to find the seed to grow a bowling ball. (See Chapter 4 for more ways.). If you get started writing and find out that it is a good path of self-exploration for you, I recommend the workbook <u>At a Journal Workshop</u> (10) by Ira Progoff, or <u>The Artists Way</u> (11) by Julia Cameron and Mark Bryan.

Chapter 2: Bypassing Your Tactics
Section 1: The Marble Defense Force

What happens when the best marble-gathering strategies that you have been able to devise don't work or stop working? Remember, if you are not able to keep the minimum requisite number of marbles in your bowl, it will feel as if you could die of it, or as if you are already a walking ghost, like you do not matter at all. What happens when, after half-a-lifespan of playing the **Marble Game,** you figure out that the game is rigged? And because you know nothing about plugging the hole in your bowl, you think here is no way to win? Having the experience that, despite your best efforts, you are losing the Game, feels intolerably frightening, defeating, or infuriating, depending on your psychological make-up. Frightening. Defeating. Infuriating. When faced with the core problem of trying to prove we matter, each of us is prone to one or more of these three tendencies: **Anxiety, Depression or Anger.** These same tendencies correspond with the reactions of the mammalian reticular alarm system: the automatic unconscious self-protection system that kicks in when an individual is at threat: Flight, Freeze, or Fight.

While there is certainly a small percentage of people in the human family who suffer from other diagnoses in the Diagnostic Statistical Manual of Mental Disorders, the majority of people who seek help from a mental health professional like me are suffering from one or more of the same three big problems. The **Big Three** are anxiety, depression, and/or an inability to manage anger appropriately. Some of my clients are saddled with an exhausting cocktail of all three. (Counseling for chemical dependency, and addictive behaviors should by rights of frequency, also be grouped with the Big Three, but in the interest of model-clarity, I have decided to address that issue separately in Chapter 7. Addiction has its own insidious role to play in the context of the Marble Game.)

The mainstream way of looking at the big three mental health problems is that they are diagnosable, discrete illnesses that can be treated with a variety of treatments (physical, behavioral, chemical, dietary, etc.) as if they were diseases of the body like diabetes or high blood pressure. And, as with the diseases of the body, treatments have been developed that have some efficacy helping people with anxiety and depression feel better, and assisting angry people in diverting or redirecting reactive responses before they occur. However, just as the traditional bent in the medical community has been treatment of the symptoms of diseases like diabetes (with insulin shots), and high blood pressure (with blood pressure medication), before looking at underlying causes to develop treatments that might prevent illness, the mainstream mental health community has had a bent towards treating the Big Three as if they are discrete stand-alone mind-diseases that need symptom-ameliorating techniques, rather than focusing primary attention and money on addressing root causes.

The majority of my mental-health colleagues treat the Big Three within the context of the medical community's traditional disease model, and the gold standard diagnostic text of my profession, The Diagnostic Statistical Manual of Mental Disorders (3), encourages that lens. However, when it comes to most people, I have come to view the top three mental health problems as simply one layer of the mind's long term **defense system**, just as the three tactics of the reticular alarm system (fight, flight or freeze) are **defense** tactics to protect the individual in a time of imminent threat.

Anxiety, depression and anger are **defensive coping tactics** for the same underlying intolerable human experience. This ongoing core problem is an experience so intolerable that there is not a person I know who would rather endure the feeling of it, than allow their primary defensive coping tactic (anxiety, depression or anger) to take over, in order not to have to experience the soul-eating feeling of:

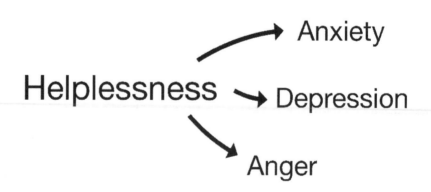

Helplessness (also known as "powerlessness"), in the face of a need that is all-encompassing, is so demoralizing that human beings will do anything not to feel it, and I do mean **anything** -- start a fight with a spouse, spend $60,000 on plastic surgery, get loaded, stay permanently loaded, read a child's diary, go home with a stranger, shake a baby, stop eating, build an arsenal of nuclear weapons that could destroy the world three times over, and/or kill themselves to keep from feeling it. The helplessness that human beings experience in the face of the biggest psychological imperative we have ("Find a way to matter!") even explains completely some of the most disturbing problems we witness on the planet. Only the determination of a desperately powerless self, that the only way to matter in this life is to strike a violent blow against an unimaginably powerful enemy, can adequately explain the phenomena of terrorism to me.

Anxiety, depression, and anger may hurt your heart, your body, your quality of life, and your family, but they are cake compared to the feeling that there is absolutely nothing you can do to influence or control a core experience that threatens your very self: powerlessness. So we slip into the coping tactic of choice, like slipping on a defensive suit, and allow the coping tactic to run our lives and dictate our choices. The coping tactics are a trap, of course; if you are spending all of your energy defending against the helplessness you feel by handing your authorship over to Anxiety, Depression and/or Anger, there is little creative energy left for growing a bowling ball, plugging the hole, and resolving your feeling of helplessness directly, so you can quit playing the Game for good.

Anyone can fall into the trap! Even me! While I appreciated none of the episodes at the time, I feel rather fortunate now, to have experienced each of the Big Three coping-tactic traps in my own life -- one major depressive episode at 15, one year of generalized anxiety (peppered with panic attacks) at 34, and several months of the opportunity to experience unprecedented of levels anger just a couple of years ago. I have even held the wish that death would make it all stop a few times when I was deeply anxious or depressed. At the time, the emotional pain felt as if it could actually **be** lethal. Now, however, I feel thankful for having been able to experience a few opportunities for feeling crazy, because I think they have assisted me mightily in my understanding of the underlying mechanisms of each of the **Big Three** from the inside, rather than by simply witnessing.

Anxiety

Anxiety is characterized by feelings of worry, restlessness, fatigue, irritability, muscular tension, difficulty sleeping, and spinning thoughts that make it difficult to focus or concentrate. I like to think of anxiety like this: Imagine that your brain is a frantic, well-meaning little hamster running on a wheel. The hamster believes that if s/he could just run fast enough, or well enough, or with enough efficiency, or get the other hamsters to run with him the way s/he wants them to run, s/he would finally get somewhere that would save his life.

Within a real brain that's talking at you, and oh, but do brains that are prone to anxiety talk to you a lot, the interior dialog would sound something like this:

(Picture the hamster.) "If only I could work harder, or faster, or keep hold of enough strings, or figure out how to be a better person, or get that person over there to change, or judge myself hard enough to quit making mistakes, or find the right path, or think about it hard enough long enough, I'd be ok. I just have to work harder at thinking." (Go back to the beginning and start the loop again.)

Anxiety traps you in your own brain, in a loop of your own thoughts, like a race-track you can't get off of. As Deborah, one of my clients, put it: "I just lie there in my bed, and I need to sleep, but my brain just keeps replaying that conversation I had with my husband over and over again as if by playing it enough times I can go back in time and make it go differently."

There are infinite themes for people's loops, but they tend to fall into 4 basic categories:

1) Replaying the past: "I want to be better! I need to figure out how not to make mistakes, so I better replay all the mistakes I ever made." Or "If I replay that disempowering incident over in my mind often enough, I will gain some power over it."
2) Role-playing the future: "I want to be better! I need to invent strategies for finding the right path, or staying on the right path, and then contingency-strategies in case of the failure of those strategies, and contingency-strategies for my contingency-strategies, in case my contingency-strategies fail, so I gain power over the unpredictable future." or "I just know disaster is approaching and I have to figure out how to avert it! (Go straight to making plans and contingency plans.)
3) Entrapment in an intolerable NOW: "I am trapped. I can't bear it. And there is no way out. I am trapped. I can't bear it. And there is no way out. I am trapped. I can't bear it. And there is no way out." <spin, spin, spin>
4) The only way I will keep myself alive is with my own thinking -- "If I stop paying attention every second to my own breath, I will stop breathing, and die." Or "If I stop thinking about my health and everything that could go wrong with it, a fatal condition will find me."

A mind that feels as if it is working on a problem, even if the work is 100% unproductive, even if the constructions of that mind exist entirely in the realm of fantasy, will not be present to its sense of helplessness. The brain cannot effectively think about two things at once. Even the best multi tasker has to flip back and forth between thought streams to keep them going. So anxiety thought-loops become a drug that temporarily puts the horrifying sense of helplessness to sleep.

On the subject of multi tasking and anxiety, I have to take a minute to say that when one's mind-space is being hogged by anxiety thought-loops, an individual's capacity for efficient mental functioning goes way down. Another way of saying that is this: "Anxiety makes you stupid." – at least it can make you seem stupid - to yourself and other people. Even beyond the phenomena of test-anxiety performance problems, and tongue-tied job interviews, just the day-to-day experience of having your mind spinning on thoughts that are irrelevant to day-to-day tasks causes forgetfulness, bad-driving, errors at work, temporarily forgetting important details like the names of your kids, etc. I have had numerous clients with school problems that turned out to be attributable to anxiety, not learning disabilities, or lack of intelligence. In addition, there have been two clients in the history of my practice who had been misdiagnosed and medicated for ADD. Turned out they were just anxious. It turns out anxiety makes it really, really difficult to pay attention!

I want to finish up the section on anxiety by talking about what can happen when an individual's spinning thoughts are the very thing s/he can not get hold of. When the flow of thoughts themselves, become the intolerable source of torture that an individual is helpless to stem, a trap that there is no way out of because it is in your own head, s/he will sometimes resort to the most disturbing tactics to "make it stop", like cutting or burning one's own skin, starving the self, and severe drug use.

While physically harming the self can seem horrifying to parents and teachers, cutting makes sense in the context of "wanting to make it all stop." Physical pain is so immediate. It drags one out of the mind and into the present moment with the body's own imperative: "Pain! Blood! Attention to the pain!" Cara was a teen 'cutter' who told me, "It happens when I feel powerless and horrible, like I don't have any power to help myself, and then I feel horrible and weak for feeling like that too, like I should be able to help myself. It's a trap I can't get out of! <Cutting> is the only thing that makes it stop. It makes me feel like nothing else matters for a minute. Like it actually helps me not to care about me or anything else."

Depression

Depression is characterized by feelings of sadness, irritability or frustration, even over small matters, loss of interest or pleasure in normal activities, insomnia or excessive sleeping, changes in appetite, trouble making decisions, fatigue, feelings of guilt or worthlessness, and/or thoughts of wanting to die. The way I think about it is this: Picture a bear that was captured as a cub, kept in a cage, hosed with water when it cried, and poked with sticks or periodically starved if it asked for help, or it was ignored for years at a time, or offered a meal only to have the food snatched away when it came over to try to take a bite, then left again all alone until it forgot how to run, or fight, and it's growl got rusty. That bear would eventually sink down to permanently collapse in a heap on the floor of its cage, cover it's nose with it's paws and just wish that death would come and make it all stop.

Depression's voice sounds like this: "I have tried and tried and tried absolutely everything I can think of to change my situation. If it is actually the case that there is nothing I can do to help or change or fix the pain of this loneliness (or entrapment, or sense of meaninglessness, or self-loathing, or feeling of worthlessness, or guilt, or physical pain etc.) then I am just **done**. And I am not just done with trying to fix this, I am done with life and God and all you people! I am going to get into my bed, pull the covers over my head and hold my breath 'til it's over." Alternatively: "I am just going to sit my butt on this

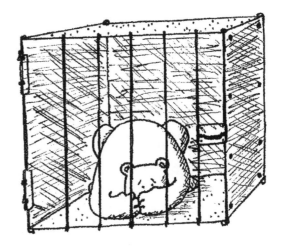

couch, plug into the television/internet, gain a bunch of weight, and attempt to drown my hopeless life in someone else's fantasy reality."

Depression scares me, as a practitioner, more than either anxiety or anger, because it is the ultimate abdication, the diametrical opposite of claiming authorship over one's life experience. With anxiety and anger there is a lot of energy there. Mostly, all I have to do, as a practitioner, is help a client redirect the energy to better uses. With depression, it is as if the sufferer's pilot light has gone out. From that person's point of view, the only thing s/he might think s/he has going for her is the capacity to never give a crap about anything ever again. "And, no one can make me!" It **is** a power, of a sort. And if that's all the power a person believes s/he ever could have in the face of intolerable helplessness, then the strategy of depression is self-re-enforcing. There is no way to force another human being to turn a face back towards life again. That person will eventually get sick of being the living dead, and come back to choose a different strategy, or s/he will just stay dead until the body goes too.

Anger

Anger, while not viewed in and of itself as a diagnosable disorder, has its own discrete segment of the mental-health treatment sector that has sprung up in order to treat "perpetrators" of violent abuse and anger management issues. A lot of the worst sufferers of uncontrollable anger end up in our prison system where they have little hope of ever getting a handle on their sense of powerlessness, and thus have little hope of ever sidestepping the trap of their anger to find peace with themselves and others. Volatile inmates often continue to act out violently when they are released, hurting or threatening someone, and ending up in prison again.

Picture a bull in the ring, encircled by a jeering crowd calling for his death, bleeding from one hundred cuts, head down and ready to charge. The voice of anger sounds like this: "What do you MEAN I am powerless!? I cannot possibly be powerless! I WILL KILL YOU IF YOU DON'T STOP!" As crazy as it sounds, every big person who ever smacked a little person in reactivity was feeling just that way. "How DARE you shove my own utterly ineffectual,

irrelevant self up in my face." Think about it, if 200 lb me is so utterly powerless in every arena of my life, that I can't even get 20 lb you to stop crying, or stop wetting the bed, or stop waking me up in the night, how fragile do I feel? The most emotionally fragile people in the population slide into violence when faced with their own horrible fear that that don't matter at all, and can do absolutely nothing about it.

While there is a often a sense in the culture that people should be able to "pull themselves up by their boot straps" to escape depression, or stop "doing it to themselves" to escape anxiety, of all the Big Three, the culture at large has the most unrealistic expectations regarding an individual's ability to 'snap out of it' when it comes to anger. People who are not able to staunch their reactivity are demonized and shamed, a response that tends to bring on an increased sense of powerlessness in the sufferer -- and resulting escalation of angry behavior. There is a strong, strong cultural fantasy that individuals should be able to keep themselves from getting angry and acting out by **force of will**. They can't.

There are members of my profession, and members of the public who will strenuously object to what I am saying, because angry reactivity and its periodic accompanying violence is just **"wrong"**. I am not saying it isn't wrong. I am simply saying that people prone to anger can't just stop their reactive behavior just because they should, or even just because they want to. The reticular alarm system* is hard-wired and people prone to violence were programmed as kids to shoot right down the "fight" side of "fight, flight or freeze" when they get to a certain level of threat. Unfortunately a human's gauge of threat-to-self doesn't stop at physical. Threat to sense-of-self can be an even more powerful stimulus to violent behavior.

Anyway, I am not saying that people prone to violent outbursts don't have a responsibility to do the internal work necessary to feel more like they inherently matter in the grand scheme of things, and thus make themselves less at risk for angry outbursts. They are responsible for doing that work. But shame-based therapies make helplessness worse, and a person prone to anger will not be able to keep from getting angry when s/he feels threatened and helpless, any more than a person prone to anxiety can will herself to stop thinking too much, or a person suffering from severe depression can force himself to look for a job.

Marble-Solicitation Strategies and the Big Three

You may find that you have dual coping-tactics, i.e. that you swing between depression and anxiety, or maybe you cope with depression for awhile and then periodically whoosh into anger. I had one client who told me, "Oh my God! I cycle through all of the **Big Three** every single day! I get up every morning full of crazy spinning thoughts about how to make this a better day, by lunchtime I am depressed as hell because none of it is working, and by the time I get home from work I am just pissed off with everybody! I do that every day!"

I would like to mention that I am aware that the examples I have chosen for anxiety, depression, and anger swing towards the intense. They may be so "out there" that you felt unable to identify with them. You certainly may not meet the criteria for any DSM diagnoses. But every one of us has a tendency towards one or more of the coping-tactics to avoid the feeling of helplessness. The way I would put it is people have "anxious tendencies" or "depressive tendencies", or a "tendency towards volatility." And people with different primary tendencies tend to be drawn to different marble-solicitation strategies.

Anxious people tend to choose more active gathering strategies: morphing, pursuing, nagging and caretaking for their marble solicitation, while people with depressive-tendencies tend to choose the more passive ones like withholding and suffering. Volatile people often choose intimidation, though I have seen a fair number of them swing between a number of other strategies and then eventually turn volatile only if they don't work. Withholding-intimidators can be particularly scary because they seem so unpredictable. (Of course, frightening unpredictability is part of the shtick.) Judging and guilting seem to be equal-opportunity marble-gathering strategies.

Getting out of the trap by bypassing your coping tactics

While handing control of your life over to anxiety, depression, or anger may be an unpleasant, yet partially-effective, tactic for temporarily managing the horrible helplessness that arises within you in response to losing The Marble Game, they are practically useless when it comes to addressing the real underlying horror of a low or empty bowl. In fact, allowing your hamster to waste time spinning it's wheel (making clumsy distracted choices, annoying the crap out of your friends, oblivious while your kids burn down the house), will tend to make your anxiety worse.

Allowing the bear to plug into the television (or the computer, or the refrigerator), hiding from the world until your spouse finally gives up trying to resurrect you, the kids finally stop coming to you to tell you their stories, and the phone might ring but it is never for you, will have a tendency to **increase** ones sense of worthlessness and irrelevancy, not improve it. Helplessness and the accompanying coping-tactic of depression will get worse.

Finally, as you may have noticed, if you let yourself be run by the bull, it can be hard to keep a good job. And you may be able to intimidate your family into not leaving you physically, but you can kiss goodbye any chance of ever having an authentic "you matter deeply to me" moment with one of them. Anger pushes people away and you eventually lose even your chance to feel like you matter to the ones you love, unless it is in a dramatic act of violent, negative impact like terrorism. "I will show you I am not irrelevant! I WILL KILL PEOPLE!"

Anxiety breeds more anxiety. Depression breeds more depression. And anger just breeds more triggers for violent reactivity. The coping tactics of the psyche are defensive **traps** within which you are digging the pit of your own unhappiness deeper and deeper, while your sense of identity grows more and more fragile, until there is nothing left in the bowl but shame and disappointment.

Section 2: The Bypass Your Tactics (BYT) Model

Bypass Your Tactics (BYT) is a model designed to help you bypass the three primary defensive tactics (Anxiety, Depression, Anger) by providing you with three alternate paths to take, paths into the bright, flexible world of conscious authorship. I always get a picture in my mind of prisoners-of-war when I think of this shift; coming out into the light from a solitary basement confinement, seeing the sun for the first time in years, eyes blinking and watering.

So how do you escape your particular trap? First you have to quit handing your life over to your coping tactic, and look past the anxiety, the depression and the anger to face the source of your pain directly, **your helplessness**. This process is not fun. Nobody likes to hang around self-reflecting on the cause of their powerlessness. While you are distracted with your hamster wheel, or hiding under the covers, or shouting at everyone else, though, you are never going to address the actual root problem.

So what is it? Are you paralyzed with loneliness? Do you feel so ugly that no one will ever choose you for a "you matter to me" relationship? Does guilt or shame from your past feel as if it paints you with unworthiness? Do you fear you are fundamentally lazy because you can't get yourself to DO anything? Or is it something more simple? "I can't leave this ugly relationship because I have 3 kids and no marketable skills." "My partner speaks to me in a tone of voice that implies that I am an imbecile, but I am too scared to stand up for myself." "I have been faking my orgasm for seven years and I will never be able to tell my husband now!"

Then **dig deeper**. Why can't you tell the truth? ("I am a caretaker who will fail in my job if I bruise my husband's ego?" "I will have to destroy my preferred identity that I am a Cosmo Sex Goddess?") Why can't you stand up for yourself? (Are you afraid that if you make a fuss he will abandon you? Are you afraid if he abandons you, you can't look after yourself?) What do you actually feel powerless in the face of? Are you going to die one day no matter how much insurance you buy, no matter how much you work out, or how many supplements you eat? I will have some questions at the end of the chapter to help you dig deep to find your core answers. This is not unlike an alcoholic finally admitting to being powerless in the face of alcohol. You must admit what the real problem is, and stop distracting yourself with secondary issues, before you can address what is really wrong. Only when you know what you are feeling helpless in the face of, can you bypass your coping-tactics and work on your experience of helplessness directly.

The first of the three bypass paths is:

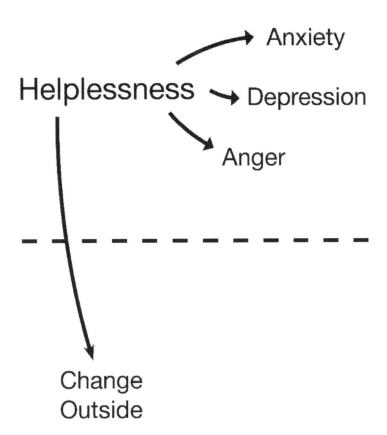

Change Something on the Outside of You

Ok. I need to admit right off the bat that this path annoys me. No, that's not right. It isn't the path itself that annoys me, it is the amount of weight that western individualist culture has put on this path as the only option for changing a dynamic in your life that isn't working for you. If your marriage looks wobbly, have a baby! If your husband is ignoring you, lose twenty pounds. If girls don't want to date you, buy a better car, make better investments, get another credit card, move to a better neighborhood! We live with a cultural mythology that if you are unhappy about something in your life, there is always something you can do on the outside that can change it. And if you are unhappy for any length of time, it must be because you are lazy or incompetent, because there is always something you can do in the physical world to change it, and you haven't done it!

It is a fallacy that there is always something material that you can change to make your problems go away, and if you just figure out what it is, you will be happy. This belief is one of the most tenacious and damaging false-paradigms people walk into my office with. It creates a sense in them that they are failures if they can't find the 'right' path, the thing they 'should' do. "I want a rule book!" said one young woman, "so I can know the right thing to do, so I don't regret it later!" There is no 'right' thing to do. There are just things to try to see if they help, and if they don't, try something else.

Ok, rant aside, sometimes (a small percentage of the time... humbug...) it is of course possible that changing something outside of you will wipe out your helplessness and your preferred helplessness-coping-tactic, all in one swoop. Sometimes, all you have to do, if you feel underappreciated at work, is quit and find a new job. Sometimes, as any number of young men can testify, you can get a new hair cut, let your sister take you shopping for jeans, learn to play the guitar and viola! The girls are all over you. And, right now the universities are full of laid-off workers getting new training to reenter the job market as more-desirable employees. Sometimes all you have to do is leave that son-of-a-bitch, ahem, sorry, I mean that person who suffers from an anger-oriented coping tactic, and everything is immediately better.

In my own practice, I do have a fairly sizable portion of my work that is dedicated to helping people figure out how to start their own businesses, divorce a partner with the least amount of collateral damage, lose weight, stop drinking, move into better living situations etc. The next chapter in this book will be a short one on some strategies you can try for changing material things outside yourself, that may help with your sense of powerlessness, and by extension, any anxiety, depression, or anger that is plaguing you.

But before we get to that, back to the **BYT** model! The next path you may be able to take to bypass your tactic is:

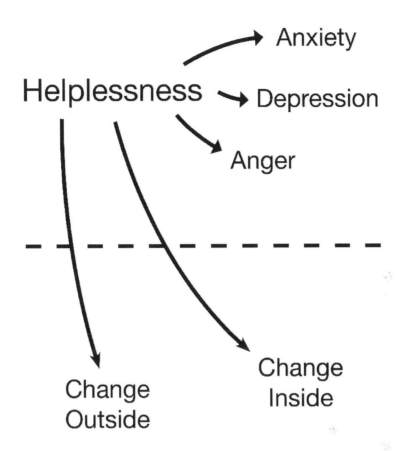

Change Something on the Inside of You

"We would rather be ruined than changed; we would rather die in our dread than climb the cross of the moment and let our illusions die." - W.H. Auden

Changing yourself on the inside is **hard**. This is not because the actual focus, labor, and practice involved in changing yourself is so hard. Internal re-programming is really no harder than learning many other practical new skills. It can take a couple of years. You feel clumsy and hopeless for a long time. "Ack! I am wasting my time!" Then one day it all comes together and you are riding on two wheels! No, change is hard is because you clutch the bowl of your identity and your marble-gathering strategies to your chest, and guard them like your life were literally at stake. Because of course it is. "Step away from the bowl!" your defense tactics say. "My whole identity is in that bowl of marbles, my whole self as I know me!"

Which of these thoughts sound familiar? You might like to make a check mark next to the ones that resonate with you. We all line up our defenses against change:

- "I am what I am. You can't change who you are!
- "Change is too hard. I will fail! And if I fail one more time in this life, I think I might just die of it."
- "If I change, how will I even know I am 'me' any more?"
- "My friends and family will be upset with me, or judge me, or humiliate me for going to therapy, or reading all these stupid self-help books if I change."
- "I'll be abandoned if I change."
- "I'll be attacked!"
- "If I let go of guarding the bowl, I will find out that everything bad in my life really was my fault all along!"
- "I'll end up being forced to be responsible for everyone else's feelings!"
- "I'll have to face that I **can't** be successful at keeping myself safe by being responsible for everyone else's feelings!"
- "If I change on my own, I will forever give up my chance of having all the pain I have suffered in my life be redeemed by someone else, and finally getting validated and loved and recognized for having suffered it. You want me to let all that go!??"
- "If it turns out that change was possible, and I could have been happy all this time, if only I had changed, all my suffering will have been for nothing. I'll find out I wasted my life."

Those certainly are a lot of really weighty reasons not to change. And **you don't have to**. Certainly no one can make you. But if you ever get so sick and exhausted from losing the Marble Game, or your sense of helplessness starts to feel as if it is going to choke you to death, or you yell at your precious baby or puppy one more time, perhaps you will decide you **want** to change.

There is tremendous, basically unlimited, potential for altering your experience of your own life through the path of internal change: from the fear-based identities, paradigms and strategies that reinforce your sense of helplessness and worthlessness, to new ones that put the power of authorship in your own hands, sometimes even in partnership with the divine creative force of the universe.

One of the most underappreciated internal shifts can be so transformational, and is so suppressed in western culture, that even though it is actually an example of "change something on the inside", I had to give it its own spot to round out the Bypass Your Tactic model:

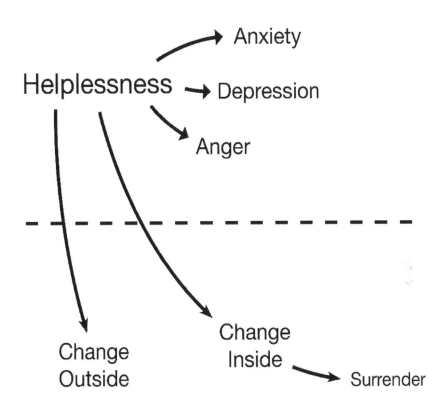

Surrender

When I was thirty-one, I experienced some difficult, though short-lived, circumstances that triggered in me a profound sense of helplessness, thus sending me through my first bout with measurable anxiety symptoms. At the height of my discomfort, a beloved friend bestowed upon me the small gift of a fridge magnet that sported a few words that made me literally shriek with resistance. The magnet said, "Sometimes, there was nothing she could do about it." Argh!!

To a caretaker with anxious tendencies, the intimation that it could be true that sometimes there really isn't anything one can "do about it" is anathema. It meant that my best marble-gathering and best marble-conservation strategies were useless in that moment. **And** my best frantic-hamster thought-loops would bring no relief from the sense of powerlessness I was experiencing. In that moment I simply could not bear the idea that there was nothing I could do about it, even though there was a part of me that knew it was true. I studied the magnet periodically for years, pondering its effect on me, until finally I was able to take the message in and incorporate it into my path to freedom in my life and practice.

Sometimes, there **is** nothing you can do about it. This is a very counter-culture idea. We Americans receive tremendous pressure not to "give up". If you give up, you are "lazy," or a "quitter"-- the cardinal sins of our individualistic pioneer-fantasy-obsessed world-view. When there is actually nothing you can do about it, the only way out is surrender. In fact surrender can be such a powerful choice, wiping away the intolerable experience of helplessness so thoroughly, that it is not only a way out, it can be a way through to a whole new view of yourself and reality.

So what does the voice of **Surrender** sound like?

"Oh. Well, if this is really the way it is going to be no matter what I do, what else can I focus my attention on, so I am no longer obsessing about my impossible challenge at the exclusion of everything else available to me for the rest of my life?" Or even, "If I really am going to be facing this reality for good, how can I use it to my advantage?" I imagine that to some readers a surrendered-shift that goes that far might sound a bit airy-fairy-Pollyanna. However, I have seen it happen. My favorite documentary of all time is called Murder Ball (2006), a movie about the 2004 American Paralympics Wheel-chair Rugby Team. (Good movie!!) Don't even think about trying to mess with the identities of any of those badass athletes by doubting that they would not "go back to normal" even if they could. Also, think about all of the transformative souls down through history who have taken a terrible misfortune and turned it into a career, or the strength to head a movement for social change. Senseless struggle is a terrible waster of human potential. Surrender and keep going!

Just a few years ago, a few other members and I were trapped in a hellish, harassing homeowners-association situation, the kind they make horror movies out of. After three years of trying (basically, from day one) to leave, I was finally able to sell my house and get out. It required a willingness to surrender to the loss of a good portion of my equity, but escape from my intolerably helplessness-engendering situation, I did! (Best money I ever spent, by the way.) Some of my dear neighbors who had also been the butt of punctured tires, up-ended trash containers, and dog feces left in very awkward locations, stayed. They didn't even try to leave. At the time, I couldn't believe it. I wanted my friends to escape with me. None of them did. Sufficiently surrendered to the situation to remain fairly peacefully within the situation, they stayed. To be fair I had the financial flexibility and sufficient faith in my future earnings that I felt I **could** pay the price to go, authentically surrendered to the financial loss rather than the living situation. People surrender only when they absolutely have to -- when, based on being true to themselves there really is no other choice to make. That is why authentic surrender to intolerable helplessness is usually the last option anyone will take.

Surrender is NOT the same thing as taking up depression as a coping tactic against helplessness!

When I initially share this model with my clients, Surrender can come off to some people as if it is the same thing as taking the path to depression. After all, "surrender" sounds a lot like "give up" and "I quit." One gets a mental picture of a fortress just recklessly opening its portal to the blood-thirsty hoards. I want to offer, however, that the act of authentic surrender is actually the very opposite of a depressive "giving up". Depression speaks in finalized statements like "I am done." "If I can't get (fill in the blank with intolerable thing) outside of me, to change, I am never caring about anything again."

The voice of Surrender speaks in questions, the language of possibility: "What next?" "Who am I now?" "What else changes when I let this go?" Surrender is the perspective of the self, shifting into a whole new field of probabilities. The individual's identity-bowl is suddenly pure-white, for a moment, full of the bowling ball of the divine creative-force of life itself.

I just noticed that when I write about "Surrender", I tend to capitalize the word, almost as if it is a living being -- a spirit that comes in to imbue the sufferer with aliveness and authorship. I do feel that way about it. I have seen authentic surrender shift a person's hellish experience of life to peace or excitement, literally in an instant. I will tell stories of powerful surrendering-alchemy in chapter 6.

Chapter 2 Questions:

I developed the **Bypass Your Tactic** model as another tool to help you begin to answer the questions:

> 1) Why am I so crazy?
>
> 2) Why is s/he driving me so crazy?
>
> 3) Why do I keep doing the crazy stuff I do... and then do it again and again!?

Now it is time to get out pen and paper again and write down what you are figuring out about that. Here are more questions to help you see yourself more clearly:

1) Which coping-tactic trap is your psyche's unconscious pick in the drive to avoid the experience of helplessness: Anxiety, Depression, and/or Anger?
2) What experiences, people, or dynamics in your life do you feel paralyzingly helpless in the face of?

Dig Deeper Regarding Each Separate Instance

Are you paralyzed with loneliness? Do you feel so ugly that no one will ever choose you? Does guilt or shame from your past feel as if it paints you with unworthiness? Do you fear that you are fundamentally lazy? Or, is it more simple than that? What dynamics in your life make your stomach turn when you contemplate them? Or cause your brain to slide right by, refusing to study them?

3) What specifically about your particular dynamic, experience or person is so intolerable?

4) What about it is so intolerable?

5) What does your powerlessness in the face of the answer to #3 or #4 mean about you?

6) How has your favorite of the helplessness-coping-tactics served you until now? Are you feeling any less helpless in the face of whatever experience feels so intolerable through your experience of your coping strategy?

7) How has your coping strategy made your helplessness worse?

8) How have your coping tactics affected those at home, or at work?

The rest of this book is designed to illustrate how bypassing your trap can be achieved through using one or more of the alternate roads offered by the BYT model. I will also be offering possible answers to two more of the questions posed in the intro: In the face of all of my flaws how do I become the person I want to be? And "How do I get that other person over there to be who I want him/her to be, and do what I want her/him to do?

Chapter 3 will offer some options and ways of thinking about changing things outside yourself in the material world, towards the end of addressing your helplessness. Chapter 4 begins to explore how it is that you can improve just about every painful experience you think you are stuck with in order to be the author of your own journey through a life full of peace, joy, and a sense of adventure. Remember I said earlier that I would explore strategies for finding the seed to grow your bowling ball? That's in Chapter 4. Chapter 5 expands the concept of Surrender. And in chapter 6, I will explore addiction and how it relates both to The Marble Game and the (BYT) model.

I challenge you. Begin to plot the hamster's escape. Start looking for a blowtorch for that bear cub. Get ready to grow wings for your bull.

Chapter 3: Changing Outside

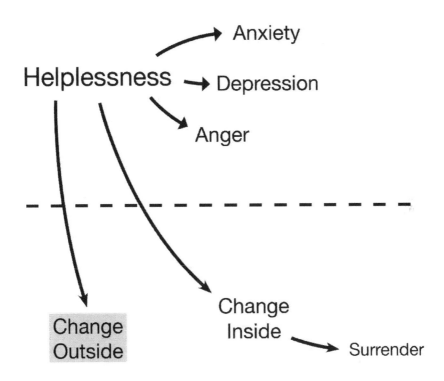

Section 1: Some Words About Paradox

80% of new clients come in to my office saying that they are looking for "tools", as in "All we need is a few tools to help with our communication." I am always tempted to reply, "Then you better go to Home Depot!" But I don't say that! Instead I say "I've got tools!" and as you will see, I do indeed have a lot of really great "tools." But unless you skipped forward in the book directly to this section, you will already know that I am pretty suspicious of the cultural tendency towards focusing all our attention on making alterations in the material world outside the self as the best course for improving how you feel about yourself and your life. We already live in a societal soup skewed towards using "tools" for "fixing" and "doing" as the only paths to change, so I feel reluctant to go along with the guilt-inducing belief that "doing life well enough", or "doing enough of the right stuff" will make you happy. Furthermore, there are countless books already published on how to change yourself, change your relationships, and change your fortune by **doing** things. You can learn to save money, start a business, have a make-over, lose weight, be your own contractor, try 1001 ways to be romantic, communicate non-violently, discipline your kids, be a skillful lover, and write your own best-seller ☺. Do, do, do, do, do.

It isn't that those books aren't useful. I have bought dozens of them. Gardening, knitting and canning are great strategies for putting my head-hamster to rest. (Tasty and fuzzy too!) I have learned to do all kinds of wonderful things out of books. It is just that getting trapped on the doing-wagon can be indistinguishable from driving down the shoulder of Anxiety's road. And, if all that 'doing' doesn't end up helping you feel better, or fixing your problems, there's a good chance you're going to end up trying to avoid the resulting powerlessness you feel by trapping yourself in a feedback loop with one or more of the Big Three coping tactics from the last chapter.

Ok. That said (again), of course there are things you can do that have been demonstrated to sometimes help people who struggle with the symptoms of anxiety, depression, and anger. Oftentimes, the way I think of the tool of "doing" is that it can be the medicine that helps weaken the symptoms of anxiety, depression, or anger, so you can generate more time, space, and energy to address the underlying problem of helplessness directly.

There are even actual physical practices that may assist you **directly** in the process of shifting who you are on the inside. Yoga, meditation, and journaling come to mind. Meditative pursuits have been found to be an effective way of addressing issues of anxiety, depression and anger. I will be discussing them as a group at the end of this chapter, these paths that humans have been developing for thousands of years in the quest to help the "doing" human mind shift out of the "land of doing," into the land of authentic being and meaning making.

I will make you a deal. If you make a concerted effort to employ firm but loving self-talk to rein in the fixing-addicted hamster that lives in your head, I will fill this chapter with useful doing-information. The whole rest of the book will also be peppered with doing suggestions, all interspersed amongst hints about shifting your being! In fact much of the rest of this book will be all about marrying shifts in doing **and** being in such a way as to maximize your ability to slip right past your own coping-tactic traps.

The Grand Paradox of Human Behavior

One of the cardinal rules of my field (Applied Behavioral Science) is that **"the strategies people adopt to help or fix a problem usually create the problem or make the problem worse."** In chapters one and two I gave many examples that demonstrate the premise that we humans are masters of coming up with strategies to address our experience of powerlessness that should work, but don't. Marble-gathering strategies, marble-conserving strategies, and helplessness-coping-tactics -- all these are strategies of the psyche that make the very problem they are designed to address worse, not better. And, we humans get stuck to our problem-solving strategies as if they were pieces of our own flesh. "This plan seems as if it should work!" we think. "I can't understand why it wouldn't work." Or perhaps, "It worked in the beginning, so it should keep working!" Also, I think our stubbornness regarding the plans we develop for addressing our problems comes from a hunger for one of the most popular of validation-marbles, the one called "being right." "No really!" we say again and again, and for a lifetime. "This really should work!"

Be suspicious of your old strategies. Be suspicious of these new strategies as well. Almost any "doing" strategy can go wrong and become a trap, in and of itself, if it is taken too far. If what you have been employing to fix a problem doesn't seem to help, stop. Change course. Remember that the hamster likes to feel as if it is doing **something** to prove that you are not helpless, even if the thing it is doing is a complete waste of time. The hamster is addicted to doing stuff in the attempt to influence, manipulate, and control the material world outside the self. It doesn't care as much about making progress as it does about keeping the hamster-wheel whirling.

Section 2: 'Tools' That Can Soothe All Three

Look after your physical body with: Exercise

Use up some of that hamster's energy by giving your body **real exercise**. Get your bear up off the couch and outside in the sunshine. Make your bull run off some of that adrenaline before you interface with the irritating rest of human kind. There is nothing like exercise to soothe anxiety, lighten depression, and take the edge off of an ugly temper. Seriously, if you have an anger problem, you need to raise your heart rate for at least a half-hour six days a week.

I just want to say right here that I have bias in favor of getting outside (in all weather, so get the proper gear!) to move around. I think we need to breathe un-recycled air, get the vitamin D, and be with trees, dogs and neighbors. Ok, I had to say it. But go to the gym if you are stubborn! Regular exercise has been found to be more effective than talk therapy or medication for improving people's subjective experience of their own lives! (12) It works both on the physical level (chemistry of the brain and metabolism), and on the emotional level (how badass you feel when you get out there every day). It is even an effective marble-gathering strategy, as you pass all the people who gaze at your fortitude admiringly, and fellow-exercisers who give you the secret signal of the regular exerciser club. Want to know what that is? You had better start working out! Ok, I am going to go all woo-woo on you here and say that I think it also works on the vibrational/energetic level. That's all I'll say about that because I don't want to freak all the scientific secular humanists out. Move your body, people! If you do, you might not even need to read the rest of this book!

I am fully aware that 76% of all you "tendency towards depression" people are likely feeling as if I am poking you in the eye with a stick right now, over and over. Hm… even starting small, is starting. I once had a client who began her quest to move her body by walking around one block every day after dinner. It helped.

Look after your physical body with: Food

Eat regular, nourishing food that comes out of the ground rather than out of a package. Keep your blood sugar level. Depressed people often eat sugar for comfort, crashing their blood sugar on a regular basis. Having regular low blood sugar, plus the weight issues brought on by eating lots of sugar, plus a tendency towards depressive coping-tactics equals one unhappy bear.

Anxious people can have a bad habit of not eating. I know this from personal experience. And, when you don't eat, your body starts to produce lots of stress hormones. Keep messing with huge swings of blood sugar long enough, and your body will start to give you a big surge of adrenaline every time your blood sugar gets low. Voila! Instant panic attack! I recommend that people prone to anxiety eat little snacks all day long (not sugary), and end the day with a small boiled egg or a handful of almonds before bed to sustain their blood sugar through the night. Don't even think about skipping breakfast if you have anxiety. Anger is a closer cousin to anxiety than either sufferer knows, so everything I just said about anxiety holds true for anger. If you struggle with anger, never try to parent your kids if you are hungry or too tired. Never let your kids get too hungry or tired either. Hungry, tired you, with hungry, tired kids, is an explosive combination.

Look after your physical body with: Sleep

Speaking of tired, even-out your sleep patterns. Most people need at least seven hours of sleep a night, preferably eight, to generate the energy needed to positively impact any of the **Big Three**. Do you struggle with sleep? Are you one of those people who can not stop checking Twitter or Facebook all day long and into the night? I had one client, Brenda, who was whacky with lack of sleep and frantic with addictive media-checking patterns. It was an absolutely crazy-making combination that was escalating her run-of-the-mill tendency towards anxiety into a full-blown panic disorder. All she needed to help her quit the habit was to start going to bed at 11:00 every night. She had been staying up half the night online! Four or five hours of sleep a night was sending her off the deep end! (That is not enough sleep, people!) She wasn't crazy, she was just too exhausted to make her hamster go to bed!

If you are anxious or angry, lower your **coffee** intake. No more than two shots a day, preferably in the morning. The systems of anxious and angry people are already revved up too high. Caffeine can make that worse.

If you are depressed, drink more coffee. That was a joke! I'm only kidding!!

Look after your physical body with: Touch

Get massage, acupuncture or reiki. Humans need physical **touch**. Babies who don't get enough are likely to just up and die. Adults can slowly starve to death without it too, it is just that we pin other names to the resulting health problems. Loneliness is a greater predictor of death than obesity or smoking. (13) Massage can help an intimidator begin to tolerate the healing proximity of another being without the stress of needing to talk to that person, see them looking at you, or having to look in their eyes.

Look after your physical body with: Getting a complete physical work-up

Have a comprehensive physical that includes blood work from a qualified and friendly doctor, nurse practitioner, or naturopath. Sometimes anxiety just turns out to be hyperthyroid disorder, or the dragging weight of depression is actually celiac disease, or a low-grade infection, or, in the case of one of my clients, colon cancer. Feeling emotionally bad is not uncommon if your body is exhausted from fighting an invisible mystery illness. (Oh dear. There go all the hamsters of the hypochondriac people!) Just get a physical, ok?

Look after your physical body with: Medication

I am of the opinion that many of the people who are currently on medication to treat regular run-of-the-mill depression, anxiety, and anger could get off of it from within a few weeks to a couple of years, if they took up the healthy habits above. (Oh dear, I think a half a dozen executives in the drug industry just picked up their phones to call in a hit on my life!) That was **not** me saying that I think **you** or anyone else 'should' get off their medication. Whether or not you are on medication is none of my business, and I don't have an attachment either way. I just think that if your issue is anxiety, depression or anger-related, then if you wanted to, and you were willing to take a couple of years to rewire your brain, then with focus, commitment, and clear intention (and collaboration with appropriate medical professionals), there is a good chance you could. (If you are diagnosed bipolar, or with any diagnoses that puts you at risk for psychoses or suicide, don't even think about stopping your meds, ok?) I just don't like the idea of people who could live and thrive without medication believing that they have a disease that will require a physician's care and chemical management for the rest of their lives, if that is not indeed that case.

Let me tell you the story of April, age 41. April's mother was on anti-depressants, her brother was on anti-depressants, and April was on anti-depressants, all of them to combat the symptoms of both anxiety and depression. When April was 17, and suffering some normal adolescent anxiety regarding where she should go to college and what she should be when she grew up, her mom told her about a wonderful new drug called Prozac. "Everyone should be on it! It makes you feel wonderful! And it has no side effects!" April's mom's doctor wrote a prescription for April and by the time I met her, she had been on one kind of serotonin reuptake inhibitor or another for 24 years. April had never really questioned the need for them, though she suffered from many of the side effects they can have, like a sense of insubstantiality, weight-gain and low sex drive. Furthermore, she was still depressed. Even though she had been on SSRIs all of her adult life, April still felt guilty and sluggish most of the time, and periodically she would have flare-ups of depression so paralyzing that she could barely force herself to answer the phone, get the mail, walk the dog etc. After she read an article on the side effects of anti-depressants, April and her doctor asked me to keep a weekly eye on her while she slowly weaned herself off of them. (If you want to try to come off of psych meds, it is usually important to come off very gradually. Talk to your doctor about it first.)

Over the course of several weeks April cut her medication in half and in half again and in half again until she stopped altogether; while I counseled her to increase her exercise and regulate her sleep-patterns better. She felt no change, psychologically except maybe a sense of victory that she was finally "facing her life" and "getting to know herself off medication" for the first time since she was a kid. Then over the next year, I worked with April on the project of growing her own bowling ball.

Now April is reasonably content, with periodic swells of happiness, and the occasional, usually short, dips into the pool of her nemesis, guilt. Best of all, she is enjoying the physical relationship she has with her husband better than she has since the first year they were married, twenty years ago. April is not the only client in my practice with a story like this.

By this time, I have probably given you the impression that I sit firmly in the anti-medication camp. I don't. While I generally prefer to see if any of the other options can have an effect first, I end up referring people for med evaluations several times a year. Medication can give a person who needs it just enough breathing room to get over the hump, so they can start the work of rewiring their brain to bypass their trap on the way to addressing the source of their helplessness directly. And I speak from experience when I tell you that sometimes, anxiety or depression hurts so much that the person suffering it feels like s/he literally could die on the spot, or would want to. I feel extremely thankful to the modern science of chemistry that rescue medication exists for times like that. And medication can be as much of a psychological comfort as a physical one. For a few of my clients, just knowing that they have a rescue medication in the cupboard can help them comfort them enough to avert a panic.

Create a basic organizational system for your money, stuff, and time

Saying "get organized" is kind of ironic given the passage in Chapter 1 on how too much organization can steal your whole life away from you. Notice an overarching theme of this book though, that many beneficial practices which can be wonderful for helping a person be psychologically healthier, when taken too far, become a destructive force: eating, exercise (which can be abused as a form of 'moving'), sleeping, recreating, 'processing' with your partner, even self-reflecting... (maybe even especially self-reflecting!) The mind has an unfortunate tendency to think that if something helps you feel better, even more of it is going to help you feel even more better.

A bit of organization is a wonderful thing. It can ease the "doing it right" thought loops of a hamster, help a bear feel less overwhelmed, and soothe some of the bull's irritation with the universe. How much is the right amount of organization is very subjective, however. You'll have to experiment. And if you are feeling utterly undone by contemplating your undone errands or growing piles, offer to trade eight hours of logistical and moral support with a friend or neighbor who is suffering from the same problem. You would be amazed at the dent that two people working all day, even while talking and snacking, can make. (If you actually want to accomplish anything though, turn the TV off.)

Give your brain other creative and constructive things to do

Your brain is the most marvelous, sophisticated, subtle and awe-inspiring structure that exists in the physical world. You are so lucky to be here and so lucky to have it. It is a tool designed to solve problems that could make a computer cry and design things a computer could never understand or appreciate. I hope you will take a moment to love your brain. But, also know this: like an unexercised Australian shepherd puppy, your brain will chew up your identity, your worth, your world, and maybe even the people you love the most, if you don't give it constructive work to do. If you don't give it work, the best you can hope for is that it will eventually give up and go to sleep when it has been beaten up and shamed enough for not sitting still. Brains are built for building and exploring.

"So what am I supposed to be building?" you say. I have no idea! However, we will cover finding your own core-truth and sense of purpose in the next chapter. In the meantime, if your brain needs stuff to do, buy a bunch of self-help books, or books on how to learn to do stuff that you want to do. Take classes. Remember what you loved to do when you were a kid and do the adult version of that. Learn to knit or fix your own car, or figure out how your family could survive on one full time, or two part-time jobs while your kids are little. Build something, design something, or design something to build. Make art. Journal! It sort of doesn't matter what it is. Creating material things, and giving birth to clever thoughts and works in the material world can tire out your wonderful brain, and might even be enough to convince your hamster, bear, or bull that you might not be so irrelevant after all. In fact, you matter!

Learn to tolerate your own company

"Ack! I can't stand to be alone!" some of you are thinking. For some of you, the discomfort of being alone stems from the fear that if you are alone ("uninvited," "not out there having fun," "not holding the hand of an adoring lover" etc) it really does mean that you don't matter. For others it is the terror of being left alone with the Australian Shepherd of your mind, which might rip you to shreds if are left alone with it. If you cannot tolerate the feelings that come up when you are alone with yourself, I don't know that there is any way that you are going to be able to do the work necessary to make the shifts on the inside of you that you need, grow a bowling ball and stop the suffering. Self-reflection is a must, and to self-reflect, you need quiet, solitary space to reflect on the interior world of you. Some of you may feel as if I have given you an impossible task, but you can do it… just a little bit at a time, just like the desensitization therapy for any phobia. We can almost always eventually face overwhelming psychological discomfort if we take baby steps, learning to tolerate our horror, piece by tiny piece. I believe in you. Note that just by reading this book, you are on the road to self-reflection!

Section 3: Special 'Tools' That Can Help Anxiety

Anxiety's Vaccine

Here is something that your busy mind can do when you notice it is trying to chew you up with anxious thought loops. Just have it repeat the word-vaccine to counter anxiety: **"I am enough."** You can repeat it over and over when you feel overwhelmed, or randomly throughout the day. Certainly whip it out immediately every time you hear your internal judging voice trying to make you feel bad about yourself. When that voice says something horrible to you, just reply: "I am enough!" Or "I am enough, just as I am." Out loud is best, though it might earn you some odd looks on the bus.

Don't like my vaccine? Make up one for yourself that really resonates with you!

Make yourself harder to reach!

The simplest technique I have offered anxious clients that seems to have helped the greatest number of people is to make themselves less accessible to the world in general. I am advising that you try placing more barriers between you and interlopers on your privacy, and energy vampires on your time, energy, and attention. I guess I should have said that this trick is **logistically** simplest. Emotionally, and psychologically it isn't simple at all. To do it, you have to bypass the faulty paradigm in your psyche that you exist to validate others, and the fear that if you quit doing that 24/7 you will be permanently abandoned. Making yourself less accessible includes ideas like: A) turn off your cell phone so you can return just the calls of the people you want to talk to, when it is convenient to you, B) check your texts and email only once or twice a day, C) say "no" to at least 50% of the people who ask you to do something for them (and ignore the ones who hint). Then, when you learn to manage your anxiety around your community's responses to these small changes fairly reliably, it is probably time to **'weed your friendship garden'** (Thank you Camille Bloom for the concept).

Weed Your Friendship Garden!

Who contributes to you? Who sees and supports your best self? Who gently calls you on your most self-damaging anti-anxiety strategies? Who generates a fair share of contact with you, not leaving the friendship-maintenance responsibility entirely in your court? These are your **friends**.

Who uses you and gives back nothing but more marble-solicitation marbles? When you feel irritable or tired after getting off the phone who was the person you were just talking to? Whose conversation is a constant stream of complaints, criticism and judgment regarding you, or other people in their lives? These are your time-sucking parasites. Oh dear. Did I say that out loud? What I meant to say is, unless they are actually physically starving, these are the people in your life who are desperately trying to get you to keep them feeling like they matter with a steady supply of marbles. Perhaps you could give them a copy of my book as a going away present. ☺ Weed them out. It is like pulling off a band-aid. It only hurts for a minute! I have seen terrified clients weed their friendship gardens one after another, feeling as if they were going to be wearing the brand of "BAD FRIEND" for life, or just simply be alone for the duration. It might be scary to do, but I have never seen the result be more painful than what was going on prior.

Ayurveda

Learn about the ancient Indian practice of Ayurveda, which works to balance the three opposing energies in the body with all kinds of interesting practices. The three types of ayurvedic energies correspond remarkably well with the Big Three coping tactics. Vata (Air/spirit energy) people have a tendency towards anxiety. Kaffa (Earth/Water energy) people have a tendency towards depression, and Pitta (Fire energy) people have tendency towards volatility. Explore fun Ayurvedic practices for grounding 'Vata' energy.

More Good Work for the Brain: Read

Start with an easy little book, by Thic Nhat Han, called <u>Peace is Every Step</u> (14). This is a good book to keep by the bed to read and reread if you get awakened in the middle of the night with a panic attack. Then, if you generally find that you are sick with anxiety, like your stomach hurts and your heart races, and you are not sure how you can stand it any more, read <u>The Power of Now</u> (15) by Eckart Tolle. If you just have anxious-tendencies try <u>A New Earth</u> (16), also by Eckart Tolle.

And when you are feeling a panic attack coming on, or you're in the middle of one:

- Put your hands or feet in warm water, and focus all your attention on the toasty, watery feeling, to the exclusion of everything else.
- Cradle a warm or hot water bottle or compress against your solar plexus.
- Drink six ounces of juice to retrieve your blood sugar, then do a bunch of push-ups, (or walk up bunch of flights of stairs) to use up some of your adrenaline, then drink six to ten more ounces of water to further dilute the adrenaline in your blood stream, and

finish up by eating a protein snack even if you don't feel like it. If it isn't helping very much, wait a half-hour and repeat.

- Try "square breathing" for at least fifteen minutes: Breath in while counting slowly to five, hold your breath in while counting slowing to five, breathe out slowly while counting to five, hold your breath out while counting slowly to five. Repeat the pattern, counting in your head the whole time for at least fifteen minutes. If your mind wanders, just bring your attention gently back to your counting.
- Watch some stand-up comedy or listen to mood-altering music.
- Write all this stuff down and post it in a noticeable area because when you are in a full-blown attack, you won't remember what you are supposed to do.

Seattle therapist Carol Gaskin's recipe for what to do if anxiety won't let you sleep:

Get a fat spiral notebook and a good pen. Drink a glass of water, and have a snack if it has been more than four hours since you had anything to eat. Get into your bed and prop yourself up comfortably, with a fat pillow on your lap for your notebook. Start to write. Write everything that goes through your mind, absolutely every thought as it is traveling through your mind. Don't worry about punctuation, or capitalization, or sentence structure. Just write the stream of words as fast as they go through your head, as fast as you can go. If you can't keep up with them, don't worry. The thought loops of your mind always come around again. You will get another chance. Write and write and write, with no judging, and no editing and no worry about performance. If you get tired, go to sleep.

If you don't get tired, then when you begin to notice that you are starting to write down the same thoughts that you already have written down, maybe two, three or four times already, as your brain travels around its hellish loop, begin to gently speak to your brain saying things like this "Yes, thanks for that. I already have that down." "Yes, you said that before, I have it right here. You can set it down now." "Yup, that one is here too, if you ever need it again, it is written right here seven times, so it will be easy to find." Let your hamster keep writing while you gently soothe the little beast, thanking it for its hard work, and reminding it that you have it all down now, all the important stuff. Write until the hamster shows signs of running down, turn off the light, and go to sleep.

The first time you do this, you might write for several hours; the second time, perhaps not quite as long. If you keep doing the practice faithfully, the time it takes for the hamster to wind down should get short and shorter, with occasional flare-ups when the world triggers your sense of helplessness.

Don't be freaked out the next morning if you read your automatic writing, and think that your ex-husband (or wife) was right, and you really are a complete whack job. Our minds collect all kinds of frightening sludge, the poisonous judgments directed at us all our lives, a lot of it generated by **us** to punish ourselves.

Most people have a huge backlog of stuff they have needed to say to various people all along the road of life, but didn't. And, legitimate things that needed to be said have a tendency to get all warped and scary over time when you squish them down deep in your unconscious. You might find that there is even a twisted, rageful and violent spirit who lives down in your unconscious who comes up to speak on paper when you finally give it a chance. Just remember, if you have one of those angry demons down there, it is down there because no one would listen when you needed to say the things that were the most important. Be kind to yourself. Be kind to your scary demon.

Your psyche may need you to hold on to the pages for a while, so you are not lying to your hamster when you tell it that it can rest because you have the important thoughts written down. But, eventually it will be time to let the pages go. Some people burn their pages ritually, allowing the ashes to fly away. Some people bury them in the garden to be composted by the earth, or shred them and spread them on the garden as mulch. I recommend that you don't keep them, though some of my clients have used them as source material for powerful poems and music. Most importantly, don't carry them with you into your conscious creation of your new identity. They are heavy with the pain of your old life, and some day you won't need them any more.

Note: The pages you have written can be extremely disturbing to your family or roommates if they find them. So I highly suggest thinking beforehand about how you are going to prevent that from happening **before** you start writing. If you are involved in a child-custody battle or might be in the future, your page-disposal plan had better be airtight! One never knows what might come out, needing to be released from your psyche, but not released to the public! The hamster is a careless and dangerous beast!

"Perhaps everything terrible is in its deepest being something that needs our love." ~Rainer Maria Rilke

Section 4: Special 'Tools' That Can Help Depression

Did you ever notice that there are two kinds of people: 1) the ones who find it easier to **do** the things they think they should (even though they don't want to) but have a hard time **not doing** the things they think they shouldn't be doing; and 2) the ones who find it easier not to do the thing they think they shouldn't be doing, but have a harder time **doing** the things they think they should. Anxious people tend to fall in the first category. Depressed people tend to fall into the second.

Depression saps your volition. "Saps your volition" is just a fancy way of saying it is really hard to get yourself to do anything at all, let alone anything new, strenuous, risky, or anything that takes you away from your computer. That said, I have seen it happen. But, to stack the cards in your favor, I just want to go over once again the things you especially **do not** want to do if you **do** want to feel better. Not-doing is your strength, remember? If you are stuck in the trap of depression, it is especially important that you do not drink alcohol (alcohol is a depressant), and that you cut your media time down to two hours a day, or less. (Television and net-surfing act as depressants on the brain too.)

Note to the depressed: I just want to point out that you might feel really bad, but if you have made it this far in the book, you are one rare depressed-specimen. Not only have you held enough volition to read this far, but I debunked all your best marble-gathering strategies in the first chapter, intimating that at some point you are going to have to let go of the whole victim-identity thing, AND YOU'RE STILL HERE!! Could I hand you a fat marble please? ☺

Depression's Vaccine

If you didn't read the part about word-vaccines in the section on "tools for anxiety," now would be the time to check it out so you know what I am talking about when I tell you that the vaccine for depression is: **"I choose life!"** Just say it to yourself periodically during the day, as enthusiastically as possible. If you say it out loud, it might make you laugh. Lord, could you use a laugh. If your internal guilty voice, or the voice inside that tells you are worthless and lazy is plaguing you, say your word-vaccine back to it gently, but firmly and often: "You are entitled to your opinion, but I choose life." Or perhaps call it out with ringing fortitude. "I CHOOSE LIFE!!"

More Work for the Brain: Read

Read <u>Way of Transition</u> (17) by William Bridges, and <u>When Things Fall Apart</u> (18) by Pema Chodron. If you are a woman get a workbook by Sark. They really should be called "funbooks."

Explore fun Ayurvedic practices for getting sludgy 'Kaffa' energy moving.

Make yourself easier to reach

Go outside. Spend at least an hour outside every day, walking around in the beautiful world, two times a day is even better. If it is ugly where you live go somewhere beautiful and **then** walk around. Volunteer for a cause you believe in, or to help someone who needs you more than you need them. Volunteering is one of the fastest ways I know to shift the sense that you are wasting space on the planet to an inner experience of contribution. It is hard to keep feeling you don't matter when it is in your face every day how much you are mattering, to the people or cause you are lending yourself to.

Take the Gluten Challenge

Don't eat gluten for a month to see how you feel. Then after 30 days, have a big dose of it and see how you feel. The number of people I know who have quit eating gluten and had the sun come out in their lives is amazing. I could really become the anti-gluten evangelist here. There is something about gluten that makes many people sludgy and irritable. You might even find that a bunch of mysterious health problems that you thought were attributable to other things magically disappear if you quit eating it. In my family, between the four of us, when we said good-bye to gluten, we said good-bye to chronic sinus infections, gum disease, chronic anemia, joint pain, intestinal issues of all kinds (that was a polite way to say that), and the growth problems of a kid who was averaged sized for his first year of life, but had slipped completely off the growth chart by the age of six. When he quit eating gluten, he caught up to his peers within two years. Finally, my partner, who had suffered a lifetime of emotional mood swings was instantly emotionally stable, once we figured out all the stuff gluten is hiding in.

Cultivate gratitude

I strongly suggest that you make a concerted effort to look for and punctuate the things in your life that are blessings. This can be very difficult, depending on the family system you came from. As I mentioned in chapter 1, some people have been programmed from birth with the paradigm that only the biggest sufferer is deserving of care and marbles. Your mind may be completely resistant to looking for what **is** working in your life, or acknowledging the people who **do** positively contribute to you. I have vats of compassion for the double bind you are in, but the marble-gathering strategy you may have been programmed with as a child is deeply flawed. It does not help you develop the feeling that you matter, if you drive everyone away with your complaining, guilting and suffering. People get tired. I suggest you get a beautiful journal, the prettiest or sexiest you can find. And get yourself a beautiful smooth-writing pen. Then every night before you go to bed write down what you were grateful for that day. Include the small stuff … that crow that chewed you out when you were pulling in the trashcans. In the morning, start the day by reading them again, and bless the world that you are still breathing.

Let's talk about thank you notes again. I said some pretty culturally-outrageous things about thank you notes in the first chapter, that I am now going to take back. Ok, no I am not! Actually, in chapter 1, what I said was that writing the thank you notes that are extorted in return for the gifts that were sent to you to procure marbles for the giver is something no one needs to feel responsible for. But when you feel authentically thankful, go for it! Writing thank you notes that help you contemplate and intentionally reflect upon the contributions that other people make to your life is a great way to reprogram your **own** suffering-prone brain. (By the way parents, there is no way to **force** or guilt authentic gratitude out of your kids, so don't take what I am saying as open season on the nine-year olds, who you think you can force to sit there "contemplating" gratitude, so they can really mean it when they write their thank you notes. Kids learn gratitude by observing **you** expressing conscious thankfulness for your own abundance.)

Pets

Get a pet. Pets can help one cultivate gratitude, because they model for us what it is to feel thankful for the simplest little things. Pay more attention to the pet you have. Take better care of that pet. (This is not an invitation to go get another pet if you are already a hoarder of pets or in danger of becoming one!)

Section 5: Special 'Tools' That Can Help Anger

Seek out…

Dear Angry Person, the thing I am most interested in having you do is the thing that is going to sound the least appetizing in the 'tools for anger' section. In fact, you will likely hate it at first. But here it is: find a way to talk to a receptive and sympathetic listener about your feelings of helplessness on a regular, predictable basis. This could look like getting a therapist, joining an anger support group, or taking a class to practice talking about your feelings in a supportive environment. I get that the last thing an intimidator or a withdrawer like you wants to do is willingly expose the truth of a deep vulnerability to anyone else, but fear of exposing vulnerability **is** your vulnerability, and it is the fear of its exposure that causes you to lash out when anyone (including you) threatens to expose it. Letting your helplessness out into the light of day in a contained and supportive situation, thereby discovering that you have faced your internal firing squad and lived, can have an immediate positive effect on your negative reactivity.

Walk away

As much as you might resist seeking out the ears of strangers and friends who actually want to hear about your feelings, your close family is generally another matter. Feeling understood by the people you are close to is so important to you, that you often stay in a heated discussion long (LONG!) past the point when you should leave the argument to cool down. Practice
walking away early. Walk away the minute you feel the Bull in you starting to rise. Leave the house. Walking away can be terribly difficult for you, because it means to the insecurely-attached kid inside you, that you are backing down and giving up all chance of getting validated.

*Here is a tip: (First, you have to walk away early enough that you have enough brain-space left to employ the tip.) Having you walk away can feel crushing or terrifying to the person you are arguing with. **They may hate arguing with you, but having you walk away can feel as if you are tipping over their whole bowl of marbles.** Inside his or her brain, the hamster says. "I am so utterly worthless and insignificant that I am not even worth fighting. So s/he is leaving me!!" Say to the other person, "I am leaving to cool down now, but **I am coming back.** I will be back *<insert specific time here>* and we can talk about this again at *<insert specific time here>.*" If you have left it too long, it may be all you can do to choke out "I am coming back later!" before bolting out the door, but that is better than nothing. Utilizing this tip makes it less likely that the other person will follow you and chase you down trying to prevent your escape, amping up your helplessness so high in the process that you lose control of your frothing lunging bull.

If you are prone to volatility, a nice thing to do is keep a pair of shoes and a jacket or sweater in your car. Hide an extra car key outside too. That allows you to leave immediately, if you find yourself in a risky situation, without having to find your keys and shoes while a rearing, lunging bull is crashing around inside of you; Maybe even when you are being followed around the house by someone else's rearing, lunging bull.

The Jellyfish Maneuver: If for some reason you can't physically leave the house, as is often the case if the person who is triggering your helplessness is a child, leave mentally. I have given this idea to dozens of parents of small children and the practice has been a revelation to some who feel utterly bowled over by the chaos of their kids. Children under six or so are just basically walking manifestations of the chaos we cannot escape from who live in our houses with us 24/7. Few things can trigger a psyche vulnerable to helplessness as much as a small child. The Jellyfish Maneuver can be so powerful for rewiring ugly preprogrammed responses in the brain that I am beginning to think it might be able to assist some people in shifting their whole relationship with the inherent chaos of physical world. I almost saved it for the end of the chapter to put it with the meditation and yoga!

It goes like this: When your toddler is freaking crazy, and you can't get a break, or you start to feel as if you are going to smack somebody, flop right down on the carpet and make yourself go limp. With the dangerous, pint-sized creatures running wild all around you, just drop and start to relax every part of you. Lie there letting the noise and chaos drift over you like a hurricane that is happening in the sky over your head, while you imagine you are safe and rocked in the bosom of Mother Ocean. I don't care if they are drawing on the walls or pouring jelly on couch, the integrity of your soul is more important than the saving of the carpet. In fact, the wilder the environment, the more residual bang-for-your-buck you will get from escaping the storm to sink beneath the waves, like a jellyfish into the infinite ocean of the present moment. Sink down in a warm ocean and let the storm rage without you.

One side effect of the Jellyfish Maneuver, is that it can be so surprising to anyone else present that they fall instantly silent and curious. "Wow!" All of a sudden the whole dynamic has shifted as if by magic wand. "What is Dad doing over there?" Some parents have reported to me that within minutes of the Jellyfish Maneuver, their toddlers are lying across the mother-jellyfish belly, limp and quiet, being little jellyfish themselves. (If you think you might be at risk for being jumped on, grab a large cushion to place over your face and belly before you sink down.)

Regularly-scheduled alone time: Individuals vulnerable to being possessed by the Bull need lots of self-reflection time to study the deeper layers of what triggers their sense of powerlessness and to practice sifting up useful information about what went wrong the last time the bull ran someone over, and why. They also need space and quiet to practice speaking firmly but gently to their internal toxic critic, and to figure out why they actually **do** matter on the planet. I like to have people who are wired for anger have a regular standing date, alone with themselves, at least two interruption-free hours each week. No phone, TV, or computer allowed. Journaling is a supportive practice that allows the writer to get more bang for their buck with self-reflection.

Write

Get yourself a sturdy book, maybe a big one with no lines, and every night before bed write a list of all of the good things that day, big and small, that you were the author of. Did you make a nourishing breakfast for your kids? Did you illicit a smile from your neighbor with your greeting. Did you offer help to someone who needed it, or fix the leaky faucet, get the bulbs planted or call your lonely grandma? Write it all down.

Also write about any episode that day when helplessness got the best of you. List the incidents of anger that arose over the course of the day, and what underlying feelings triggered a volatile coping-tactic. How did you get from point "a" (regular well-meaning you) to point "b" (the you that you wish that no one had seen or heard today, and that no one would ever see again). Where would you have wanted the situation to go instead? Pose alternative options you could have tried that might have headed off the experience of helplessness altogether, or addressed it in a constructive manner. How could you have authored your **own** contributions to the situation differently in order to maximize the probability that you could have gotten where you actually wanted to go with the interaction? What could you try next time, when you feel your Bull start to bleed and snort.

Anger's Vaccine

If you didn't read the passage on word-vaccines in the section on "tools for anxiety," now would be the time to check it out so you know what I am talking about when I say the vaccine for anger is: **"I am ok."** (Or **"You're ok. I've got you."** if you want to speak directly **to** your panicked and frothing bull.) People who slide easily into anger tend to have been wounded very young, so the simpler the self-talk the better. "All is well. I'm ok. Nothing really bad is happening." -- the kinds of things one would say to a terrified child who was hiding under a table threatening to bite anyone who reached out to him.

More Work for the Brain: Read Sitting in the Fire (19) by Arnold Mindell, and Anger (20) by Thich Nhat Hanh.

Explore fun Ayurvedic practices for soothing 'Pitta' energy.

Watch stand up comedy, the kind that is clever and funny, not ugly, and keep a collection of mood-altering music to listen to.

Make something important

I have found that it is especially important for people who struggle with anger to have both the meditative experience that can come with physical work, and the result of seeing the work of their hands. Try taking up a substantial constructive physical project like growing food for your family, knitting hats for the homeless, working on cars, or building a boat or a house. Don't expect though that your family is necessarily going to come on board and be your project slaves or validate you by being as interested in your project as you are. The aim is to give **you** something in your life that is really worth doing, not just another stage on which to play out your sense of relational helplessness. This is **your** practice, your project. Let **them** ask if **they** want to help you, or if they are too scared of you to ask, only invite them if you see them hovering around looking hopeful.

Section 6: Doing Tools, that Support Changing on the Inside

In preparation for the next Chapter: Changing on the Inside, this is the section where I talk about practices in the material world that assist the practitioner in putting their helplessness-coping-tactics to sleep so they can address the challenge of building a bowling ball with less interference from defensive parts of the mind. All of these practices in this section fall under the umbrella of cultivating more attention to, and presence within, the present moment. I am referring to "mindfulness."

First, I have noticed that when it comes to both talking to my clients about these options, and having them follow through on the things I suggest, people tend to evince a good deal more resistance to some of the options in this section than they do to more mundane practices, like reading a book, exercising, or getting more sleep. Clients who will dredge up the energy from somewhere to get to the gym three times a week, often seem as if they will do anything to keep from sitting in meditation. My hypothesis about the trend that my clients have a harder time getting themselves to commit and stick to regular journaling or yoga than they do regular dog walks or creating an organizational structure, is that their minds are unconsciously fearful of the changes meditative practice might bring to their identities. That is, the practice of meditation has a good chance of eventually making your hamster, bear, or bull obsolete. And, from the point of view of your psyche, the Big Three are there to keep you **safe**. Your unconscious believes you could die without your defenses! So, it will try every trick it knows to keep you from succeeding at meditative practice. That is not what my clients say about why meditative practice is so hard though. What they say is "I already tried that one time." "It was too boring." " My mind kept wandering. I couldn't concentrate." That is The Bull wanted action. The Hamster got twitchy. The Bear fell asleep.

Of course you couldn't concentrate! Of course it seemed to boring. Your mind is accustomed to working furiously at the thinking-thing every waking moment. The hamster will fiercely and manipulatively use every sneaky trick at its disposal to get you to go back to tending the thought-loops it thinks you need to survive. From a hamster, bear, or bull's point of view, meditative practice threatens your bowl of marbles. And your psyche thinks you could die if your coping-tactics were not vigilantly standing in defense of your bowl... because in a sense you will. Your current fear-based identity will die. You may barely need marbles at all when you have plugged the hole in your bowl, and the marbles you end up wanting may not be the ones you want now. So from the point of view of the coping-tactics in your mind, the 'you' you could become is a potentially threatening, unknown future self. I have even had some of my clients, for whom this fear has surfaced all the way into their conscious mind say, "Who will I be then? Will my family even like me?" "Will I like myself? I don't even know that person." "What if I am 'selfish'?"

In chapter 4, I will talk more about bowling ball transitions, and gentling the people you love into relationship with the new you the best you can. It can be scary or unnerving to people around you when you change, particularly if they are no longer going to be able to count on you for the marbles you used to produce for them. But, in my experience, the ones who really love you get used to it **if** you handle it in a way that is both kind and utterly certain. I will talk more about how that looks in practice in chapter 4. Right now, all you have is my word for it... and perhaps your own hunger for peace. If you are lucky you may also have the certainty that continuing down a life-path that is run by your defensive coping-tactics is a hell that you don't want for yourself. You may even know deep down that what I said in chapter 1, about authentic generosity only coming from a full bowl is true. If you want to be able to be a force for real giving in the world, you will commit to growing into a person who can look after your own hamster, bear or bull, instead of expecting the trapped and unhappy creature to look after you.

Meditative Practice

This section will be very brief, but the time I spend on the subject is not commensurate with its value or importance. It will be brief simply because there are such good books already out there about these subjects, and such skilled teachers promoting them, that I feel embarrassed, like a poser, writing about them. Honestly, in my own life, I have three primary meditative things that work for me, and I will dabble in a few other areas just for fun, but I, myself, am in meditative-practice grade school. Please purchase and read the beautiful books from the masters of meditative practice: Jack Kornfield, Parker Palmer, Pema Chodron, Thich Nhat Han, Deepak Chopra, Echart Tolle.

Self-Reflection is key, and I have covered a bit about it in the sections above. Writing (journaling) is an enormously effective aid to self-reflection, both automatic writing (see above) and the writing directed by the questions in this book. Answer the questions that your own curious mind begins to generate when you finally allow it the space to wonder/wander. Please, when you are self-reflecting, summon the kindest, most understanding part of yourself to do the asking of the questions.

Some people use the terms "meditation" and "mindfulness practice" interchangeably. I am not sure that there is an authority to ask regarding the "true" definitions. When I use those words, the way I mean them is this: **Meditation** is the practice of trying to empty your mind completely, as if it is an empty vessel. **Mindfulness** is the practice of having your mind concentrate on one thing to the exclusion of everything else: your breathing, a sound, your heartbeat, a candle, or this present moment etc. For the remainder of this book, when I use the term **mindfulness practice**, I will almost always be referring to the practice of attempting to **focus on this present moment to the exclusion of everything else that your brain tends to want to focus on**. Everything else in your brain that tries to get your attention: stories of the past, stories of the future, and stories about what is or could be happening right now is put aside for the moment. Mindfulness practice seeks to quiet all thinking other than the noticing, listening and responding to what is actually happening **in this present moment**. It is integral to the process of growing your bowling ball, so I will be exploring it further in chapter 4.

If one uses my definitions, and I have no attachment to you doing so, then the most common form of meditation, a **seated meditation** focusing one's attention on one's breathing, is a mindfulness practice. It is my personal belief, that if a particular form of meditation is torture for you, just try another kind, at least for awhile! Westerners have especially busy minds, so choosing a mindfulness-based practice tends to be an easier place to start, than trying to empty your mind completely right off the bat. Choose a place to start where you think you can succeed.

I highly suggest **sound meditation** for new practitioners, particularly people who are very auditorially oriented. You can sit and listen to wind chimes to the exclusion of everything else, or strike a chime every minute or so and listen intently until the sound is completely gone. Then listen to the silence in between the sounds for a few seconds. **Chanting** is another sound option. I particularly love the practice of chanting for people with severe anxiety because there is something that feels so good about vibrating a horribly tight chest with sound, from the inside out. Don't feel intimidated. It isn't difficult. For anxiety, just slowly chant the tone "Ohhhhhhhhhhh" or "Ohhhhhhhhhmm" in as low of a pitch as feels comfortable to maintain for a full exhalation. Keep it up for at least fifteen minutes or so, as you empty all the air from your lungs with each Om. Play with the "o" of your mouth until you hit the shape that supports the best chest-vibration. Ahhhh relief... at least for some people. Some of my clients who are not able to sleep at night due to busy brain-loop problems find that chanting right before bed helps enormously.

Fifteen years ago, at the beginning of my own meditative practice journey, I had heard of **walking meditation** (walk slowly, with your full attention on the rhythm of your feet, or anything else integral to the action of walking), and I tried it after several unhappy attempts at seated meditation. With walking meditation my western brain was still bouncy as a puppy. And I finally invented my own practice of **running meditation**, giving the puppy some real-time bouncing, while I focused my full attention on the rhythm of my feet. Regular running meditation was the practice that really helped me settle my mind down and tame the Hamster. Other more active mindfulness practices that may offer the promise of settling down the busy mind, so you can begin to grow a bowling ball, are:

Yoga
Tai Chi
Martial arts
Hand drumming/shamanic drumming
Ecstatic dance

How well or how long it takes for meditative practices to begin to impact your mind depends a lot on how they are taught. Some yoga is taught strictly as exercise, for example, and some martial arts classes strictly for defensive skills. Impact on you will also depend on how often you practice, and how well you maintain your own 'learning to stay in the present moment' intention.

I don't want to leave this section without talking about a practice that is the most important and effortless meditative option for many people. Spending time alone **connecting to the natural world**. Many people, myself included, feel more connected to themselves in this moment, and every living thing in existence, when they spend adequate, regular time in the company of the wild. Nothing gets me into this moment faster and more deeply than the natural world... except perhaps the practice of doing therapy.

Chapter 3 Questions:

This chapter is designed to begin to help you formulate answers to question #4 from the Intro: **"In the face of all of my flaws, how do I become the person I want to be?"** I focused on tools and changes in behavior, primarily intended to create material shifts in the system of your physical body and the human relationship systems around you. I offered the possibility that if you stick to the practice of them, many of these "doing" tools will begin to affect the system inside your mind as well, preparing you for the work of making fundamental shifts in your identity and paradigms, on the way to growing the bowling ball to fill your bowl.

If you had not done it before this, I am hoping that after reading this section, you have purchased a notebook that you really enjoy writing in, and the best pen you have ever owned in your life, in order to take a crack at the following questions:

1) Which section fits best with your primary helplessness-coping-tactic?

2) What practices have you already tried? What has helped and why? Which ones have seemed less useful and why?

3) What new tools might you like to try, or try again, and why are those the ones that appeal to you?

4) If you were to give two types of meditative practice a try, which ones sound the most appealing to you and why?

5) What kind of support might you need to assist you in maintaining a steady practice of the doing-changes that you think will help you the most?

Chapter 4: Changing on the Inside

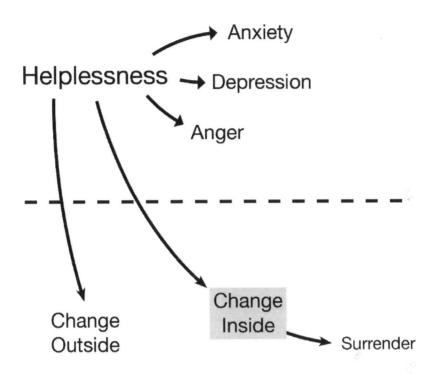

In Chapter 1, I asserted that until you are able to successfully address the core problem of plugging the hole in the bottom of your bowl, the fear that you don't matter will tend to make a slow but inexorable conquest of your life. Chapter 2 offered the **Bypass Your Tactic Model**: a way to re-frame **Anxiety, Depression**, and **Anger** as your psyche's well-meaning but misguided attempts to rescue you from the intolerable helplessness you experience when your Marble Game strategies don't bring victory in the world competition of "who matters more?" Chapter 3 explored the first option for **Bypassing Your Tactic**: Making changes in the material world outside of you, as one means to avoid getting trapped by the any of the **Big Three**, so you can work on addressing your helplessness directly.

This chapter addresses the second path that **BYT** offers: **Making Changes on the Inside of You**. For the next few chapters I will be offering you various means to address your helplessness directly by **growing your own bowling ball**. We will explore the malleable nature of the Self, and of reality, towards the end of making you the author of yourself and your experience of life.

Section 1: What is Identity?

"And so it is with every name we take – Democrat or Republican, mother or father, employer or employee, every name we take as our identity colors and shapes the way we walk, and way we feel about ourselves and the people we meet." - Wayne Muller

Who are you? If I were to ask most people that question, the answer would be a name, for example: Gaelen Elizabeth Billingsley. Perhaps the name would include a title, as well, to give the asker even more information: Dr. Deepak Chopra, General Colin Powell, Secretary Hillary Clinton, Queen Elizabeth. Those **are** the names and titles belonging to those people, and they evoke associations that you carry within your own mind, but how much does the name tell you about who those people **really** are? How much does your name express about you?

For much of human history, before the American rise of the cult of the individual, a name was a huge signifier of identity, because name often pointed to class and clan. Individuality was not very important then. What mattered most, for much of human history, was the group you were affiliated with. These days, however, while names still sometimes carry information regarding an individual's class or race, a name conveys only a tiny percentage of what is most important about a person. If one includes a title, a bit more about level of education or career track can be illuminated, but that's about it. Unless you are part of the teeny minority of people who change their names, you didn't even have a say about the name you currently wear. It was bestowed upon you, along with much of the rest of the identity you currently wear, by the family you were born or adopted into.

So who are you really? What is your "identity"?

"I don't know", is the most common answer I get when I ask this question of a client. But you must know a good deal about who you are, because you have spent a good portion of your life up until now defending a bowl of marbles that validates what you hope is true about yourself, and trying to hide the things you believe about you, that you think would attract the judgment that might pop all your marbles like they were soap bubbles. So take a minute to stop and think… what would you say to someone on a first date? Add that to what you hope that person will never find out about you, and you will find you do know quite lot about your identity. But how is it that you know the things you know? Really stop and think about this.

We are all born with an individualized nervous system: left-handed/right handed, level of sensitivity, etc. So that aspect of our self is hard wired. But then for a long time, everything else about our sense-of-self gets collected from what is reflected back to us, about ourselves, from the facial expressions and attentiveness of our caregivers. Are our bids for care and connection answered consistently? Are our caregivers capable of and interested in sharing regular, fully present, "you matter to me" moments with us? If so, we may absorb, **"I matter to my family."** Do they consistently hear and respond to our calls for care and attention in a timely fashion? If so, we will absorb, **"I must matter because my needs get taken care of when I cry for help."** However, if we miss these important developmental interactions, our early sense of our own worth and the paradigms we create regarding the basic security of the universe get a different stamp. That is, All the outside reflections we see as babies tell us about ourselves, and are then absorbed and believed by us, forming the underpinnings of our identities and the size of the holes in the bottoms of our bowls.

In the next phase of childhood identity-development, almost everything we know about ourselves comes from the things people **tell** us about ourselves, and the stories we overhear our parents and teachers **telling others about** us: "Jack is my trouble maker." "Piper likes things her own way." " Logan can't keep track of his own shoes." These are the definitions kids absorb without knowing it. Are the things that you heard about yourself actually true? Or entirely true? How much about what you heard about yourself arose from accurate observation, and how much of it was colored by what your parents and teachers wanted to believe about you, or what kind of marbles they needed you to produce for them (how powerful or satisfied they needed to feel) in the context of their relationship with you?

Like all parents who observe their kids, by the time I was 3 my parents had observed many things about me, and they had formed their own ideas regarding my identity. I was hearing on a regular basis: "Gaelen is very sensitive." "She doesn't trust people." "She is stubborn!" "She spends a lot of time in her own world."

And like all parents, as I got a little bit older, my parents began intentionally reinforcing the aspects of personality and behavior that they hoped for, for their daughter, while unconsciously also reinforcing, through punishment and judgment, aspects of identity that they wanted to stamp out. Soon, in addition to "sensitive, non-trusting, and stubborn." I was being intentionally reinforced around, "confident, tough, and intelligent", and unintentionally reinforced around "sneaky, impermeable, and emotional." Was I really any of those things? Identity starts to get fuzzy very fast after you pass early infancy. The older you get, the more colored by parental and peer viewpoint it tends to be. Was I sensitive, stubborn, and untrusting, the earliest identity labels placed on me? I think so. Was I "confident and tough"? I don't know, but I learned to look confident and tough to get marbles, because that was what was valued in my family. "Intelligent?" Yes, though my early school grades did not really reflect it. "Sneaky, emotional and impermeable?" "Emotional," I am not sure about. Emotional displays made the grown-ups in my family system nervous, so even modest displays were discouraged. I am not particularly "emotional" now. "Sneaky and impermeable?" These ones I feel as if I can comment on because I actually can remember a bit about my "sneaky and impermeable" evolution. I don't know if I started out with a bent towards "sneaky" or not, but I do remember that the more judgment I received about anything I did, the sneakier I felt I needed to be. And the more pressure I felt I was under to be transparent, the more impermeable I got. It was a family-systems reinforced feedback-loop. Every family unintentionally reinforces a wide variety of behavior and identity-themes with feedback loops like that one. My family was not even especially flagrant with regard to unintentional negative-identity reinforcement.

How much of what you were told about yourself growing up was true, even then? How much of what you think you know about yourself was programmed by caregivers, either intentionally or unintentionally? And how many of the stories your family continues to tell about you, to support their right to continue to define your identity, are accurate reflections of who you have become? What were you labeled with as a kid that still colors your view of yourself? Were you: lazy, clumsy, selfish, stupid, ugly, a loser, a liar, a user, a prodigy, the golden child, the bad seed, the one who would never grow up, the one who would never desert them, the one who would never amount to anything, the one who would make all the money? Do you want to be any of those things? Are you any of them? How can you know, when your "identity" is nothing more than a bunch of stories about the past that you and the people around you replay inside your heads?

The people who were close to you collected stories about you all of your young life, tales whipped out as proof to back up assertions regarding who they think you are. Some of that story collecting is still happening, but mostly a family has decided who they think you are by the time you are an adolescent, if not before. Then you take over the job of maintaining that identity. If you bought the family stories about you, and most people do, you keep retelling them to yourself, and also begin collecting new stories that fit into your old identity collection. You have been collecting and replaying stories about yourself all of your life, stories that tell you who you are.

Here is the thing though: No one keeps and replays the memories of everything that has ever happened to them. You unconsciously select which stories to store and replay from your life experiences. You unconsciously decide, with your indifference, which ones to forget about and leave behind, just like your family did when you were growing up. We all have a bent towards remembering and repeating stories that reinforce both the "good" things we believe are true about ourselves, and the "bad" things we are afraid are true about ourselves. Data reinforcing the "good" makes us feel as if we matter. Data reinforcing the "bad" we store to feed the internalized shame we think we need to teach us to be better people, and keep from making mistakes. Data that does not fit either collection gets unconsciously tossed out. What I am offering here is the possibility that identity is not the life-sentence you think it is.

Identity strings of story beads

I think of the stories that you have collected to tell yourself who you are as beads on the strings of your identity. You wear a different string of collected story-beads for each theme of your identity: one for "I am clumsy", one for "I am hard-working", one for "I am crazy", one for "I am not trustworthy", one for "I am the hot commodity", one for "I can't keep a job" etc. You wear one string for each major theme you think is true about yourself. We tend to wear these strings of story-beads 24 hours a day, replaying and replaying the identity-stories in our heads, whether they become us or not, even if they weigh us down like grave stones, or feel as if they are choking us to death. We wear our strings of story-beads like a life sentence that we simply must learn to endure because that "is just the way I am."

It isn't. You may have some history that you cannot rewrite, or have made a string of "mistakes" that you think will permanently define you, but you **can** rewrite **your part** in the story, and you can recast your mistakes, if you learn from them. You have a choice about the stories you hold on to and the meaning you ultimately make about those stories. I will show you what I mean.

I have a woman walk into my office and she says to me: "I was an abused child. My mother was on drugs and would leave me alone for days at a time. Sometimes I would run out of food. When she came home she would bring scary drug-using guys with her who messed around with me when she was passed out. Now I can't get my life together. And walking down the street I feel as if I have a big blinking light over my head that reads, 'Abuse this woman.' because I am always taken advantage of, and I always get into relationships that victimize me."

I could have a woman with an **identical** life experience walk into my office and say: "I was an abused child. My mother was on drugs and would leave me alone for days at a time. Sometimes I would run out of food. When she came home she would bring scary drug-using guys with her who messed around with me when she was passed out. I should have died. Lots of people would have committed suicide. But I survived. Now no one messes with me. And when I walk down the street, everybody can tell that they had better not try, because I will freaking kill anyone who does."

Same life experience, two different collections of stories and meanings collected - to produce two very different identities. Could it really be that simple? It could. You are wearing dozens of strings of story beads **yourself**. Your caregivers clipped on the first strings when you were little, but now you are a grown-up person. Do you like the strings you have? If yes, great! Do you hate the strings you have? Then just snip them. Snip the ones that hurt you right this minute and let all those stories roll away onto the ground. You don't need them anymore. All of those things happened long ago. The only thing that keeps those stories alive is the retelling and retelling of them, with their ascribed meaning. Stop telling the stories, and those identities die.

In the real world snipping, your string looks something like this: "Huh… I thought I knew who I was… It has just occurred to me, that a lot of that stuff I thought I knew, people with their own motives and biases told me about myself. I guess I could have attributed lots of different meanings to my life experiences if I had known I had that power. I guess I don't really know who I am right now. Perhaps I will start to study the me I am now. Perhaps I might even decide who I want to be and start cultivating the me who is going in that direction."

It really could be that simple. I have witnessed occasional breakthrough therapy sessions that allowed an anxious, depressed, self-shaming individual to snip the old strings of their identity, look back to select a different collection of important life stories, make a new fundamentally different meaning of what they can remember, and voila! Brand new strings of beads! Brand new person. I have literally seen an individual walk out of my office a new person, with different strengths (and problems). Sometimes it really is that easy.

Community Response to Your Changes

Sometimes it really can be that easy for **you**, that is. But it is often pretty nerve- wracking for the community of people around you. Your friends and family can be extremely resistant to letting go of the identities they pinned on you as a kid, for all the Marble Game-related reasons I have already explored in this book. They may also react negatively to the simple fear that if you change, they won't know you anymore, or the new you might not like, love or need **them**. Families in particular, can be resistant to seeing you grow up and survive without them. Family resistance to allowing adult children to let go of childhood-identities is a particularly common experience for the youngest adult-child in a family. Does your family still expect you to forget to bring a dish to Thanksgiving, avoid helping with the dishes, or believe you can not be trusted to produce an appropriate Christmas gift for your nieces and nephews, even though you are thirty-five? Then you know what I am talking about!

Your community will eventually adjust. Your family will eventually adjust, although that can be a difficult road. In chapter 1, I already told you about one parent who kept threatening to have a heart attack when his adult children made bids for independence. Even that Dad ultimately surrendered to his daughter's new identity. The vast majority of families do eventually adjust, and learn to love the new you. So do your real friends. In fact, changing your identity from one that causes you suffering, to one that is in support of your health and future happiness, is a great way to discover who actually loves you, as opposed to who has only been hanging around to squeeze you for marbles. The people who really love you want to see you happy and successful, more than they want you to continue to play the role you have always played.

So who do you want to be? I invite you to start thinking about it, but don't decide right away. There is no reason you need to. "I am not sure, and I am claiming my right to be in a state of flux while I ponder the question" is a perfectly acceptable answer, although it can make the people around you nervous. Taking time to study the question is in your best interest, and I will be exploring ways of cultivating new identities in later sections.

When I begin to speak to my clients about snipping the strings of identity that they don't want to carry anymore, a certain contingent always comes back with statements like, "You can't do that! Real life doesn't work that way!" Really? What is "real life"? Who gets to decide what is "real?"

The Jump is so frightening between where I am and where I want to be...
Because of all I may become, I will close my eyes and leap!
- *Mary Anne Radmacher-Hershey*

Chapter 4 - Section 1 Questions:

1) What elements of your protected, preferred identity are you accustomed to defending from judgment, because you think you must be 'that way', or you won't matter very much?

2) What elements of your secret, shameful identity have you been hiding because you fear exposure?

3) What were the primary identity stories you were told about yourself as you were growing up?

4) Which of the stories that you were told about yourself seem like they were true about you then, and which don't?

5) Which identity stories continue to feel relevant to you, and which ones don't?

6) What aspects of your identity do you think were reinforced intentionally, and why?

7) What aspects were reinforced unintentionally, and why?

8) Which of the stories your family continues to tell about you are accurate reflections of who you have become?

9) What are the themes of the identity-strings you want to snip?

Section 2: What is real(ity)?

Seriously. What is real? What do you think you know? What can you count on as undeniably true about the world around you? Are you sure? Even at the physical level (up/down, colors, textures, time, and solidity of objects, etc.) the world you perceive through the system of your senses gets translated, sorted and interpreted by your brain. Everything you think you see, hear, feel, taste, and smell is just your brain's individual interpretation of reality. None of us has any idea if my interpretation is the same as yours. We just assume so. But every brain is a little different, and every brain undergoes a completely different process of growth and evolution, even the brains of kids raised in the same family. So, no brain can have a perception of reality that is exactly the same as someone else's.

What you believe in, as **"the nature of reality"** (also known as **"the identity of the universe"**), gets interpreted by some even bigger string of beads that you unconsciously wear, not unlike the strings of identity-beads you carry to remind you who you are. These "paradigms regarding the nature of reality" strings hold the stories your parents told you about how the universe works, along with stories you have collected from your own experience, to form your understandings about reality and the rules by which life itself is governed. And, just as you will let some memories fall by the wayside if they don't fit with the themes on your identity-strings, the data that you encounter that does not fit with your "view of reality" gets left behind and forgotten also. Further, if any of the data you encounter feels actively threatening to any paradigms you cling to because they help you manage your personal brand of intolerable helplessness, the data may be rejected with gusto. "That's just crazy!" you say.

This brings me back to the question, "What is real, and how can you know?" I note that most of us assume we know what is real without really considering the question carefully, and we brand other people who don't agree with us "crazy".

What does "crazy" really mean? In the introduction, I said I thought that people use the word "crazy" to describe both behaviors that don't make sense to them and people who are exhibiting those behaviors. I also said that everyone makes sense. If you were to get to know any person well enough, inside and out, that every person would make sense. (Is my assertion that 'every person makes sense' "reality"? That is a good question. I will look at it again towards the end of the chapter.) "Crazy" has also been used to describe the behaviors of mentally ill people, and those people themselves. By this time, you will have gathered that I find the terms "anxious", "depressed", and "angry", when used as diagnoses, only moderately useful. I also find the rest of the diagnoses in the DSM only moderately useful. Diagnoses are a convenient shorthand, but they can't really address either the uniquely complex make-up of each and every individual, nor shine a light on the simple root causes of most of the unhappiness that affects our species.

"Craziness" exists as a spectrum across humanity. There are not "crazy people" and "sane" ones. Everyone has some craziness. I like to say that we are, every one of us, about five nights lost sleep away from a psychotic break. That is not a very wide space between me and hallucinations and paranoia. I also know that I, along with many parents, are one diagnosis of a child's major illness away from an "anxiety disorder", or one child's death away from a "major depressive episode." Every person has a limit on what they can take, and not come out "crazy". How many soldiers with solid identities and solid views of "reality" come away from war with a broken bowl, and no idea how to put it back together?

Chapter 4 - Section 2 Questions:

1) In the family you came from, which alternative views of reality (paradigms) were branded "crazy"?

2) Which of those "crazy" paradigms still seem crazy to you? Which ones don't?

3) Were you ever called "crazy"? What were you doing to threaten the paradigm of that judger?

4) Can you think of any paradigms you have that seem true to you, but really hurt you or your friends or family members?

Section 3:
The Unconsciousness to Consciousness Spectrum

In my own practice, I think in terms of "mentally ill" less and less. What has been proven a far more useful mental-health paradigm for my practice can be illustrated by this simple spectrum:

Imagine all of humanity lined up along a continuum that goes from unconsciousness to consciousness. I have to stop here and wince because those particular words often bring up for me mental pictures of 1960s flower-children, high on acid and staring at the sun. Bear with me folks. I have thought about this a lot and there is no better way to describe what I am talking about.

Unconsciousness

I visualize the entire family of Humanity lined up on the **Unconsciousness to Consciousness Spectrum** based on each person's capacity to be present to the shared reality of this present moment, as opposed to being lost in the self-created "reality" of his or her mind. On one far end, next to "unconscious", are mental disorders that trap individuals so deeply in their own minds that they are rendered catatonic. Someone like this is so lost in his or her own mind that s/he does not even register anything that is happening in the outside "reality". I.e. One might clap one's hands right in front of that person's face and s/he would not even blink -- profoundly unconscious.

Psychoses, disorders that have a direct affect on the individual's perception of consensus "reality", are just a little bit farther up on the scale towards "consciousness". Unmedicated, psychotics are walking dreamers. Their eyes are open, and they can speak and move around and see you, but if they were sitting across from you, they might be convinced that you were an invader from another solar system, and every time you opened your mouth, you might be speaking in an alien tongue while clicking horrible insect-like mandibles. Someone at that level of consciousness can take in some information about what is going on outside their own mind, in the present moment, but outside information is primarily used as source material for an inner dialog being generated by that person. I.e. mostly s/he lives in the world of his own mind, completely buying the stories and images his mind is sending him about "reality".

If you come up a bit farther on the consciousness scale, you will run into some of the personality disorders. People who fit the diagnoses of, say "Borderline," or "Narcissistic," have suffered an attachment breach within the first few years of life that made 'reality' simply unbearable. The message they got in babyhood was that the universe they had been born into was not a place that would ever take care of them reliably, so each of them invented a fantasy universe, and a **fantasy identity** for themselves in that universe, an identity that made them **The Star of the Movie of the World**.

Someone with severe Borderline Personality Disorder can see you sitting across from her, and s/he can generally hear what you are saying, but if what you are saying doesn't go with the way s/he has scripted her internal story line, really unusual things can happen. S/he might radically twist the words you are saying in his/her mind to mean what s/he wants them to mean. S/he might completely and unconsciously eject the conversation from memory, literally remembering nothing about the conversation, since it didn't fit with the script in her head. (This is kind of what any average person does with information they receive that is counter to an established view of reality, but on a grander scale.) The level to which a person with a personality disorder can just eject vital consensus-reality information from a "personal reality" is startling. Another thing that could happen, if what you say does not go along with the way **The Movie of the World** is supposed to go, is that you might get cast as the "bad guy" in the story. Now everything you do and say is interpreted and reinterpreted through the lens of the **bad guy mask** that has been placed on you by that highly "unconscious" person.

For someone at that level of "consciousness," there is no real sense that you might have your own movie going on as well, with a fully developed story line that matters just as much to you, as the story line of the **Star of the Movie of the World**. And, if you leave a scene you were playing with the personality disordered person, you become almost completely irrelevant, like you only really exist when you are playing a scene with him or her.

They are walking dreamers similar to a person with delusional psychosis; seemingly awake, but spending most of their "waking" hours actually lost in the solitary confinement of their own minds. In that mind-world they are never wrong. They never make mistakes. They are always the heroes/victims of the scene, and all the rest of us are supporting characters in the hero's story. They don't know they are trapped and they can't help it. It isn't their fault, any more than it is the fault of a delusional person that s/he is delusional. They are simply profoundly unconscious and almost completely disconnected from what the rest of us are sharing in the outside world.

Unconscious and feeling as if we matter

So how do these ideas play out for the rest of us? In the context of **The Unconsciousness to Consciousness Spectrum** I use the term "unconscious" to mean: "trapped by the tendency to keep your attention on your internal mind-world, rather on the actual moment", and "running your choices and behaviors from pre-programmed reactive responses, rather than conscious, creative intention". So what does unconsciousness in a regular life look like?

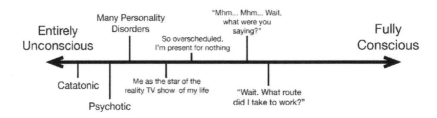

The entire first half of the section on **Bypassing Your Tactics** explored three different coping-tactics we slip into when we can't tolerate our in-the-moment experience of helplessness. Having Anxiety, Anger, or Depression assume control of your volition is one example of how we can all go unconscious and get trapped in the mind-world of our own internal dialog. If you slip into any of the Big Three coping-tactics, you temporarily lose the capacity to be awake to creative possibility in the actual present moment. In the grip of a coping-tactic, the Hamster's reality is the only reality.

What about day to day, though? How does unconsciousness look when there is no current threat to the identity-bowl of the self? Here are some very common examples of every-day unconsciousness:

-   Your kid is trying to get your attention. You are really busy and making little noises as if you were listening, but not really having any idea what he is talking about. Kid walks off feeling as if he doesn't matter much to you.
-   You told your kid you would get off work early enough to see the soccer game, but something came up and it slipped your mind. Your kid ends up feeling as if she doesn't matter to you very much.
-   You promised your spouse that you would start putting your dishes in the dishwasher right after use, but this morning your mind was already at work while your body was

still at home eating breakfast, and you left your bowl of oatmeal on the coffee table. Your spouse ends up feeling s/he doesn't matter to you.

- Your body comes home from work but your mind is still at the office, so you walk right by your spouse with no greeting. Spouse ends up feeling as if s/he doesn't matter very much to you.
- You have an agreement with your spouse that you will call if you are going to be late from work. You don't remember about that until you arrive home to a frightened, livid spouse. Your spouse ends up feeling s/he doesn't matter very much to you.

In the context of our relationships with other people, humans share a tenacious fantasy paradigm that goes like this: "If I really mattered to you, you would stay permanently awake to my needs, and the agreements we have made." I know this is yet another unpopular bubble-pop on my part, but that is NOT ACTUALLY TRUE. Will alone, cannot keep any person conscious. Love alone will not keep any person conscious. And unconsciousness is not intentional. We want so much to believe that if we were loved enough, the people around us would remain in a constant state of mindfulness regarding our needs. We think that if our loved ones forget the stuff that feels important to us, it is because they don't **choose** to remember, ergo "I don't matter enough for them to keep my needs in mind."

Do kids forget to hang up their coats when they get home because they don't give a rat's about what you want? NO! They are simply unconscious when they walk in the door, either still at the school in their minds, or already lost in the mind-world having a snack! Do they keep losing their keys because they are irresponsible? Do **you** keep losing **your** keys because **you** are irresponsible? You keep losing your keys because you lose conscious-connection with the keys, and get lost in your mind-world, before you have disposed of them with conscious intention.

90% of the things that we all do, or don't do, that get interpreted to mean that other people don't matter to us, come straight out of the fact that most of us are lost in our fantasy story-worlds, the vast majority of the time. We are unconscious, rather than present to ourselves and each other in the moment. Unconsciousness isn't on purpose. It is no one's fault. It is just the world we know. Most people have never even really considered that there is a difference between the world in their heads (that is made up of unquestioned stories, judgments and interpretations), and the actual world that is happening outside of them right now in this moment.

Here is the saddest thing: The only place we **can** ever actually meet and matter to each other **is** this present moment. Yet being present to each other is an experience that happens more and more rarely in the technology-mediated millennium world. Nobody is taught this. So people grow more and more lonely without understanding why, and more committed to marble-gathering strategies that don't work.

Unconsciousness is contagious

Furthermore, unconsciousness triggers more unconsciousness. We all find the unconsciousness in people around us so irritating, and so alienating, that other people's unconsciousness tends to trick us into leaving the present moment, to fall into the trap of our critical judgement. Unconsciousness spreads - triggering escalating, out-of-control stories like a plague. Personal interactions then become driven by the scary, ugly stories we have about: how little I matter to you and thus how deserving you are of my judgment rather than about what is actually happening. And, the more we fight, the truer the stories feel.

If you want relationships that are more conscious, **be** more conscious. Individuals who can stay present to the actual world tend to both attract people who are more fully present and start pulling unconscious people into the present more often. Furthermore, if you can stay conscious in the face of someone else's unconsciousness, rather than having your reactivity knock you straight out of the actual world and into your story-mind, the possibility exists that you could help other people wake up, to join you in the actual world. I will talk more about strategies for helping other people wake-up in Chapter 5.

The Trap of Failed Expectations

People with personality disorders are not the only ones who get attached to their ideas regarding "the way the story is supposed to go". The more time you spend buying in to the artificial reality that you are spinning with the thoughts inside your head, the more vulnerable you are to the jarring emotional dissonance that happens when the actual world doesn't cooperate with your plan. Almost everyone suffers from failed expectations occasionally, but the more unconscious you are to the fact that "the way things are supposed to go" are really just your stories, the more likely it is that you will be tremendously judging of the "uncooperative" world outside yourself. The more judging you are, the more you get carried away by your thought loops, and so on, and so on, getting sucked more and more deeply into unconsciousness. Ever pound a steering wheel in traffic, or punch a hole in a wall? You know what I mean, then.

"Because the sick person does not perceive his own distortions, he feels that ills in life and functioning come from the outside. The sicker he is, the more he feels that his troubles are caused by outside forces." - Zweig & Abrams

What Makes You More Unconscious?

All behavior that pulls you out of the present moment and into the fantasy universe of your (or someone else's) mind fosters unconsciousness. In our world, the more time you spend watching television, surfing the net, fighting with other people spinning in your thought loops, the more unstuck from the actual world you will tend to be. Unconsciousness-fostering behaviors tend to turn the mind into a passive recipient rather than an active participant in life. To be clear, I am not saying that any of those activities are "wrong" or "bad". I am simply saying that they do not support you learning to be present to your actual life. Can you begin to cultivate a balance for yourself? Could you learn to choose consciously when you want to get pulled under, say to watch a movie, as opposed to checking out reflexively, reactively, and without even noticing?

Perhaps nothing fosters a person's slide down the spectrum towards unconsciousness like addictive patterns and behaviors. Addiction is an internal-world need that you carry, that can eventually eclipse **all** the real-world needs you have. The thought-loop of addiction is a self-made universe in and of itself, a reality so powerful that it can skew the addicted individual's perception of the actual world into shapes and meanings as delusional as a psychotic's. Addiction is such a powerful force for unconsciousness that I have worked it into both the

Marble Game and the BYT model, and have dedicated an entire separate chapter to it later in the book. (Chapter 7)

Can you reduce unconsciousness-engendering activities? Can you balance the activities you pursue that put you under with more activities that wake you up? Any activity that puts you in the driver seat of life, any creative, constructive, planning, planting, moving activity offers you the opportunity to join yourself in a present moment of mindfulness awareness.

Consciousness

Let's pause for a moment and go way up to the other end of the spectrum to the land of complete and total consciousness. Who inhabits that end?

I don't think I personally know anyone way up there at the "fully conscious" end of the spectrum. I would love to though, so I could seek that person out to ask about it. What I think, however, is that people who were way up there would spend virtually no time spinning around in their mind-world, telling and retelling the stories of their past, lost in fantasies and judgments about the world, or trying to anticipate the future. Their attention would be focused on what they are noticing in this present moment. And, if someone like that chose to be sitting across from you, you would feel as if the pleasure of making a connection with you was the only purpose that existed for that person in that moment. For that someone, the only moment that would matter would be the present moment they were sharing with you. What you had done in your life previously would be irrelevant. They would not care who you were yesterday. "That's over", they would think. "It only exists as stories in your head. You are only what you are this moment, born fresh every second."

"Who are YOU?" that person would ask. "Come out of the collection of stories inside your head-universe. Come out and join me in the real moment. What do you know about the self you are NOW?" And if you were able to bring yourself out of the head-universe, to join that human being, fully present in the NOW, what **would** you be? What would you be right now, without all your judgments about other people and yourself, without your past, and your bowl of marbles, without your worries and plans about the future? What are you really? I am so curious.

As I said, I do not personally know anyone who is way up there at the tippy-end of "fully conscious," but I have met some people who seem pretty close, at least in certain circumstances. Very conscious people have a presence that radiates peace, strength, and profound compassion. They see opportunities for shared humor and creative, playful interaction everywhere. They don't take their "identities" very seriously, yet their words have tremendous influence. I bet the great teachers of humanity would have occupied the space at the very conscious end of the spectrum, and that is why their presence was so moving, their words so powerful. If you too were able to set down all of the things you think you know about your "identity" and "personality" to fully inhabit this moment of your life, your presence too, might calm, settle and move the people around you.

I imagine that Ghandi was one such as this -- a little man, unconcerned about his "identity", who moved a nation and ultimately the world with his presence. Down at one end of the spectrum of consciousness, you have the unconscious people who are so lost in the worlds inside their minds that they literally cannot take in information that is counter to their manufactured "reality". Up at the other end you have, say Ghandi, who was so at ease with what he was and what he was for, that he peacefully undermined the confidence of the most powerful imperialist nation on earth. Ghandi had to have filled his bowl with an extremely stable bowling ball to bow out of the Marble Game to the level at which he did. Dare you to aspire to be like Ghandi?

You have already begun moving up the consciousness spectrum just by asking yourself the questions in this book: questions about you, your **Marble Game Strategies**, your **Coping-Tactics**, your **identity**, your **reality,** and your **level of consciousness**. Holding open-ended questions with authentic curiosity starts to break up the unquestioned and unconscious stories you have had about who you are and "the way the world works." Asking yourself questions about the nature of who you are and why you are the way you are, and questioning if the nature of your reality serves you, begins to awaken in you a self who can fly outside the delusions of the mind-world, to consider a wider possibility for reshaping your reality and you. Above all, the more time you spend fully present to this moment of your life, connecting to the actual self you are right now, inhabiting the actual world around you right now, the more effortlessly conscious you will become.

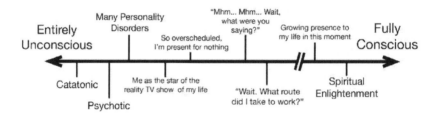

Chapter 4 - Section 3 Questions:

1) Where would you put yourself on the spectrum from unconsciousness to consciousness?

2) When are you most in the present moment, and how long do you stay there?

3) What are the most demanding thought loops or stories in your head that pull you out of the present moment?

4) Where would you put each parent on the consciousness spectrum? Can you remember times when your parents were fully present to you? What was that like?

5) Are there people in your life now who are fully present to you sometimes, and/or who you can be fully present to? What is that like?

6) What kinds of unconsciousness in the people around you, irritates **you** the most, and why?

7) What kinds of unconsciousness exhibited **by you**, irritates the people around you the most, and why?

6) Are you ever fully present to your partner? Is your partner ever fully present to you? What kinds of interactions between you cultivate mindfulness?

7) Can you be fully present with your children? How do they respond to you when you join them in the present moment?

Section 4: Core Truth and Finding the Seed

Mindfulness and the Actual World of this Moment

I am going to ask you again, who are you? I am not asking your name. I don't care what you do to make money. For right now, I don't want to know about the strings of beads around your neck, or the stories the beads represent. I am not asking about the coping tactic you turn your life over to when you cannot bear your helplessness, and I don't want to know about the kinds of marbles you hunger for. In this moment, I am asking you to step into a moment of mindfulness.

Remember my definition from chapter 3? "Mindfulness" is the practice of focusing on this present moment to the exclusion of everything else that your brain tends to want to think about. What is left when you set all of that down - to sit in the real world of the present moment outside your own head - and witness what you **are** without all of those mind-stories?

If you just took a minute to try it, perhaps you were successful, but most likely you were not, at least not yet. It seems hard! "My mind won't cooperate!" It can even be scary. I get it. Your mind has been constructing an armor of unconscious thought loops since you were a kid. I think one fear can be: "What if I **were** to set aside all that stuff that I **think** about me, only to find there wasn't anything left that mattered?!"

If "mindfulness" were as easy as just wanting to do it, we could all be Yoga masters the first day we set foot on a mat. However, in spite of the challenges, you may actually know more about who you really are than you think you do.

In your life there probably have been interactions or events that **did** draw you fully in to the land of the present moment without you even trying to get here. There have probably been times when the present moment was so absorbing that without even thinking about it, you temporarily set down your internal story-universe and dropped 100% into the actual world, even if it was just for a few seconds. In that moment, what was true about you? I am going to put forth the premise that in those times when you were fully present, those were the moments that wiped away all of the history and the stories of the self-made mind-world, to reveal vital information about the core of your real being.

Note on "mindfulness" - *Gaelen's pet peeve is the use of the term "mindful" as an imperative that means "pay attention!" or "watch it!" I.e. "Be mindful of your manners!" or "I want you to be mindful of your grades this quarter." "Mindfulness", as a concept, is so important, that I hate it when its meaning gets skewed and watered down, and also when it somehow gets tangled up with external criticism. Mindfulness is about full presence in this moment. There is no room for judgment in the present moment – literally. Judgment requires a perception of time - so one can compare a former desired state, or future desired state, to the current undesired state. So there is no room for judgment within the context of "mindfulness". Argh.*

Adam's Story

I have to tell you a funny-sad story. I had a client once, a young man named Adam who suffered from debilitating anxiety. His anxiety was so bad that he was forced to withdraw from all of his classes that quarter when I met him because he had missed so many of them. When social anxiety and his critical internal voice got the better of him, he couldn't leave his dorm room. It was hard for him even to come to therapy when things were bad. After I had worked with him for just a few weeks, we discovered that for some reason, he was a mindfulness prodigy! This is pretty unusual for someone with such a toothsome head-hamster. But Adam could really get into the present moment. All he had to do was go outside and hook in to the natural world. It even worked in the city, if he went to a park. He told me he would get the feeling that the trees wanted his attention and he would just focus on the movement of the leaves, and get absorbed.

Here is the thing though. Adam felt guilty for spending time in the present moment even though, after a few minutes of full presence to the real world, he experienced terrific relief from the clenched stomach, racing heart, and tight throat of anxiety. Though it felt completely wonderful to him to get out of his mind and in to the moment, he felt guilty. He said this: "I feel as if it isn't ok for me to be spending so much time hiding from what is 'really' going on."
"Hiding" from what was "**really**" going on?!

What was **really** going on was that the leaves were gently wiggling under the eternal sky. That is the only thing that was really going on. What Adam meant though, was that when he left his internal-head-world and came to inhabit the actual world, the worries and stories that were the most solid fixture of his internal story-universe felt neglected. He feared that something even worse than what he normally worried about could happen if he didn't constantly tend his anxious thought-loops like a garden. Adam's collection of internal stories felt like the real "real world" to him, while what was happening in the actual present moment felt like an escape-fantasy. The irony was both tragic and funny, though it was months before he was able to get enough perspective on the irony to laugh at it himself.

Your worries are not "real". Your history is not "real". Your identity is not "real". All of those things exist as nothing but thoughts in your head! You give them a kind of reality only when you think you "know" them.

"Stop!" a client said to me the other day, "What do you mean?! Cancer **is** real!" Yes, cancer is real. It is **your worries** that you might get cancer that are not real. They are only thoughts. They don't give you cancer, and they don't protect you from cancer. "But, what if I have cancer?!", he asked. Does worrying about cancer keep cancer from happening? Does worrying about it serve you in any regard? "No… except maybe it makes sure I get check-ups!" Do you really have to worry about getting cancer constantly to ensure that you schedule a yearly check-up? "Ok, but what if I **did have** cancer. I could die of it!" Would your worrying about dying of it keep you from dying of it? Would your constantly thinking about dying of it keep it from happening, as if the possibility of death is a pot that you must keep watching so it doesn't boil over?

When you are able to raise your **consciousness** about the difference between the stories in your head and what is real, something amazing becomes possible. What if you were to fully surrender to the truth that maintaining your identity-bead-strings is your responsibility, and it is up to you to manage them as you see fit. What if your accountability and authorship allowed you to develop the freedom and flexibility to single out one central truth about yourself, an unassailable reality about why you matter, to hold on to all your life long? Raising your consciousness regarding yourself as the author of your identity can allow you to snip the strings, and let the beads you don't want roll away to leave only what is real about you in the present moment.

Finding the Seed to Grow Your Bowling-Ball

How do you know what **is** real about yourself?

As I mentioned in the beginning of this section, there have probably been people, environments, and experiences in your life that **did** suck you fully into the present moment, without you even trying to get there. There have been times when the present moment was so absorbing that without even thinking about it, you temporarily set aside your internal story-universe and came 100% into the actual world, even if it was just for a few seconds.

You can do this. Remember what I said in chapter 3 about fragile parents sometimes being able to raise kids who feel a solid sense-of-self? If fragile parents are able to do that, it is at least partly because those parents were able to sink into the present moment to share a "You matter to me." moment with the baby. How about you?

- Have you ever stared into a baby's eyes and had time stop?
- Or watching your children playing in the yard, were plunged suddenly into the moment, struck by how perfect they are, or how perfect is the afternoon light?
- Have you ever stared into the eyes of your love, and had time stop?
- Or played or sung music with a group of people and gotten into a creative zone when the flow seemed so effortless and the sound so amazing, that it was almost like you **were** the music?
- If you were, or are, an athlete, remember that moment when all of a sudden everything came together, and time seemed to slow down as the universe partnered with you to create the magic goal/dive/leap/score/basket/play?
- Were you ever buried in a creative project so deeply that six hours passed before you looked up to realize that you had missed lunch?
- Or have you ever been on a walk in the woods and had all the stories judgments, and worries drop away, supplanted by the sound of the water and the smell of the trees, and the mystery of life?

If you said yes to any of those, or recognize the feeling I am describing, in that moment, you got out of your story-head, and were 100% present to the actual world.

Halt! If none of that resonated with you, don't give up! Don't start thinking* that you are so broken that there is no way you will ever be able to find your seed, raise your consciousness, or grow yourself a healthy bowling ball! If none of what I said about the experience of "full presence in the moment", resonated with you, all it means is that you are going to have to pay extra attention to the meditative practices at the end of chapter 3. You are going to need to give yourself lots of opportunity to fall into the present moment, so you have a chance to grasp what I am talking about. It isn't as if there is some sort of time pressure. Neither God or a panel of judges is assessing your speed or your performance. Don't forget, if you are exploring the questions in this book, you have raised your consciousness already! Being "on the road to growing a bowling ball", is a hell of a lot better than being utterly unconscious of the fact that you are even playing the Marble Game. (If you continue to struggle with getting into the present moment, even after trying some of the tricks I offered in chapter 3, I recommend you find yourself a real live be-in-the-moment mentor -- a therapist, a meditation teacher, etc.)

*Thinking about it doesn't help, by the way. Thinking about it just puts you straight into the comparative (i.e. judging) mind, like "Am I here, or am I there? Am I here, or am I there?" **There is no way to be here if you keep comparing here to there.**

The Relationship Between Doing and Being and Finding The Seed

With all the fuss I made at the beginning of chapter 3, about you not getting all trapped in your head-stories about being able to find the "right" thing to "do" in order to finally feel like you matter, I might have given you the impression that I think we should all sit around on cushions meditating all day, and not do much of anything. (I don't think that, by the way. I love having a physical body, and all the cool stuff I get to do and build and make happen with it.) Both of the stories I am about to relate are about people who found the seed to grow a bowling ball in the context of doing something. But they didn't find it because they had chosen the "right thing". They found it because they allowed themselves to sink into full presence in the moment, to be all that was real and important to them in that moment.

Your Core Truth is the Seed

The clearest look you can have at who and what you really are comes when you analyze what you were in those times of perfect presence in the moment. Study the moments that have called to you so clearly that you came out of your mind to be fully present to the actual world.

If this is difficult to conceptualize, another way I sometimes ask that question is: **"When were you the You-est You that you have ever been?"** Stop now. Get quiet and remember. Remember the time(s) in your life when you felt utterly tapped-in and connected. Remember when you just were you-in-the-flow-of-life-and-existence. What comes to you, about those moments? What was obvious and self-evident to you about reality and your self?

If you sink into what you experienced and learned about yourself in those moments, and when you think about it, it gives you a profound sense of being moved, or grounded, or rung like a bell, or connected to all things, then this is your core truth. You have the seed to grow your bowling ball.

Star's Story

Star loved to climb. When I met her she was an intense, graceful and articulate 27 year old. But I soon learned that she had been an awkward, clumsy, introverted kid who had been born to a big, gregarious, team-sport-oriented family. As you might imagine, Star grew up feeling like an alien, both in her family system and in her own body. She could not catch or throw a football. Nor could she generally get a word in edgewise at the dinner table. And even if she did get a chance to speak, what she said always seemed to confuse and discomfit everyone, so she learned to just keep quiet. As a young adult, Star struggled with depression, anxiety, and a profound experience of purposelessness. Then, by chance, she found climbing. For the first time in her life, Star was really good at something physical. And when I asked her the question: "When were you the You-est You that you have ever been?" She told me that she felt as if she met her real self while climbing. She said, "I was born to climb."

"I was born to climb" was Star's core truth. Those were the words she used, but what she was really recalling to herself when she said them was an experiential moment of profound mindfulness that would occasionally happen when she was climbing. She told me: "I am way up high, clinging to the side of this huge mountain. My fingers and toes are imbedded in cracks and

I feel like a tiny speck, like a bug on side of a mountain. No, it's more than that. I feel like I am a tiny speck clinging to the side of the whole earth in space… utterly insignificant... while at the same time I feel like I AM the earth. I am connected to everything." In those moments Star could not doubt that she mattered. She felt a profound connection to everything, almost as if she **was** everything.

I told this story to a client one time and he said, "But how can that be someone's core truth? If she fell and broke her back and got stuck in a wheel chair, she wouldn't be able to climb, and then her life would be pointless. That can't be a core truth!" Remember though that I said that those were the words Star **used**, to remind herself of a **feeling** she sometimes experienced in the present moment, the feeling of profound and mysterious connectedness. Even confined to a theoretical wheelchair, Star could say her core-truth words in moments of stress or doubt, to bring back a little piece of that knowing, a little piece of faith about her real self that could bring her out of the mind-world and more into mindfulness in any moment. It is a knowing about her own existence that climbing had brought to her that she never lost.

Alta's story

My grandmother loved her husband very much. His name was Gordon: a petite, asthmatic, brilliant, red-head. I should say Gordon and Alta loved each other. She always told to me that that was all she ever really wanted to do with her life, love him, and be with him, and travel with him, and dance with him. She closed her eyes to remember the feeling, "We danced and danced!" She told me the stories again and again. As a little girl, I had loved to spend time in their room, where she kept a closet full of a lifetime of dancing dresses, all different colors. There weren't any from the 30s, although there was a pair of white kid gloves from that time, because my grandparents had been very poor back then. (She said everyone was poor back then. You just danced in what you had.) But there were a couple of dresses left from the forties, a lot from the fifties and sixties, and even a few from the seventies, in all the bright flower prints and colors Alta loved. They kept dancing all through their marriage until he became ill from Parkinsons and died in 1986, at the age of seventy-two. My Grandmother outlived Gordon by twenty-two years, but she never stopped telling me about the dancing, the music, the swirling people, the wonderful places where they danced, and what a beautiful dancer my grandfather was. If I had asked her the question, "When were you the You-est You that you ever were?" Alta would have answered, "When I was dancing with your grandfather. I was born to dance with your grandfather." She would have said this at ninety-four even though he had been gone for twenty-two years. Gordon's death did not rob Alta of her core truth. Whenever my grandmother would close her eyes and remember dancing with Gordon, she brought herself home to **the truth of her connectedness:** to him, to the music, to all the happy people, and to dancers everywhere who love their beautiful dancing-partners. To the end of her life, my grandmother could remember how much she mattered, how connected she was, by remembering, "I was born to dance with your grandfather." No one and nothing could take that away from her, not even the loss of him.

Did my grandmother need to find dancing, to find her core truth? Would Star never have met her real self, if a friend had not challenged her to come climbing with him for the first time one day? I have to believe that my grandmother would have found another thing to do with my grandfather that would have put her in touch with the same core-truth feeling experience, even if she had lived in a culture that didn't allow men and women to dance together. And Star would have found something else: horses, or drumming, or yoga, or skiing that helped her fall into the true nature of herself in the present moment.

The Core Truth of The Marble Game Itself

For most of human history we lived on the edge of subsistence. The fact that we mattered was in our faces every day. Back then, if individual members of a group did not contribute to the family or clan, there was not enough to eat, blanket weaving did not keep up with the cold, there was not enough wood to keep the fire going, and babies cried but were not comforted. Every person's contribution to the group counted as human culture was evolving. We used to see the direct result of the work of our hands and **know** we mattered. But, in wealthier parts of the industrialized world that is, in large part, no longer true. We have become isolated and alienated from our work, each other, and our significance to the real world. No wonder so many of us seek connection and proof of our significance in the virtual world of social media.

I believe that we are all searching for the same experience of profound connectedness, the inarguable self-evident experience that we matter. But, if you are ready, it can find you. Do something. Do the thing that feels like it might allow you to hedge your mindfulness bets, but most importantly do something to give the actual world the opportunity to connect to you in the present moment. It is here and now that you will meet your Self.

What is so true about you that no one could take it from you? You could be in a room full of 100 people, and they could all be pointing and shouting at you "That isn't true! We know the truth! You are a liar! You are deluded! You are crazy! We know you better than you know yourself!", but the judgment would roll right past you. What is so true about you that you could stand in the center of that doubting, judging, attacking crowd and create a place of perfect peace inside of yourself, a quiet place of refuge to allow you to hold your self firm and solid against any storm of judgment, and against any invalidating attacks on your identity. What is so true that in the face of all those people trying to define you for their own purposes, you could define your own self. This is your core truth. And it is the seed from which you grow your bowling ball.

If you know what you are and why you are here, then you will know when the judgment of other people fits you and when it doesn't. If you know what you are, then unwarranted attacks from judgers don't weigh very much, because if you **know** something is not true about you, being accused of it doesn't bother you at the core of what you really are. If you know what you really are, then you know your own value in your own eyes. You don't need marbles from other people reinforcing a fantasy identity that you thought you needed in order to matter. If you know what you really are then you can stop getting trapped in thought-loops about all the things you are supposed to be 'doing', and 'doing right'. You are you, right now, just as you are.

It is possible to have more than one core truth, but it is likely that you won't have a dozen, or even six. If you think you have that many, then there are probably common themes among them.

So what are you? What is your life for? Why were you born?

Section 5: A You Who Fits

Letting Your Fantasy-Self Die

Now that you are starting to work on what you are, what aren't you? Your fantasy self is composed of two different kinds of beliefs:

> 1) the stuff you really want to be true about you (because you think it makes you matter more), but that isn't particularly true and
> 2) the stuff you try to hide about yourself (because you are afraid it makes you matter less) that also isn't particularly true.

Not only does it require a tremendous amount of work to shore up aspects of identity that are not particularly true, but the ever present possibility of being found out makes your head-hamster very busy. So, it is time to start letting your fantasy self die. You are not going to need it anyway. Once you have a bowling ball, there will only be room for two things in the bowl of your identity: your core truth(s), and the elements of identity that you have decided to adopt just because you want to – aspects that serve the vision you have of who you really want to be.

Once you have a reliably solid bowling ball, and are thereby finally able to rest on the faith that you inherently matter, you will have the luxury of taking on other secondary aspects of identity more lightly and with humility. These would be aspects you decide to cultivate for fun, adventure, personal growth, or just because they make your life feel more meaningful to you. There is no need to defend these secondary aspects of identity with Marble Game conserving strategies, because you will know you don't need your secondary identities in order to matter. You'll have an unassailable core truth established in the bowl already.

Right now, I have "I am a writer" in my bowl. That is fun for me, and kind of exciting, but I don't need "I am a writer" in my bowl to feel ok or good about myself. If someone were to say to me, "You aren't a writer. You have never had a book published!" I would say to them, "That is true, if that is your definition of what "writer" is. But to me, I am spending a lot of time writing in my life right now, so that makes me a writer, to me." Will I still have "writer" in my bowl a year from now? I don't know. I hope I will. I really like having it in there now. But I might be more interested in having some other elements of identity in there next year, so "writer" might get bumped. I don't have an attachment, or a need to defend that identity.

Alternatively, if someone attacks one of my core-truths, there is no need to defend those either. I might not want to hang around a person who is attacking one of my core truths, because it is not an enjoyable experience to be with someone who is trying to shore up his or her own sense-of-self by attacking mine, but I would not be particularly threatened or upset. As I said, real core-truths are virtually unassailable.

Telling New Stories and the Shaping of Reality

How do you snip the strings of the identities you don't want, and take up the new ones you do want? Stop repeating the old stories to yourself and everyone else, and start telling new ones. That's it.

For some of my clients this turns out to be really easy. They have a revolutionary moment, sometimes in a session, sometimes in a moment of self-created mindfulness, wherein they realize that half of the way they have been seeing themselves was completely bogus, or perhaps a major paradigm they were carrying around, about "the way the world works" was completely false. Voila! All of a sudden, they are a new person living in a new universe with new rules. That isn't to say all their problems disappear, but perhaps they get a new set that comes with the new self. I had a moment like this in grad school when a colleague helped me realize that, while I had been given messages all my young life that led adult-me to believe I was a 4 on the Enneagram (a popular personality-typing system), I am actually a 5. All of a sudden, I made sense to myself in a completely different way, a way that allowed me to have compassion for myself at a level I had never experienced. I have felt more comfortable in my own skin, ever since. Simple basic shifts in perception can have big, systemic ramifications.

For most of my clients, though, learning to stop telling the Self old stories and start telling new ones is a more gradual process. **It takes a rise in consciousness, the waking up in the present moment to the you who is repeating an identity-story and the conscious and intentional reframing of that old story (or the replacement of it) with a new one.** Waking up to an inner voice retelling you identity stories and to your physical voice telling other people old stories about you is a process that can take some time. But, if you decide to do it, and commit to raising your consciousness around it, it is completely in your reach. Some of my clients wear a bracelet to help them remember, or keep stickies on the bathroom mirror, in their car, or on the computer with little reminder notes about who they are becoming.

Shifting central identity themes and paradigms that feel so true to you can seem impossible. "How can I be other than what I **am**!?" "How can reality work other than the way I **know** it works!?" It is often hard to stand back far enough to see yourself, and your unquestioned beliefs, with a new perspective. If it **is** difficult to come up with new stories to tell yourself about you, that support the identities you want to wear, getting a therapist who can help you "reframe" the life you have had, and give you outside perspective on the negative paradigms you carry about "the way the world works," can be really helpful. Sometimes friends or clergy can help too, though you have to be awake to any unconscious motivations of the people around you, their own biases, and Marble Game strategies.

If it is your intention to adopt some aspects of identity that are completely new to you, you are going to need to create opportunities to live completely new stories, to collect on your new string of beads. For example, if you have always been timid, and are sick of wearing that string, but you can't find any "courageousness" in your history, even after much searching, it is time to get out there and do some brave stuff. If you have always seen yourself as driven by money or ambition, and want to be more balanced, but you can't find stories to support your new identity, start making choices that lead to different kinds of events happening in your life: take vacations, leave work on time, hang out with your family with no plans but to be present to them in the moment. Collect the new stories you have been creating as identity beads.

In the beginning, the change will probably feel like a lot of work. Even if you are wearing a bracelet, setting an alarm on your phone, or even papering your living space with reminder-stickies to help you remember who you are becoming, staying conscious to your in-the-moment behavior is challenging! We are wired to spend most of the time lost inside our mind-universes, while our outside behavior runs on automatic programming. The good news is, the more you stay awake to the present moment, consciously constructing your new identity, the more the constructions begin to reinforce themselves. It won't be the case that you will have to work this hard for the rest of your life. If you are committed, eventually you can and will reprogram your brain. (8)

Another problem you may run into is the issue of feeling like you are a big faker - pretending to be something you are not. Frankly, you may be right. In the beginning you **may** actually **be** a big faker. So what? What does that have to do with anything important? I was a big faker the day I sat across from my first client in the therapist chair. I was pretending to be a "therapist", but I was terrified. If I called myself a "therapist" the first day, did that mean I **was** one? If not, when did I become one? Would it have benefited my first client, or me, if when we sat down together for the first time, and the first words out of my mouth were: "I am not really a therapist yet." Are you a "parent" the first second someone hands you a baby? Are you a gardener as you dig your first hole? There is no one who can answer those questions for you, but you. Me claiming "therapist", you claiming "mother", or "doctor", or "kind", or "good listener", or "brave", is only ever a statement of faith and intention on the first day. But it is also a statement of intention, and the inalienable right to define the self.

Eventually all successful beginners grow into their identities. We fake it until we make it. That is how we change who we are.

Chapter 4 - Section 5 Questions:

1) When were you the **You-est You**, that you have ever been?

2) What comes to you about the moments in your life when a magical something pulled you right into full presence to the Now. What was obvious and self-evident to you about reality and your self?

3) What is your core-truth? What is the in-the-moment feeling experience you can recall to yourself when you say the words? What are the words you use to recall the moment to you?

4) What are some secondary aspects of your identity that you want to keep in your bowl?

5) What are some aspects of your identity that you want to release?

6) Do you want to change those things because they run counter to your core truth? Or are they actually aspects of your identity that require surrendering to, because there is not really anything wrong with them. And it is your judgment about them that needs releasing, not the aspects themselves.

Section 6: Shifting Paradigms

Reality is Shifting All Around You

"You can't do that! Real life doesn't work that way! You can't just change what you are by pretending you have changed, and acting differently!"

Maybe that is true, but I say you **can** change who you are, by pretending you have already changed, and then just **being** different; making choices from then on that are in accordance with the change. How does it benefit you to keep the paradigm that "People cannot change who they are." that **you** cannot change who you are? What do you get out of it? Do you really want to hang on to a belief about the way the universe works that traps you into the small box of your own helplessness? Do you need to hold on to that paradigm in order to trap other people into continuing to produce marbles for you? Wouldn't you rather believe you **can** adopt an identity that you can love and embrace? Or do you need to be "right" about your belief that you can't?

In my universe you can change who you are and what you believe. If I did not believe that what I just said was true, I could not do the work I do with my clients. If I did not hold open the possibility that they and their lives could be different, I would only help them stay the same. The truth is, I see people make amazing changes all the time. A big part of the reason why is that **I know** they can.

"Alice laughed: "There's no use trying," she said; "one can't believe impossible things." "I daresay you haven't had much practice," said the Queen. "When I was younger, I always did it for half an hour a day. Why, sometimes I've believed as many as six impossible things before breakfast."

- From <u>Alice in Wonderland</u> by Lewis Carroll

But are the realities we choose to adopt "true"? Hm... Sometimes... A lot of times. If we believe in them... I guess my final answer to this question is: "I don't care if they are true, if they are working!" Is it the absolute truth that people who want to change can? Maybe it isn't the absolute truth about all people, but it is a truth that works for me. I will say that people who don't think they can change are caught in a trap that guarantees that they will stay the same. Knowing you can change is a prerequisite to successfully adopting a different identity, and I see people make changes all the time that they once thought were impossible.

Change Your Lens

Change your lens to create your own reality. Do your beliefs about the way life and the universe "work" serve you? If not, I invite you to do some research about an opposing belief, that could help you change your mind. Also, I invite you to embrace being wrong! And laugh! It feels good! Here is my all-time life-favorite quote!

Since things neither exist nor don't exist,
Are neither real nor unreal,
Are utterly beyond adopting and rejecting -
One might as well burst out laughing.

> --*Longchen Rabjampa (1308-1363), Nyingma Master and Scholar*

What do you wish you could believe? Here are some examples of realities that I choose to adopt because they work and because I choose to live in the kind of universe that these beliefs support. And perhaps, because I believe in them, they seem to virtually always come through for me. Some of the reality beads (paradigms) on my string are:

1) "If you were able to know any person well enough, s/he would make sense."
2) "Every person does the best s/he can, based on what s/he knows."
3) "Every person inherently matters."
4) "Being happy is a much easier goal to reach than being right."
5) "Mistakes are only mistakes if you didn't learn anything."
6) "Suffering exists to draw your attention to a thing that needs to change."
7) "Unconsciousness sucks!"

Are any of those paradigms true in the absolute? In **this** context, the question is irrelevant. They are true to me. And there is no panel of judges, and no figure with more authority to rule on my paradigms than me. **There is no one with more authority to evaluate your paradigms than you.** So what collection of truths about the way your universe works do you **want** to start collecting as reality-beads? **You choose.** If you start researching information that supports a new belief you want to adopt, and hanging out with people who already accept the paradigm, you may be surprised how painless it is that you have been wrong all along.

The Hamster's Escape

"Thus unpredictability, chaos, wildness lie at the heart of the universe. We do not live in a predetermined, clockwork, mechanistic cosmos. The door is always open for revelation, emergence, newness, and transformation." - David Spangler

I recommend you begin to make peace with unintended and unforeseen effects of your changes. Get ready to champion, in your life and in your relationships, the intent to continue to alter your identity based on new information and new perspectives as you encounter them. The more time you spend in the present moment, as opposed to your internal story-world, the more authentic your identity will be. And the more authentic you are, the more you will continue to learn and change and grow. Your core-truth may stay solid, but some of the aspects of identity you are cultivating right now are transient. You will be a different person tomorrow if you stay open to the aspects of yourself that the present moment is calling for now.

The actual world is not like a hamster wheel, but it is inherently unpredictable. **Chaos* is the Core-Truth of a physical, temporal reality.** That is part of the magnificent adventure of real life. If we knew absolutely who we were, and who everyone else was, and if our responses were completely consistent, and everyone else's responses were completely consistent, and the universe's responses were predictable, we would be meat machines living in a mechanistic universe. No thank you. Your hamster might believe it longs for predictability, but certainty is soon just another horrible wheel to escape from.

So how do we cope? How can we tolerate the helplessness we feel when there is no solid ground in the universe but the faith we find inside ourselves? In the interest of assisting you in adopting realities that bypass powerlessness and support your authorship, I would like to offer you a paradigm I have named "**The Hamster's Escape.**" This shift in reality begins with one of the most important questions I ever ask my clients:

What is the only way to feel comfortable existing within a universe that is inherently chaotic and unpredictable?

The Hamster's Escape is a two-part answer, and it is the most fundamentally important "reality" I have come to about the way the human experience works best.

1) Surrender utterly to the truth that that is just the way that it is and it will never be any different.

2) Know you are up for it.

There is no way to make yourself safe from pain or the unexpected while you are still alive. We are not safe. Being alive is not safe. Loss is inherent to change, and change will find you no matter what you do to hide from it, no matter what "right" path you think you have found, or what "right" view of reality, you adopt. Chaos comes. All we can do is the internal work necessary to replace helplessness with **authorship** by remaining flexible and present to each moment so we can change ourselves as required and adapt.

Chapter 4 - Section 6 Questions:

1) What are some of your fundamental beliefs about the way life and the universe work?

2) Which of your paradigms serve you well? Which are hard to live with and would be great to be "wrong" about?

3) If you wanted to be wrong about those paradigms, what could you do to expose yourself to new information and new ways of thinking?

4) What do you wish you could believe? How could you gather supporting evidence for those beliefs?

*Definition: Chaos Theory – The branch of mathematics that deals with complex systems whose behavior is highly sensitive to slight changes in conditions, so that small alterations can give rise to strikingly great consequences.

Section 7: Growing Your Bowling Ball

Integrity is Your Fertilizer and the Rudder for Your Boat.

When it first dawned on me that the picture of reality that was making the most sense for both me and my clients dictated that there simply was no way to tame the wild universe, I felt for a period of time I as if I was walking around with a great gaping nothingness under my feet. It felt like no one was running THE show, and perhaps **nothing** mattered. Maybe the universe made no sense. It was a bona fide existential crisis. Then I read <u>Man's Search for Meaning</u> (21) by Viktor Frankl. His book chronicled his experiences as a Nazi concentration camp inmate, and described a method for finding a reason to live even under the most extreme circumstances. His conclusion was that it is up to you. It is not up to your parents, your children, God, or the universe. No one outside of you can hand you a reason to **be** here. It is up to **you** to find **your reason**.

Life is about learning to manage your anxiety while you surrender to chaos, fully inhabiting the present moment so you can perceive the infinite possibilities -- learning to play with them as if they are a box of cosmic art supplies, thereby turning your life itself into a magnificent mixed-media experiential art project!

Sounds fun, right? No? Sounds dangerous?!

"It's hard to be brave, when you're only a Very Small Animal." – A.A. Milne as "Piglet"

How do we not get swept away by all of the overwhelming catastrophic forces of the Chaos that is the ocean in which we swim? Every brave voyager needs a rudder.

In section 3 of this chapter, I offered you an avenue for discovering **the seed** of why you matter. Then in the last section, I said **"There is no one with more authority to evaluate your paradigms than you."** I will go further now to say that the only thing we can ever truly **have** authority over in this existence **is** our paradigms. Even your physical body can be controlled and enslaved by someone else. Paradigms, perspective and attitude are the spin-offs of core-truth, and they are the only things you can have 100% power over, the only things you can be 100% true to.

The core-truth seed is what you know you are, something that can never be taken from you. Now I offer you a path for growing that seed into a full blown and stable bowling ball, for plugging the hole in the bowl of your Self: **Integrity**.

When I say "integrity", I am not referring to a common usage for the word, "living your life steadfastly adhering to high moral standards." Whose morals are those? What panel of judges came up with an outside list for you to measure yourself against? What I am referring to is the integrity that arises in response to a list of personal ethics dictated by a you that is in alignment with your own core-truth. Integrity is you being true to yourself, rather than being true to what other people have downloaded into you in order to keep you producing marbles for them. When we make choices in our lives that are in alignment with who and what we really are, our seed grows bigger and more solid until it finally plugs the hole in the bottom of the bowl. When we make choices that are counter to our integrity, we start forgetting why we matter, and our bowling ball shrinks. Sometimes, if the breach of integrity was particularly bad, our bowling ball pops altogether, just like a soap bubble, and we have to start all over to grow a new one.

Fear is Integrity's nemesis

The most common reason you might violate personal ethics (make choices that are not in alignment with who you really are) is fear:

- Fear that other people won't give you marbles any more if you become someone who makes sense to you, more than you make sense to them
- Fear other people will pop the marbles you have so carefully collected in your identity bowl with their negative judgments, or tip over your bowl altogether
- Fear that in setting down the old paradigms that used to govern your actions, so as to adopt new ones that fit you better, it might turn out that you cease to matter when measured against the old rules
- And, if you are embroiled in the super-trap of an addiction, fear that if you turn away from the master coping-tactic of your addiction, all the pain and all the emptiness, and all the self-judgment that your addiction promises to keep at bay, will come rushing back like a tsunami to completely obliterate the bowl of your self

When I begin to suggest to clients that they might leave behind being directed by the paradigms that were programmed into them by other people in favor of living a life that is directed by their own personal integrity, the most common fear my clients voice sounds something like this: "Wait a minute, won't that be **mean**? Isn't that's **selfish**? Won't I **hurt other people's feelings**?!" It is tempting to spin off now on a review of chapter one, and why it is that it is not actually possible to be authentically generous towards another person if you are not sporting a full bowl. Instead I want to tell you a story. This story is called:

What Does Real Kindness Look Like?

Once upon a time I had a client I will call Stewart, Sarah, James, Jason, Becky, Roland, Susan, Martha, Kendra, Abigail, Timothy, Lindsey, Bob, Tracy, Travis, Darnell, and on and on. I actually think this might be the story of 57% of the people who walk into my office with a hamster in their head. So let's call him Darnell.

Darnell's mother (dad, girlfriend in Florida, ex who swore to "stay friends", sister, and so on and so on) **loved** Darnell. Darnell loved his mother too. But, Darnell was working towards standing in his integrity, out surfing the edge of chaos, and trolling the present moment for possibilities to weave his life into the most magnificent mixed-media experiential art-project possible. Mom was a part of that picture for Darnell, but not a **large enough** element from Mom's point of view. Darnell did not call his mother enough to make her feel as if she was still central to his story line. In truth, the fact that Darnell was spending so much time in the present moment, rather than in his head-world retelling himself stories about what a great mother he had been blessed with, was viewed as further evidence that **she did not matter** to Darnell any more. He disagreed. Darnell loved his mother.

She called him a lot. She left messages. Sometimes she left messages daily. Sometimes she texted, message after message. "Call me." "You haven't called me" "You never call me." "Why don't you call me." When Darnell did call her, the first words out of her mouth were, "So you finally decided to call me." Darnell's mother really really wanted him to call her more often. Even more than that, she wanted him **to want to talk to her** more often.

Darnell wanted to call his mother. But even more importantly to him, he wanted to have the space to be able to **want** to talk to her. But, she nagged him to call so often, and was so critical when he did call that the authentic wanting on his part had been all squeezed out. Darnell was no longer able to want to call her. And though in the magnificent mixed-media experiential art-project-life that Darnell was building, "authentically wanting to talk to my Mom" was part of his picture, his mother was not cooperating.

Darnell consulted his integrity and realized there was only one thing to do. And, it was super scary. It broke a half-dozen paradigms about "the way the universe works" that had been programmed into him by family, and school, and the dominant culture, all of his life. Darnell called his mother and told her this: "Mom, I love you. And I really really want to want to talk you. But somehow there has been this terrible dynamic set up that prevents me from having what I really want. So from now on, **I am only going to call you when I authentically want to talk you.**" Darnell's mom (dad, girlfriend, ex etc.) freaked out! "But that is so selfish! It's mean! You have hurt my feelings!"

Stop for a second. What does real kindness look like? Is it kind to call someone out of obligation just so you don't hurt their feelings and they can get a hollow marble for their bowl, **rolling your eyes or watching TV as they are talking**? Is it kind to go out with someone even though you know there is no chance you would want to be with them, just so they don't have to experience you being "mean" by turning them down? Is it kind to text your sweetheart back when s/he texts you every five minutes, while you grit your teeth with annoyance at the incessant interruption? Is it kind to pretend responsiveness to his or her sexy invitation in order to keep the peace, disassociating from the present moment the minute you hit the bed?

More than she wanted Darnell to call her, Darnell's Mother wanted him to **want to talk to her**. She was trying to force him to want to by nagging him, thereby ensuring that neither she, nor he, could get what they both wanted. Acting from his integrity, Darnell ultimately did the most kind thing he could do, the thing that was most in support of the relationship they both wanted in the long term. Being "true to your self" is not "being mean". It is respectful. It is you treating the other person like an equal partner in the relationship. It is telling the truth.

I have had clients who are so run from "not being selfish" and "not hurting feelings" that their families don't know them at all. They buy greeting cards in bulk, filling them with meaningless platitudes, and sending them out faithfully when the calendar says to. They even show up for weekly marble exchange dinners where nothing real is ever said, because that might make someone uncomfortable. Everything looks pristine. But no one is seen or known. Is that kind? Is hiding and pretending and faking kindness until there is not a speck of authentic connection left between you and the people you are supposed to love "kind"?

I am going to maintain that in your intimate relationships, unless you risk physical danger, **it is never a mistake to act from your personal integrity and be real.** In being real you may incur temporary hardship. You may bother someone, make them mad, hurt their feelings, break the rules, or get abandoned, but, ultimately, if you are not real, you can not be known, and if you are not known, you can not be loved. If you are real, the people around you will tend to become more real over time as well, so they too can have the experience of being known and really loved. It is scary but it is worth it.

Darnell's Mom eventually did adjust to a son who lives his life from his personal integrity. It turned out he really did want to call his mom, and they have the best relationship they have ever had. It's real! Mostly, my clients' families, partners, friends, and exes eventually adjust. Most people who start out scared to death by the unpredictability of an authentic connection, end up loving how "real" feels! And, if the people around you don't, that is a very important thing for you to consider. What does it mean if someone in your life really cannot get over the fact that you are not any longer the person s/he demands that you be? Is that kind of resistance to your core-truth, which is the soul of what you are, a dynamic you even **want** in your life?

The fear programmed into us as children is a powerful motivating force that can drive us away from integrity, consciousness, core-truth, and each present moment in the actual world. Every decision we make that is driven by fear is an attempt by the self to avoid suffering. But, somehow the life choices we make that are sourced out of fear never seem to avert the pain we are trying to avoid. **Not living your life in accordance with your personal integrity causes more suffering than it averts**, e.g.

- A young man thinks that being cool is more attractive than being real, so he plays cool and loses the quality real-girl of his dreams to the guy who **is** willing to be real.
- A young girl stands back and says nothing in defense as friend is teased and tortured at school, day after day. Friend commits suicide. Girl comes to my office twenty years later, after half a lifetime of suffering guilt and self-recrimination.
- A personal assistant knows the boss is up to something illegal, but does not report anything out of fear of losing her job, so she gets taken down with the boss and prosecuted in the sting.
- A teen is afraid of being ostracized from his social group if he objects to getting into the car with a driver who is drunk, so he climbs in to the passenger seat and ends up paralyzed for life from the accident.
- A woman all full of self-loathing, determined to make the judging voices in her head shut up, dresses up and goes alone to a bar. She picks up a stranger and goes home with him just to feel wanted. The next morning the self-judging voices are louder and more toxic than they were the night before.
- A mother is afraid of getting in the way and making it worse when Father is angry, so she leaves the room and is not there to intervene as her child is beaten.
- Bystanders fear the power of the 3rd Reich, so they hide their eyes and stand by as millions of people are wiped from existence. The victims' pain ends with death, but the bystanders and their children live with internalized-guilt for generations.

When you make choices based on anything but being true to yourself, you bring suffering on yourself, and sometimes to other people.

I am not an airy-fairy idealist. I get that living from personal integrity is scary, and just because you make a choice that is true to who you are does not mean that nothing bad will happen to you as a result. The young girl who stood by might have been tortured as well if she intervened. The young man who got in the car might have been ostracized if he had refused. The mother might have sustained a concussion if she had stepped in. And some of the Germans who tried to help their Jewish neighbors were executed. A life sourced from integrity is not a pain-free, but it **is a** life free of the soul-torture sourced from fear. If you make your choices based from integrity, you may still lose your friends, your partner, your reputation, even your life. But if you make choices based from fear, there is no guarantee that you won't still lose all of those things, and there is a guarantee **you will end up losing your Self.**

I am also not GOD. I do not have a personal attachment to you making choices based from your personal integrity. You are on your own path. But I do know this: If you choose to go against your integrity, then you will engender suffering for yourself; the greater the breach in your integrity, the greater the suffering that results. But that's ok. Your suffering belongs to you. When I listed out for you a half dozen of the paradigms that make up my reality, I remember saying something like, **"Suffering exists to draw your attention to a thing in your life that needs to change."** So suffering too, is, in and of itself, a valuable thing.

If you make choices that are not in alignment with your integrity you will not grow a bowling ball. A healthy, solid sense of self comes from living in alignment with your core truth. But that too, is on you. No judgment called for. If you do not live true to yourself then the one who suffers the most is you. There are no mistakes, only choices. Mistakes are the choices we don't learn from. So we just make them and suffer again. There are choices that are in one's integrity, and choices that are not. Choices based from fear will induce suffering, but they are not "wrong." They just provide further opportunities for learning. Suffering creates the pressure for you to make choices based out of integrity. Suffering is your mirror, and your compass. It nudges you towards a full-bowl future.

Chapter 4 - Section 7 Questions:

1) When have you suffered the most from making choices that were not in alignment with your personal integrity?

2) When is it the most hard to be real now? With whom is it the most hard?

3) What are the dueling imperatives that are in your way in those moments?

4) Where in your life do you know you most need to bring your personal integrity to bear, instead of being run by fear?

Section 8: Change's Nemesis, Judgment

The Puppy Story

Once upon a time, you decided that you wanted to be getting more exercise, and hiking could be a good path to try. (In addition, walking in nature provides one with a good opportunity to practice mindfulness. I had to throw that in!) Anyway, it then occurred to you that if you had a dog, you would have even more of a reason to stay committed to your new hiking practice. Dogs need to go for walks, and you realized you might have a tendency to be even better to your dog than you might be to yourself. "Eureka! A dog it is!" You were so excited that you hopped right into your truck, drove to the Humane Society, and picked out the puppy of your dreams! The next day, determined to begin your new practice immediately, you got the puppy in your truck and drove straight to the base of the mountain to have your first hike together in the great outdoors.

Now the puppy had been in a kennel since she was born and the big outdoors was pretty big, so she was a little nervous when you got her out of the truck and put her on the ground. She sat down and sniffed the air. "Ready to go, girl?" you said to her. Then you got right behind her and began to push your new puppy up the hill. Her eyes rolled back to look at you, but she did not budge. You stopped for a minute, stood up, scratched your head, and examined the dog … <What the heck? Puppies love to go for walks…> "Come on girl, here we go!" Back down you got behind her, and began to push the puppy up the hill again, harder this time. She was resisting you strongly now. Her skinny legs braced against the slope, little doggy toes gripping the earth, pushing back against you for all she was worth. "What the hell! Bad Dog!" you yelled. The puppy, pulling away from you sharply, went and ran under your truck.

Ending #1: You charged over to the truck. "Bad! Bad Dog! Puppies love to go for walks! You are broken and defective! It just figures, I get the one freaking defective puppy on the planet!"

Ending #2: "Oh sweetie, are you nervous? It **is** a big world out here. Let me get down with you and scratch your ears while you sniff the ground. See nothing bad is happening. Come on now. Follow me. You're ok! Good dog! Good girl! You're doing fine!" And you began to slowly walk up the hill. She took a couple of steps, listening… then a couple of more… "Good dog!" And after a minute she was trotting towards you, and before you knew it, she was tearing up the trail, tail wagging with doggie excitement, with you charging up the hill behind her. "Wait for me!"

Most people live their lives as if they are trying to push a puppy up a hill. Only the thing is, **the puppy is you**. And it is really true; puppies **do** love to go for walks. All they need is a bit of practice getting to the present moment and some reassurance as they learn to manage their anxiety in the big chaotic universe.

We are taught from childhood that change is hard. Having the life you want is hard. You have to work hard to fight your natural inclinations for laziness, disorganization, procrastination, pleasure-seeking, and selfishness to **force yourself** to do the **"right" thing**, and make yourself **do what you should do**, what you are **supposed to be doing**.

However, what if it just isn't that hard to make life happen if you are creating a life for yourself that you actually want to live, and spending your time doing things that were truly meaningful and interesting to you? Puppies love to go for walks. It is in their nature. Humans also love to explore new frontiers, make connections, follow their curiosity, invent things, build things, grow things, sew things, knit things, play music, write music, listen to music, dance and hold hands. Humans love to look into the eyes of the ones they love and share a perfectly mindful "You matter to me." moment. If you don't love the things that are inherent to your human nature, I can tell you why. They were judged, shamed, guilted, ignored or scared out of you. It is possible to teach a puppy to hate walks.

"But I need my self-judgment, or I won't learn!"

The paradigm that children won't learn without critical judgment is deeply pervasive in our culture. And by the time we are adults, the paradigm has been internalized by most of us as **guilt** and **self-judgment**. I have client after client answer the question "What is self-judgment for?" with "It helps me learn.", and "What is guilt for?" with "It helps me remember what I should be doing, and keep me from doing what I shouldn't do." Oh really? If guilt kept people from doing the things they shouldn't be doing, the news would not be full of the sex scandals of politicians, priests and televangelists, to say nothing of domestic abuse.

Critical judgment, both external and internal, does not in fact help people learn better or faster. Research has demonstrated just the opposite, in fact. Kids' performance on tests goes down as level of external criticism goes up (22). Adult job performance also goes down (23). This result makes sense, if you think about it, because self-judgment and guilt engender anxiety. And, anxiety sucks up brain space with its escalating thought-loops, like a hungry hamster. Anxiety makes you stupid, so guilt and self-judgment make you stupid.

If anxiety makes you stupid, where does the idea that "criticism, guilt, and shame help me learn" come from? I have a hypothesis about that. Being subjected to criticism, guilting, and shaming as a child, does "help you learn" two things. They help you learn to produce marbles for the bowls of your parents, and they also help you learn not to trigger their intolerable parental feelings of helplessness that produce negative reactions.

External judgment, shame, and guilt are tools of power and control. They get a foothold in the psyche when a young child is still in the developmental phase of requiring outside care-giver reflection for positive self-definition. Remember "Spare the rod and spoil the child?" While the physical beating of children has become less societally acceptable, the emotional "rod" of critical judgment remains the most popular and little-questioned method for getting kids to do (and appear to be) what parents want... and it works reasonably well, at least temporarily. Chapter 1 is full of examples of how individuals use judgment as a way to protect their bowls, extort marbles, and even train other people to become marble producing machines.

External critical judgment is so painful to a developing self, that the mind tries to come up with strategies to head it off before it arrives, i.e. "I am going to figure out ahead of time what will draw critical judgment from the outside, and shame myself for it **before** anyone outside of me notices... so I learn not to be bad. That way I will stay safe from external judgment." That is how self-judgment, as an anti-anxiety strategy, is born.

The Paradox of Shame

The paradox of shame is this: a self-judging voice comes into existence to try to protect you from making mistakes, and learn to be more "perfect", yet it hurts so much to be criticized, even by an internal shaming voice, that we have a tendency to defend against really looking at and evaluating our relevant contributions to results we do not like. This makes learning difficult or impossible. Self-judgment hampers personal growth. It is a poison that keeps you stuck in the same trap, going around and around the same thought-loops, **not** learning much, so you make the same mistakes over and over.

Sandi had spent most of her young life bouncing between her addict mother, her grandmother's house, and the foster care system. One of the primary lessons she had learned through the experience was "don't cry". Crying had been shamed deeply and consistently by many of her caregivers, and Sandi had effectively learned to put that feeling and that behavior swiftly away whenever it wanted to emerge. As an adult she had not thought much about it until she herself was a young mother, and found that she could not tolerate it when her baby cried. She came to me because the overwhelming feelings and the violent thoughts she was having when her baby cried were really scaring her. She was afraid she might be capable of hurting her daughter.

It was difficult for Sandi to even talk about the possibility that there could be a connection between her inability to cry and her overwhelming response to the cries of her daughter, because the intimation that she might need to make peace with crying herself, to get over her reaction to her baby, was so frightening to her. Sandi was horrified by what it would mean about her if she let herself cry. Her self-judging voice was loud and poisonous. "You wimp! You cry baby! You'll be asking for it! YOU MAKE ME SICK!" Every time she ever felt like crying, that was what her internal judging voice would say to her to keep her from crying, and it worked! She would "freeze" inside, just go cold and hard.

Sandi was afraid of that voice, afraid that it was speaking the truth about her. Crying would mean that she was weak and pathetic and deserved whatever bad thing was coming her way. What her critical judgment meant to her own personal development, however, was that she had never learned to comfort herself, nor allowed anyone else to comfort her when she was hurt. So Sandi had never processed and gotten over any trauma. Her self-judgment would not allow her to look at her own vulnerability, let alone reflect on it enough to learn anything about herself that could have made her authentically stronger. All of her wounds were as fresh as the day they were made, just ready and waiting to bleed some more. She might have **felt** tough, but Sandi was one of the most fragile people I have ever worked with. Her baby's cries put her instantly in touch with a lifetime of raw pain that had never been considered at all. And when her daughter cried, Sandi's self-judgment stuck her into a mind-loop so small that it eventually consisted of only one word. "This must stop This must stop Must stop Must stop Must Stop Stop Stop **Stop Stop Stop!!!**"

In her case, it did indeed ultimately end up that going through the long process of learning to cry, while simultaneously countering the internal self-judging voice with compassionate word-vaccines*, **was** just the practice Sandi needed to make it possible for her to hold and love her crying daughter.

*I covered "word vaccines" in Chapter 3.

Judgment vs Discernment

As I said earlier in the chapter, critical judgment, both external and internal, does not, in fact, help students learn better or faster. What is equally interesting, and perhaps less intuitive, is that student performance on tests goes down in response to personal **praise** as well as criticism. (8) It seems that putting people into a judging frame of mind and **tying performance to self worth,** whether the judgment is positive or negative, seems to reduce performance and hamper learning.

If the two most commonly-practiced strategies (judging and praising) to encourage learning and change don't work, or at best work temporarily, what does work? How do we learn from our mistakes? How does learning happen? How can we make it happen?

Once I had a client say to me "You are always talking about self-reflection, and how it is so valuable, but then you are always trying to get me to stay in the present moment. How am I supposed to self-reflect and learn from my mistakes if I am supposed to stay in the present moment, instead of looking back to figure out what I did wrong?"

It is indeed at least a partial paradox, but a false one. On the one hand, the more attention one focuses on the present moment of the actual world, the more conscious intentional influence one can exert on that world and the self. On the other hand, if we never look backwards or forwards, how can we sift through the results of our actions in order to learn to chart a future course towards a desired direction? The way out of the trap is to realize that **getting in to the present moment is what allows an individual to look backwards and forwards in life from a position of conscious curiosity and creativity, rather than with the judgment that skews data and engenders unconsciousness.** Yes, we can learn from the past, but a backwards view is useful mostly to discern the results of our actions, rather than to define who we are. Past results can help reveal whether we are creating for ourselves what we most want, or if we are using stories from the past to shore up a collection of identity beads that distract us from being who we want to be now. **The key to conscious mining of the past for useful feedback about one's self is in not tying past performance to self-worth, but instead to desired results.**

Mei's Story

After having been single for a long time, Mei was dating a man she really liked, Tom. It made her nervous how much she liked him, and she often felt afraid that he had the advantage because she didn't think there was any way Tom could like her as much as she liked him. The Hamster in her mind was primed to look for evidence of his intention to abandon her, and when Tom was reluctant to introduce her to his kids until he and Mei had been dating for more than six months, she took it as a sign that he had doubts about the relationship. And, when he went ahead with vacation plans he had made with friends before meeting her without her, she took that as another sign. And when he wanted to spend some nights alone in his own house, that seemed suspicious, and Mei began to complain about it all. She regularly asked Tom for reassurance and explanations, but she never felt quite satisfied. Soon her complaining and criticizing would begin again. Tom had liked Mei very much too, but after awhile, her assaults on his boundaries grew too heavy for him to want to bear, and he broke up with her. "I can no longer tolerate how hard it is for you that I need time alone sometimes, and that I feel a duty towards my kids not to introduce them to new people I am dating until the relationship feels as if it is on a solid footing."

Mei was beside herself. She was so sad and disappointed. She disappeared into the following two styles of thought-loop:

1) "I knew this was going to happen! This always happens! I am so stupid, I should have known better! I do this every time. I know how annoying it is to go after a guy nagging all the time. I can't stand the anxiety, and I do it anyway. I drove him away, just like I always do, and I am alone now. I am going to be alone for the rest of my life, because this always happens!" (Go back to the beginning of the loop and go around again. And again. And again.)

2) If only I could go back to do it again! If only I could do that conversation over I would say ------ instead. Then he would say -------, and I would say ------- and maybe I could have gotten another chance. Or if only I could replay that one time about the kids, I could try saying ---------, and then he might get where I was coming from, and he might have said --------, or --------, and that could have sent us in a whole new direction. Or that one time we had that house argument, I should have said------. (Go back to the beginning of the loop and go around again and again and...)

The previous two dips into the past are thought-loops that trap Mei in her own mind. She goes around and around replaying the past with personal judgments of character and fantasy scenarios about a past that never happened as she drifts deeper and deeper into unconsciousness. Contrast those with the following dip into the same past:

3) "Wow! I am suffering so much right now! Tom repeated again and again that he liked me very much but that he needed me to respect his need to protect his children from a not yet stable situation, and himself from getting so rapidly sucked into our new relationship that it threw his whole life out of balance. I know I want to be a person who is really present, and listens to the people I care about. I also know I want to be a person whose fear of abandonment does not overrule my intentions. What can I do to move towards that Me right now?"

In that scenario, there is no self-critical judgment. There is just a) the important past details, b) seen from the vantage point of the present moment, c) through the lens of Mei's integrity, d) in the interest of learning.

Mei begins with what is most true for her in the present moment. "Wow! I am suffering!" (Remember, suffering exists to draw your attention to a thing in your life that needs to change.) Then she dips into the past for important, behaviorally specific information that she can use, to see more clearly how she created for herself what she most didn't want. Then she brings that information back to the present to consider what she would like to be cultivating for herself right now, in order to create what she does want. In the 3rd scenario, Mei does not get trapped in her mind by critical self-judgments. She looks back in self-reflection, but **only in the interest of discernment**. "Where was I out of my integrity? How did being out of my integrity lead to my current suffering? Where do I step next in order to get back into alignment with myself **now**?" She is back in the present moment.

We do live in a temporal universe. There is no way we could conceive, plant, build, and grow our lives without looking forward and back. And without the perception of time passing, life would be a lot less interesting. But a life lived mostly in the moment, directed by glances back into the past for information to help orient the direction of forward motion, has far more influence and authorship than one spent lost in the thought loops of the mind.

Section 9: Why Do People Change?

If Mei figures out how to begin to dip into the past for information to direct her learning, instead of for information to fuel her unconscious thought-loops, she may very well change in the direction she wants. But **why** might Mei change? If people don't change from self-judgment, what causes them to change, and stay changed?

Mei's friends warned her that she was pushing Tom away. I too asked her if she thought she was falling into old unconscious fear-patterns of relationship. But no one outside her could reach her with their "you need to"s, or their "shoulds". People don't change because they should, or need to, or are supposed to, or to keep other people from being mad at them. **The only reason people change, and stayed changed, is that they want to.** They want something else more than the benefits they think they receive from staying the same. If Mei wants to be true to herself more than she wants to escape into unconsciousness, she will change.

"Should" is just another word for judgment.

Wyatt was a very talented musician. He had been writing his own music and playing for five or six years, and his band was starting to get some attention in the local press. Wyatt and his wife, Janice, finally decided one summer that he would quit his day job to pursue taking his music to the next level. Janice agreed to take over 100% of the responsibility for supporting the family financially while Wyatt tried to "make it". Wyatt quit his job. They turned their garage into a music studio and bought a lot of very expensive recording equipment. It was time to go to the next level!

Very shortly thereafter Wyatt stopped being able to write music. His wife was undergoing the stress of supporting the family alone to make sure he could make music. He was supposed to make music. But, all of a sudden, writing music, a process that for Wyatt had always been a fluid joy, was like pushing a puppy up the hill. Pretty soon, he found he could barely even stand to enter his music studio. Wyatt's head was full of judgment. While Mei's thought-loops had focused on replaying the past, Wyatt's thought loops trapped him in a fantasy horror-future. "Oh, my God, I am going to fail and here's why!" "I just know Janice is resenting me. If I put her through this for nothing, she is going to hate me! I just know it!" "I am supposed to be writing, but what if I can't write anymore?!" "What if I have ruined my life, quitting my job! What if I am going nowhere?!"

All twisted up in the should-universe, there was just no room for joy inside Wyatt's head. He had disappeared from the present moment, where all creation emerges, into the trap of his mind. No one makes great art from "should"! No one sustains movement from a place of "supposed to". Wyatt's music was not able to find him again until he found a way to let himself off the hook of "have to". He couldn't write until he authentically got to the place inside of himself where **not writing** was perfectly ok. As soon as his judgment was gone and he quit trying to push his puppy up the hill he was free to follow it where it authentically wanted to go, and up the hill it ran!

We are, every one of us, born as artists in the present moment, into life as a giant box of cosmic art supplies. When we are focused on **results**, and the critical judgment of our results, just like Wyatt, the pressure to **produce** kills our creative drive. Life becomes drudgery – pushing a puppy up the hill. What do you **want** to be? Be it now. Can you look inward and say to yourself, with loving kindness: "It doesn't matter what I have done in the past, I will be here for me now anyway." "It doesn't matter what I do in the future, I can change course if it doesn't work for me."

What is on the line between the stuckness of fear and the forward movement of "want to"? Judgment. Sometimes fear wins out and deadens (dead-ends) us, but when you take the pressure off, and let life happen just because you want to, aliveness pours back into you. Making a life that is art is not about product or results. It is about the making of it, the living of it. There is no right way to do it, no right result from it. Critical evaluation kills the drive, just like it does with sex. If you make creation happen in your life in the moment, when it wants to come out, for no other reason other than that it wants to come out, **that** is when you are true to yourself and that is when you are an artist. A life of authorship is about process and integrity, not product and judgment of that product.

The Tragic Irony of Sin and Judgment

For thousands of years, swayed by the ideas of various religious hierarchies and establishments, parents and clerics have thought to save their charges from "sin" with judgment and punishment. Sin was such a danger, and posed such a risk of eternal suffering, that chastisement was viewed as a small price to pay in the interest of saving a loved one from hell. Guilt was instilled as a vaccine against sin. Yet "sin", in the original Greek, actually meant "to stray off the course and miss the mark" (24). So, in early versions of the bible "sin" had a very different meaning, from what it came to be associated with in later interpretations.

So here is the irony: Judgment is the thing most guaranteed to cause us to stall or to stray off our course and miss our mark, because it triggers the unconsciousness that keeps us from waking and listening to our personal integrity. I think the early versions of the ancient writings must have contained some understanding of the connection, which is why "Judgment is the Lord's". Judgment must belong to God alone because in the hands of people it begets only "sin."

Compassion is the opposite of judgment. Being in alignment with one's integrity in the present moment, while having compassion for oneself and other people, is what really keeps a person "on course", "moving towards the mark" and out of "sin". Thus integrity and compassion are what engender and support change. Can you have compassion for your self? Can you be stringently real and have compassion for who you were, what you have done, and who you are now? You will need to if you are to maintain the gains you have made growing your bowling ball.

Chapter 4 - Section 9 Questions:

1) What does your internal judging voice say to you, that has a tendency to set off thought-loops of unconsciousness?

2) Can you trace one of your thought loops around in a circle, until the end becomes the beginning again?

3) Where in your life are you trying to "push a puppy up the hill"?

Another way to ask that question is: Where in your life has fear and judgment bogged you down with stuckness, deadening you to the energy and creative potential of the present moment?

4) What interests you these days?

5) What are you loving about your life right now?

6) What do you wish you had more time to explore?

7) What would need to change, inside and outside of you, if you began to allow yourself to follow your natural curiosity and interest to pursue a life sourced from what you actually want?

Section 10: Maintaining Your New Identity

Change is a bumpy process. In my ten years of practice, I can think of only a couple of clients whose vector of evolution was a fairly smooth upward sweep. The vast majority of the people I know who want to make something different happen in their lives have a **trajectory of change** that looks something like this:

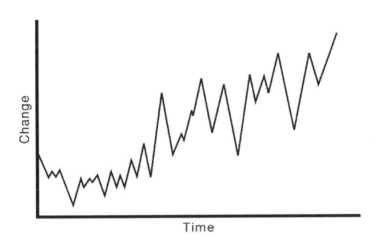

In the beginning, notice that it looks as if nothing much is happening. The individual makes little forays into change, and falls rapidly back again, up down, up down for quite awhile, feeling as if they aren't making much headway. Then s/he'll have a substantial noticeable gain, often feeling as if s/he has finally "gotten the hang of it"! ... only to fall back down again. (Unconsciousness is a tenacious beast, full of wily tricks!) Often the individual feels as if s/he has to start all over again, swimming up into the free air of consciousness from the depths s/he has sunk to.

Often, having plunged back down, it feels as if you are back down at the beginning again, having done all that work for nothing! When you are feeling trapped at the bottom of a dip, it might even feel as if the gains you had made were all self-delusion, and nothing is changing at all! But, that is just how it feels down at the bottom of a dip, trapped in a mind-loop. Unconsciousness is closely aligned with helplessness in most people.

I don't know that we ever evolve so much that we quit being vulnerable to falling into dips of unconsciousness completely. Positive change is just a general upward trend full of ups and downs. Over time though, when we do fall down, it takes less and less time to get back up again, and when one has gotten up enough times, we are able to hold on to faith a bit better so being in a dip is not as overwhelming as it once was.

"Success is just going from failure to failure without losing enthusiasm!"

- Winston Churchill

Dips into unconsciousness are not usually dangerous to a vector of change, unless you give them too much of your creative energy. Buying the "reality" of a plunge into unconsciousness can stick you back in the **Marble Game,** though. Hopefully, if you found your way out of it once, you can do it again. Here are the top six reasons why people on a path of personal integrity and authorship start buying into a dip, giving unconsciousness their creative energy, and reverting back to playing the **Marble Game**.

1) Your community (partner, family, friends, children, church, or co-workers) threatens to punish or abandon you if you continue on a path that is based on your personal integrity.

2) You are afraid that by continuing to change, you will hurt, betray, abandon, or frighten people you care about.

3) The work of fostering in-the-moment consciousness feels too hard, or not even possible. (The bouncy vector of change is too disheartening.)

4) The seductive voice of addiction suckers you back into unconsciousness.

5) You make a "mistake" that is counter to your integrity or new identity, and then allow that mistake to redefine you rather then put yourself back on the path of integrity and consciousness.

6) You experience some kind of trauma that you believe redefines you from the outside, and you don't go back to the path of consciousness and integrity.

As I said at the beginning of the section, almost everyone has a bumpy vector of change. We are all vulnerable to different aspects of the siren's call of unconsciousness. And, reading through the top six most common pitfalls, you may be able to immediately recognize the ones to which you are most susceptible. Let's look at each of the top six reasons that people go back to playing **The Marble Game** one at a time.

The top 6 pitfalls back into unconsciousness

1) Your community (partner, family, friends, children, church, or co-workers) threatens to abandon you if you continue on a path that is true to you.

To greater or lesser degrees, this experience is almost inevitable when a person begins to walk the path of consciousness and integrity. For, while not everyone on the consciousness path is at the level of wanting to quit crystal-meth, or escape an abusive relationship, even letting your partner know that you don't want to watch so much TV anymore, or you don't want to attend the yearly Family-Christmas-Disaster, or you want to quit your job to go back to school, can trigger a response that makes your psyche feel as if Armageddon is upon you.

The people around you are accustomed to you being the way you have always been: 'marble producer', 'target for judgment', 'buffer against anxiety', or just 'not too much bother'. Change in you tends to make the people around you uncomfortable, even if they say they don't like the way you are now! At least the you they don't like is a you they have experience dealing with. If you change, you could become anything! You remember the old proverb "Better the Devil You Know than the Devil You Don't"? It is at play in your family and community, whether they realize it or not.

I spent some time in chapter 4 discussing how difficult it is for the people around us when we change, so I won't repeat all the reasons not to fall into the "I might get abandoned" pitfall here. Just remember Darnell who wanted so much to be able to authentically want to talk to his mother. Remember what real kindness looks like? In my experience, your community will usually adjust. I have never met a person whose core-truth search and ventures into living a life with more integrity ultimately made them **less** generous, **less** understanding, or **less** interested in connection with the people they love, assuming those people were not abusive. Change is scary to the people around you, but in due course it will allow you to bring them a you who is more forgiving, less judging, and more interested in knowing who they really are (and therefore more interesting).

2) You are afraid that by continuing to change, you will hurt, betray, abandon, or frighten people you care about.

Many of you were trained from birth to become marble-producing machines on behalf of your parents. They didn't do it on purpose. They had no consciousness about it. But it can feel to them as if you do not love them anymore, as if you are slapping them in the face and betraying the family, when you quit playing the **Marble Game**. The same dynamic can also exist in your love or friendship connections. Client after client talks to me about taking on roles that make other people happy or comfortable, and then getting stuck and stifled within those roles; but witnessing the pain, fear and anger of people you care about can be so distressing that you decide that being true to yourself isn't worth it. It is too hard on the people around you.

Once again, I ask you what does real kindness look like? If you give yourself away, and end your bowling-ball-growing mission in the interest of continuing to provide the people around you with marbles, you are effectively supporting their continued participation in the **Marble Game** – a Game that is impossible to win. It is kind of like being a drug pusher, if you stop to think about it. The **Marble Game** distracts humanity from the path of consciousness and authorship. It keeps people asleep - lost in a bad dream they don't even know they are creating. You can't win unless you don't play. If you play marble pusher for the people you love, after you have awakened to how ugly the game really is, then **you** are part of the problem. You are part of what is in the way of your friends and family waking up.

On the other hand, if you learn to be true to yourself, remaining tuned to your integrity, chances are that your consciousness will spread. Your changes make room for others to change. Your authentic rising consciousness makes it difficult for the people close you to stay the same. When you bring **yourself** differently the unconscious programming that exists between you doesn't work any more. Others must come up with new responses to your surprising new way of being.

"An analogy might be useful at this point: If one regarded an observed tennis rally as an undesirable interaction and therefore wished to end it as rapidly as possible, it would only require that one player not return the ball." - Fisch & Weakland

I am not saying that this is a peaceful process! Sometimes people **flip out**! It can be a very uncomfortable process, but it is a holistic process, if you can hang on to yourself while the people around you learn to manage a new generator of chaos impinging on their view of reality: You! Imagine, rising consciousness spreading like a virus around you, with you as the vector.

Once more let us look at kindness. While I don't know a way for you to materially change without creating ripples of discomfort in the community around you, I would like to enthusiastically point out that there is no reason not to exhibit compassion for the feelings that will arise as a result of your changes, in the people around you. In fact, compassion for other people's suffering is most likely in alignment with your personal integrity. (I have actually never personally met anyone for whom this was not the case.) Many of my clients initially have the idea that being true to themselves must be all about setting and maintaining "boundaries". But, that is only partly true. Hiding behind rigid boundaries and ultimatums and punishing or cutting off from people who feel negatively affected by your changes is often **out** of alignment with integrity. A path that is stringently clear and real, and at the same time appreciative of the confused, fearful, sad, even angry feelings of the ones around you, tends to be the path that integrity calls for. It isn't easy. It requires a high level of consciousness to enable you to maintain enough perspective to see the unconsciousness of others and not fall into judgment yourself. Too many times, individuals buy a family's initial negative response to change and cut off from them in an effort to protect themselves. Staying in relationship and maintaining a clear, firm, and compassionate stance is the best way that I know for assisting the people around you in adapting to your changes.

Thus far in this section, I have been coming from the position that most families and communities adjust. And based on my experience, from watching over three hundred individuals and couples make journeys into the land of rising consciousness, most of the time that **is** the road that families take, friends too, but not as consistently. I have worked with people leaving the church they grew up in and gay clients who had been raised in an evangelical faith. It sometimes takes years, or the birth of a grandchild, but even they had families who eventually adjusted. But what about when that does not happen? Occasionally, it is true that the people around you, your family, your friends, your church etc, are so invested in you not changing that they are never able to tolerate it (i.e. your change is too much of a threat to their identity or paradigms about "the way the world works" for them to remain connected to you). It can feel devastating when that happens. I guess it **is** devastating, for a while. But, living a life **that is not true to who you are is more** devastating. Is a life spent unconscious, at the mercy of the Marble Game or your coping-tactics, even **your** life at all?

Not all family is made when you are born. If you lose yours, or if yours becomes consistently abusive to you when you show them your real self, I advise you consciously seek out and generate a new one. Plenty of people have.

More than once I have had clients begin to get the sense, as they become more conscious, that they are not going to fit into their current community any more if the keep at it. Perhaps their community engages in habitual unconsciousness-fertilizing behaviors, or just simply is not able to join them in the present moment to make an authentic connection. Feeling as if you are "outgrowing" your partner, or closest friends, can be terrifying enough to cause many to wonder if relapsing into unconsciousness might not be a less painful option. What if you wake up to the actual world, leaving everyone you loved behind you lost in the **Marble Game**, and find yourself alone in a strange new world?

… You will live. You will ultimately thrive. Thriving only happens in the real world! I have seen people go through this process again and again. It is true that once you start spending time in the actual world, sometimes you don't like your friends anymore. Perhaps you wake up to the fact that you were mostly a marble machine for them all along. Or it might not be that you dislike your friends exactly, it is more that it just isn't very interesting to hang out with unconscious people when you are awake.

Your friends are on their own paths. You can't save them from their internal worlds, but your emergence into consciousness may rub off on them. If it doesn't, and your relationships stop fitting you anymore, or you can't pretend to like an unconscious lifestyle any longer, you can make new friends who do fit you. Put yourself in environments that tend to attract people with rising consciousness, and you will find a new home community.

3) The work of fostering in-the-moment consciousness feels too hard, or not even possible. (The bumpy vector of change is too disheartening.)

The Marble Game, and the Big Three coping-tactics we adopt to escape the intolerable helplessness we feel when we can't find a way to win, combine to create a powerful drive towards unconsciousness. Judgment also oozes a magnetic, seductive pull away from the actual world. Even just staying conscious to the intention that we have set to work on **being** more conscious can feel as difficult as staying awake at 4:00 AM in hour 22 of a 24 hour road trip. Consider the following thought loop: "Ack! I was supposed to be focusing on the present moment and I drifted off into my head again! I am hopeless at this! I can never seem to do what I set off to do and I blah blah blah (go back to the beginning of the loop)."

When you discover that you want to raise your consciousness, it is hard to stay awake in the beginning. It is difficult even when you are alone, with no outside **Marble Game** pressures conspiring to drive you under, let alone when you are locked into a round of the Game with someone you are close to. Every one of us is full of triggers and vulnerabilities that trip us into unconsciousness:

- In solitude, if you try to stay in the present moment, but tie your self-worth to mindfulness **performance**? Whoops! Negative judgment of your performance puts you further under every time you slip.
- In relationships, someone threatens to pop your marbles with judgment? Or threatens to kick over your bowl? You leap into a defensive stance and down you go! Or someone backs away, and it looks as if you might be abandoned? You leap to pursue and you're instantly unconscious!

If you add judgment for the slip on top of the slip and go spinning off into a mind loop (like the ones above), finding your way back to conscious-intention may take a long, long time. Remember the jagged vector of change. That is just the way change happens, particularly a change in consciousness. Babies are born with perfect mindfulness. It took years to program unconsciousness into you. It may take years to undo the damage. There is no hurry. This isn't a race. No panel of judges is perched above your head grading your rate of change. Forgiveness and compassion and patience are the ways of being that are most in support of rising consciousness. When you slip, just wake as soon as possible. Get back to the present moment.

4) The seductive promises of addiction suckers you back into unconsciousness.

The **Marble Game** itself is an addiction. It is the first addiction, the one that primes us to search for other ways of filling our bowl from the outside of us when the marble solicitation strategies we have developed are not up to the task of keeping our bowls filled. Addiction promises an end to suffering. Addiction promises that we can matter, that we do matter -- if we just keep drinking more, taking more, watching more, buying more, collecting more, we will stop feeling as if we don't matter. It's a nasty trick. This pitfall is so pervasive, and runs so deep, that I have dedicated an entire chapter to addressing it. I'll be looking at addictive behavior more closely in chapter 7.

5) You make a "mistake" that is counter to your integrity and then allow that mistake to redefine you rather than putting yourself back on the path of integrity and consciousness.

In #3 I talked about the mind-loops that judgment can trap you into if you slip out of the present moment when you are trying to practice mindfulness. I noted that judging your mindfulness performance drives you **farther** away from consciousness. If the mind is prone to slipping down into further unconsciousness when it experiences a minor breach like that, imagine how prone we are to losing our way indefinitely when we make a major breach in personal integrity.

I see it all the time:

> - After promising herself not to do it any more, a mom screams at her kids. Her self-judgment sends her into a mind-loop of shame and helplessness, making her more and more prone to screaming out of helplessness, and less and less likely to hold on to herself.
> - An alcoholic is dry for three years, then gets laid off from his job and drinks to assuage the fear and shame he feels. He goes on a bender that makes it impossible to find another job. His wife leaves him. So he drinks more and more.
> - A woman who feels distant from her husband has an internet affair. She breaks it off after awhile, but still feels guilty. She withdraws further from her husband, both into fantasy stories about what it might have been like with the other guy, and also in alienation that she has done something in the context of her marriage that feels unforgivable. They eventually divorce.
> - A man makes certain he isn't "taken" in his divorce by hiring the shark attorney. He ends up with a greater share of assets than his integrity says is fair. He feels guilty so he projects on to his former wife that she is "making him feel guilty". He is rude to her and uncooperative regarding co-parenting their child. This makes him feel even more guilty, feeding the cycle of unconsciousness as he sinks deeper into resentment and self-made unhappiness.

Any of these people can wake up at any time. Any of them can get back to the present moment, make amends, and keep moving towards growing the bowling ball that makes all of the mind-loops of suffering unnecessary. As I said there is no race, no panel of judges is perched above your head grading your rate of change. Forgiveness and compassion and patience are the best ways of being, most in support of rising consciousness. When you slip, just wake as soon as possible. Don't buy the "slip reality" as "real". Re-commit to your integrity and get back to the present moment. We all get an infinite number of chances to be our real selves.

6) You experience some kind of trauma that you believe redefines you, and you don't go back to the path of consciousness and integrity.

Sometimes life hurts so much. Your partner leaves you. Your business fails. Your partner of fifty-one years dies of Parkinson's. Your child is diagnosed with a terminal illness and ultimately dies. Trauma can send you into a tail-spin of unconsciousness. "What did I do wrong?" "How could I have prevented this?" "How will I ever find a way to want my life again after this?" Trauma, particularly ongoing trauma, triggers every strategy your mind ever came up with to make the pain and the intolerable helplessness stop. Trauma can even propel us into an existential crisis, throwing into chaos all the things we **knew** were true about who we are and how the universe is supposed to work. "How could God do this to me?" "But I did everything right! How could this happen?!"

Yet even in the face of the greatest losses that life has to offer, your mind loops are no help at all. In fact, they make helplessness worse. In the face of loss and suffering, the only place to escape **is** into the real world of the actual moment, e.g.

-   A woman whose partner left her is trapped in thought loops about what she could have done differently, how to get her back, how to get back **at** her, how worthless she must be if she could be abandoned after twelve years of partnership. The only relief she can find is when she is able to get out of her head into the real world of this moment: watching her dogs playing in the yard, listening to live music in the park, connecting with friends over a beautiful meal. She eventually finds herself again.

-   The business passed on to a man from his father fails. It had been his grandfather's. He gets trapped into thought loops about what he could have done differently, how he failed his father, and how corporations are driving independent business into the ground. He is too old to start again! The only relief he feels is when he is able to get out of his head universe and into the present moment: allowing his wife's comfort and support to penetrate his heart, writing letters to congress and the newspaper about the plight of the small business owner, and gathering with other small business owners to network and organize on behalf of themselves. He eventually finds himself again.

-   An elderly lady's husband of fifty-one years departs their life together at the age of 72. She outlives him for 23 years. In the beginning, she is trapped in thought loops about how she will possibly manage without him, how she can want to live, how she will get through each day. The only relief she feels is when she can get into the world of the present moment: watching her grandchildren search for the matzo, and playing bridge with the women she raised her children with. Finally, after a while, she realizes that if she tunes in to the present moment very very, closely she can sense her husband around her. Is it in her head, or is it real? She doesn't care! Now when she gets very quiet inside herself she feels as if he is there around her and she talks to him about all the things that are close to her heart, just as she always did, and feels comforted.

- Now, for the hardest one. The mother and father with a dying child. The parents' hearts bleed. They are trapped in thought-loops almost every moment of every day: "This can't be happening. This has to stop. Please God let me wake up. I will give anything. Take me! I will give anything! S/he is so lovely, so perfect, so innocent, s/he has to grow up!" For them, even the present moment is full of pain. Every time blood is drawn and the child cries, it feels like a knife to the heart. Every time the child gasps for breath the parents feel as if they could die from the pain of it. Yet even here, the only refuge available **is** the present moment. Escaping from it into the hell of the mind makes everything worse. Children, especially young children, are naturally mindful. They don't collect pain and replay it again and again, carrying it around the way that adults do. This moment is **the** important moment for them. If you can join them in this moment they feel your presence, and you feel theirs. If you are lost in your head, they can't feel you with them. After they are gone, you will have wasted precious real actual-world opportunities lost in the world of your mind. You need to be there. You need to be there, so you can know why it is good that your baby was born, so your judgment cannot convince you that that precious life was a waste. You need to be there for each other. That is where comfort lies. Even with this one, you can eventually find yourself again.

The Existential Crisis

Traumas like those above, and even just major life transitions, can be so destabilizing to a self that the most firmly established bowling balls melt away, leaving empty bowls behind them. These are the thought loops of a full-blown existential crisis:

"Everything I most depended on is gone." "Everything I believed I was, and everything that seemed to mean that I matter is crap!" "Everything I thought I knew about the universe and the way reality works is crap!" "Nothing matters!" "Nothing makes sense!" "What is the point to anything?!"

The pain of an existential crisis is debilitating just on its own, let alone after facing a catastrophic loss. Sometimes we lose not only our most beloved connections, but ourselves as well. But if you do suffer an existential crisis, and almost everyone does at some point, all it means is that you need to go back to the beginning of this section of the book and start again. Your identity and paradigms have been wiped away. It is time to get into the present moment, as much as humanly possible, and rediscover who and what you are.

I know I said that real core truth is unassailable. I stand by that. But it is unassailable from the outside, not the inside. An existential crisis calls upon us to reconfirm, rediscover, or redefine the things we thought we knew about ourselves in order to come to a greater depth of understanding and solidity of identity. Your core-truth recall-experience may change. The words you use to bring an echo of the profound-connection-feeling-experience to you may change, but the fundamental truths revealed by a core-truth experience don't change. We just lose hold of them sometimes. I will look at trauma and the existential-crisis phenomena further in the next chapter of this book: Surrender.

Chapter 4 - Section 10 Questions:

1) Which of the six most common pitfalls that trigger an unconsciousness relapse are you most vulnerable to?

2) Where and how are they influencing you in your life now?

3) Have you done "unforgivable" things that are still defining you today? How are your judgments about those events causing you to sink into the unconsciousness that reinforces negative aspects of your self now?

4) Have you ever suffered a tragedy and felt as if you will never recover? What are the thought-loops you have around that experience? What would it mean about you or about reality if you ever were able to recover from your suffering?

Chapter 4 Questions:

This ends **Chapter 4: Changing on the Inside.** Think back for a minute to the intro and check in with yourself to examine what you have learned about the following five core human questions that I posed back then:

1) Who am I and why am I so crazy?

2) Who is s/he and why is s/he driving me so crazy?

3) Why do I keep doing the crazy stuff I do… and then do it again and again?!

4) In the face of all of my flaws how do I become the person I want to be?

5) Why bother to ever do anything? What is the point?

6) Finally, what do you notice about how you are have changed so far?

Chapter 5: The Power of Surrender

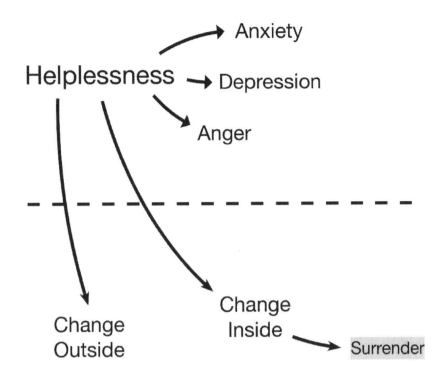

Sometimes there is nothing you can do about it.

Sometimes you have tried everything you can think of to materially change the circumstances outside yourself, but there simply was nothing **to** change, or change was not possible no matter how willing you were to face down your fear of the cost of acting. And sometimes no matter how hard you have tried to change yourself on the inside, to shift your perspective or your paradigm, or adopt a new identity that serves you instead of working against you -- sometimes in spite of all you have tried, there is nothing you can do to counter an intolerably painful force in your life. The resulting helplessness feels overwhelming, of course.

In that moment when the realization finally hits, that there is nothing you can do about it, you have two choices: A) reject your life entirely, to live in bitterness and resentment for the duration, or B) Surrender, and find out what else is left for you when the battle is over. Surrender and regroup.

Dan Leahy, one of my professors from grad school, was fond of saying: "It's not what you do that matters, it's what you do next!" I always think of this when I am contemplating the practice of surrender. As I said when I was introducing the concept in chapter 2, surrender is the kind of "giving up" that makes space for the rest of your life to happen, not the kind of "giving up" that is you giving up on your life.

Your Grid of Probability

In my mind I am picturing a field of probabilities in front of you – the immeasurable morass of all the things that could ever happen to you in this lifetime. The field is three-dimensional, however, more like a cloud, as far as you can see. Just take a minute to close your eyes right now, and picture yourself standing at the edge of a cliff. Before you as far as you can see out into space there is a 3-D geometric cloud of probabilities, each one represented by a shiny red cherry. Let's say they are spaced about eight inches apart. When you look up the grid goes up as far as you can see, when you look right and left it is the same, and when you look down there is no ground, just in an infinite shiny grid of bright red cherries: the grid of your probabilities.

The grid represents everything that could ever possibly happen to you in your life, as a result of every possible choice you could ever make. Some of the cherries are within easy reach, but others are not reachable unless you choose some of the closer ones and put them in your pocket. It is the act of you **making something happen** by selecting a cherry that causes the entire grid to reshuffle so that some of the probabilities that were far away now come a little closer, as a result of your choice, and some that were closer are now out of your reach. Every time you reach forward and choose to make something happen, the whole grid reshuffles, offering you whole new bunch of cherries.

The kind of "giving up" that exists down the road of depression, when you reject future possibility entirely, is you turning your back on your grid of probabilities so your life remains static and your experience of your existence will be pretty much the same indefinitely. However, surrender is the very opposite of that kind of "giving up". An authentic surrender **is** you reaching forward to make a choice, the choice to be done with trying to change an aspect of your life that you are helpless in the face of. When you reach forward to choose surrender and put that cherry in your pocket, your whole grid of probabilities reshuffles, offering you new avenues for making choices about your life. It is what allows you to let go of your helplessness to ask yourself the question, "What next." or "What's left?"

Launi's Story

In 2000 my friend Launi had her ankle crushed in a car accident. When I use the word "crushed", I am not exaggerating. I am not sure that there was a bone left in the ankle that wasn't broken. Over the next eight years she had surgery after surgery first to repair the ankle, and then in the attempt to address the pain. The pain went on and on. It was debilitating. And the medical interventions went on, year after year -- five surgeries, seven surgeries, nine surgeries – along with countless therapies. Nothing helped the pain for long. The eventual diagnoses: peripheral neuropathy.

Here is the definition I pulled off of Wikipedia: "**Peripheral neuropathy** is damage to nerves of the peripheral nervous system, which may be caused either by diseases or trauma to the nerve, or the side effects of systemic illness. Pain associated with the condition is described in various ways such as the following: burning, freezing, or electric-like, extreme sensitivity to touch." That is, the nerves can't calm down. They are permanently stuck in the "on" position. Ugh. Chronic pain.

It was hard to enjoy life with a leg that felt as if it was literally burning with fire a lot of the time. And sometimes it hurt so much it was hard for Launi to want to keep living at all. I remember the horror I felt several years in to the experience when she told me that if she could have her leg amputated just to stop the pain, she would. I had had no idea about the level of her discomfort until then; that the pain was slowly eclipsing her life, that the joy in many of the simple things she had taken for granted before the accident (kid's soccer games, working in her garden, helping an elderly neighbor, and her loving connection with her husband etc.) was slowly being eroded away, until the only cherries Launi was able to perceive in her grid of probability represented **more pain, and trying to figure out how to get the pain to stop**. "Person in pain" was beginning to become a central identity as well, and many of the aspects of herself that she most loved were falling by the wayside: humor, optimism, and patience.

Launi and her care-providers tried everything (every change they could think of on the outside) and every change she could contemplate on the inside. The trying went on for eight years. Nothing helped. Finally one day, as I understand it, Launi surrendered. She called me up to say she was done trying to make the pain go away. "I am a person who lives with chronic pain. That's it." As hard as it was to hear it, as it is terribly difficult to contemplate a surrendered lifetime of pain for someone I care about as deeply as I care for Launi, I could almost immediately hear some small amount of relief in her voice. Something heavy had been released: the impossible task of trying to figure out how to make the pain go away. And letting go of the single-minded pursuit that had taken up so much space in her life had suddenly made space for a "What next?" Launi was looking at a whole new grid of probability.

What that looks like in real life is that now Launi has the space to notice that she has good days and bad days, without judgment. On the good days, Launi loves working in her garden, cheering for her kids, and working on behalf of her many charitable organizations. On bad days, she lies on the couch with her foot in a bucket of ice water, reading a good book and not feeling the least bit self-critical about "not accomplishing anything". She's got her sense of humor back, and is such an expert on surrendering to what she cannot change that she sounds like an enlightened guru sometimes.

Here is another thing. Since Launi surrendered to the fact that she will always live with pain, the pain has gotten better. "Why?" is an unanswerable question, though I have some hypotheses about it. Maybe all that focus on the pain made it loom huge in her life in comparison with everything. Maybe now it is experienced in perspective with everything else. Or maybe being busy with the rest of life is simply a distraction from the pain, so she doesn't think about it as much. Or maybe the nerves are finally calming down. Or just maybe once in a while something magical happens when a person is able to authentically surrender to an intolerable experience to release her sense of helplessness to ask "What next?"

Collateral Effects – The Mysterious Magic of Surrender

Newton's third law of motion states, "For every action there is an equal and opposite reaction." Kurt Lewin, one of the modern pioneers of the psychology of organizational development, applied Newton's lens to the study of the psychology of change, and developed his Force Field

Model as a way of expressing how the third law of motion applied to human social systems. He noticed that a range of "driving forces", which exert a pressure for change tend to be balanced by a number of equal and opposing "resisting" forces that keep the change from happening. (25)

What I have noticed is that sometimes an authentic surrender from one side of a struggle can act like a martial-arts move that takes the energy of the resisting force and redirects it shooting off in a new direction. The movement that can happen as a result is unpredictable, but from the outside, sometimes the shift can look like magic.

I have seen spouses successfully lose weight only after their partners stops nagging them about it. I have seen kids do better in school after parents finally give up trying to make them successful. I have seen husbands, after years of trying to get close to bitter wives, say "I am done trying to trick you into wanting me. I guess we are done with sex in this relationship" only to have their wives say "Wait! I want another chance at this!" And, I have seen exhausted, martyred care-takers finally give up trying to take care of everything themselves, only to find that when they do step back and "give up" they make room for other people to step forward. It is no sure thing, but it happens.

Veronica's story

When I tell Katie's story to my clients, most of them are able to grasp the central message, and see clearly how "giving up" the possibility of ever escaping chronic pain was the very thing that freed Katie up to enjoy her life again. Sometimes however, the surrender that is called for involves another person, and for some reason that type of surrender usually looks a lot muddier to the outside observer, or even like a betrayal of your very self.

Veronica was madly in love with her husband Ezra, even after twelve years of marriage. She was just crazy about that guy. The two of them just had one terrible, reoccurring fight between them. Ezra was a smoker, and Veronica really <u>really</u> wanted him to quit. That was the thing that landed them in my office.

Veronica had a list of really great reasons why Ezra needed to quit:

- Even though he smoked outside, his clothes smelled like smoke.
- He had smoker's breath when he came in for a kiss.
- Because they shared a closet and his clothes smelled like smoke, her clothes also eventually ended up smelling like smoke as well.
- He was always getting up in the middle of important family moments to go outside and have a cigarette.
- It was a waste of family resources. "Have you any idea how much of our money goes to that habit?! Do you ever think about what we could do with that money?!"
- And worst of all, Ezra was condemning her to a long period of horrible suffering in their later years, as she was forced to care for her incapacitated darling husband, as he slowly choked to death from lung cancer or cardiopulmonary disease.

For Veronica, Ezra's continued smoking was proof that she simply did not matter to Ezra as much as he mattered to her. How could she matter, when by continuing to smoke, he was setting her up for such a horrifying event in her life, an event that was entirely preventable in her eyes.

Ezra had tried to quit. He wanted to quit. In fact, he had quit several times for days or weeks at a time. He just couldn't seem to stay quit. For him, his smoking had nothing to do with his love for her, or lack thereof. Ezra adored his fiery Veronica. He just couldn't seem to successfully fight the nicotine. It even haunted him in his dreams! Sooner or later, after each attempt to quit, she'd find him out behind the garage lighting up, or he would come into the house after a day of work, looking all innocent, and she could just smell it on him. "Argh!" They went around and around in my office with the escalating issue, the fighting getting more and more heated, until Veronica was at the brink of divorce. "If you don't stop smoking, it means you don't give a crap about me **or** my happiness!" she wept. "How can you make me leave you like this!"

The trouble, of course, was that he wasn't actually making her **do** anything. He was simply smoking. He had even cut it down to eight or ten cigarettes a day. And she desperately did not want to leave him. Veronica loved Ezra. She finally realized that while she was bugged by some of the day-to-day impacts on her life due to the smoking, it was the stories she was making up in her head **about** the smoking that were intolerable: "This is proof that I don't matter to Ezra". "I am looking at an intolerable experience of old age." "Ezra's smoking is forcing us apart." Finally, rather than be parted from the only one she could ever even imagine wanting, Veronica reached forward and put "surrender" in her pocket. "I married a smoker. What next?"

Once the surrender was past her, there was a new grid of probabilities before her, and Veronica could begin to address the effects of his smoking that were actually negatively impacting her real day-to-day life. If Ezra was going to keep smoking, he needed to keep his clothes in the guest room closet, so Veronica's did not get contaminated. If he wanted to get into bed with her, expecting to be welcomed into her arms, he needed to shower the smoke smell off of him and brush his teeth thoroughly. The solutions they came up with after her surrender were largely a matter of logistics, and Ezra was eager to collaborate if it meant he got to keep his Veronica.

This particular example is often harder for my clients to swallow than the "Launi's ankle was crushed" example. I often hear, "But Veronica just gave in!" "She was right!" "How is that going to help her when she is an old lady having to take care of an invalid?!" My response goes like this: Veronica was miserable in the face of her helplessness before the surrender, and now she is all smiles and full of possibility. Did she betray herself? Apparently, based on the result, it was truer to Veronica's integrity to stay with the man she wanted, even though he was a smoker, than it was to leave him and live smoke-free. What she decided was not the "right" choice, it was simply the choice that freed her up to be the author of her own life-experience again, so it was the choice that felt right to her. Another person might find that his or her integrity required a surrender to the loss of the partner, instead of surrendering to one's choice of partner, in order to be true to his or her own life's vision.

For now though, some day it may very well turn out that Veronica finds herself married to an invalid who is slowly choking to death with emphysema. There are a lot of probabilities in her grid between here and there, but Ezra is making choices that may bring that one closer to Veronica, so it **could** happen. However, even if Ezra doesn't figure out how to quit before then, or even if he doesn't die suddenly of something else before then, and even if he is not protected by great genes or chance, Veronica can always retain the power to keep choosing her probabilities and making things happen. She does not get stuck unless she turns her face away from the grid and "gives up". Some day she may decide to choose to take care of an invalid husband. But some day she may choose not to.

So what about magical collateral effects? Did surrendering to being married to a smoker eventually lead to Ezra's successful cessation of smoking, like surrendering to being in pain helped the pain dissipate for Katie? I wish I could say it did, but I don't actually know. They did not need me very shortly after Veronica's surrender, so I did not get to witness what might have happened next. I have my fingers crossed for both of them.

Note: One more thing: The magic doesn't work if you are just pretending to surrender. "Just pretending" to surrender is usually nothing more than an ultimatum in sheep's clothing. How many times in the history of the world has a person screamed at his or her partner: "If you don't (fill in the blank), I'm leaving you!" Ultimatums rarely work, and even if they seem as if they are working, the effects rarely stick. (I will talk more about ultimatums and why they don't work in chapter 7.) The magic collateral effects of surrender can only sometimes be evoked if the surrender is authentic. And there is no way to force a surrender to be real if it just isn't. The only thing that makes an authentic surrender real is if the choice is precipitated by your personal integrity overcoming your fear when there simply is no other choice for you.

No One But You Has the Right to Judge Your Decision

Watching you surrender can be hard both on the people who love you, and anyone who has trained you to be a reliable marble-dispenser. If you are contemplating surrender, the people around you may feel as if they will lose you, or as if you might die! Here are few examples of what I mean:

- A high-school basketball player deduces that he may be pretty good, but he will never make the pros, and wants to focus his energy on other things. Dad responds, "NOOOO! You can't give up! (I.e. I needed the marbles I get out of having a son who is on his way to sports stardom!)

- A teen-child of an active drug abuser tells her parent, I am not going to cover for you anymore. I am done lying to people. Parent says "No! You have to protect me until I get better! I am trying to get better! I brought you in to this world, so you can't do this to me!" (I.e. You **must** reinforce my preferred identity to people **for** me, because I am unable to do it any more, and you **owe** me.)

- A stroke victim decides to stop spending six hours a day in physical therapy trying to get out of her wheel chair, because it is taking up too much of her remaining years of bridge-playing, bird-watching, and emailing her enduring high-school buddies. Son responds, "Noooo! You can't stop trying!" (It scares me too much to experience my own helplessness in the face of signs of your impending demise, and ultimately, my own!)

- A heavy young woman tells her mom she is never going to diet again. She is sick of having food at the center of every waking moment of attention. Mom cries "No!" (If you give up the dream of being thin, you will never be happy, and I will judge myself {and other people might judge me} a failure as a mother!)

- A relapsing chemotherapy patient decides he is done with the therapy. He doesn't want to spend his remaining months in a present moment so steeped in struggle and discomfort, that there is no room for the joy of living the life he has left. Every person who loves that man cries out, "NO!! There is always HOPE!" (Please don't stop trying to keep from leaving us! We can't face your death! We don't want to be here without you!)

Ultimately, when and if you surrender in the face of a life experience that has overwhelmed your own desire to fight it anymore, it is no one else's business. Your life belongs to you, and you alone. Be as kind as you can to others, though. It is often a terribly difficult thing to gracefully allow people you care about to surrender.

The thing I want you to remember if someone else in your life goes down Surrender's path is that no one knows what it is like to live someone else's experience from his or her point of view. As such, we cannot know, for someone else, when it is time for that person to finally let go of the very last hope. It is an act of profound respect to gracefully step out of the way and support a loved one's right to surrender.

Surrender and humility go hand in hand. We love to think we know what is best for people, but we don't. Perhaps the hardest spiritual practice to master is surrendering our attachment to the delusion that we have the right to judge someone else's life choices. Even I don't pretend to know what is best for people, and I have made my life all about the study of human behavior and the motivations behind it. I am just one small mammal trying to figure all of this out, just like you, and the best I can do is tell you what I have noticed about what tends to lead to suffering, and what tends to ameliorate it, as well as illustrate ways of being that I have noticed tend to get in the way of you having what you say you want. That's it. I never believe I have the right to judge a client's self-made suffering as "wrong", like it shouldn't be happening. Too often in my own life, suffering was the best and only thing that lead to me learning what I needed to know to make it stop, and not just make it stop, but to transcend it to create some wonderful change. Every one of us is on his or her own individual adventure path, traveling towards something I don't pretend to understand.

The 2nd Biggest Sacred-Bubble Pop in this Book

I am about to put in writing the 2nd most outrageously unpopular and counterculture thing that is contained in this book (after the "I absolve you of writing any more thank you notes for stuff you are not thankful for). Here we go:

'Hope' is the fantasy story that undermines me from either embracing the actual life I have now, or changing it myself.

In my mind, I just heard the sound of countless pages fluttering, followed by a rain of thumps, as 85% of the print-copies of The Marble Game were thrown across the room!

Still reading? Dear brave souls! ☺ Hope is the sacred cow of humanity, the passive, fallback position of the desperate, trapped masses. But not only that, people -- hope is also the enemy of surrender. Hope is the marble-conserving withdrawer-fantasy that some day something on the outside of me will magically change so I can finally be free, be loved, be well fed, or have a bowl full of marbles. Hope allows most every person to abdicate accountability for his or her own experience of life. It gives you the illusion that you can bypass your tactic by 1) changing the world with your wishes; 2) changing yourself with your wishes; or 3) surrendering your authorship to a higher authority. It is the 'blue pill' from <u>The Matrix</u> (2008). It is also the con that has kept helpless people disempowered, and oppressed people oppressed for thousands of years:

- Sedentary people hope that their health will get better.
- Aging men with urinary dysfunction don't go for prostate exams in hope that there is nothing wrong.
- Lonely people sit at home hoping for love to knock on the door and find them.
- Exhausted workers quietly hope for a raise.
- Battered women in misogynist cultures clutch at the hope that a superhero will save them.
- Citizens of the world hope other countries will lower their emissions.

Hope will not keep you safe from illness or abuse. It won't bring you love nor money. It won't vanquish your oppressor and free you from slavery. And, it won't keep our species from making the planet an impossible place to live.

"My hope kept me alive that time, though!" I have heard people say. "I would have given up without it!" Well, what kind of a life was that? Does breathing mean you are alive? Hope helped keep you a slave to whatever situation you were in that required a steady diet of fantasy-food to distract and divert your attention from real changes you could make to alter the situation. The only groups of people I can think of who should apply to a steady diet of hope are people who belong to groups that have so little influence over the experience of their own lives that a fantasy-future story inside their brains may actually be the only option. "Ok, but if I give up hope, what do I replace it with? What on earth gets me through the times that I just can't stand?"

The answer is faith, and I don't mean the "hope that someone else will save me or understands the meaning of my suffering" variety of faith, but faith in yourself. Faith that you will keep making your way forward through your grid of probabilities and authoring your own life, regardless of what happens or does not happen as a result.

Your practical choices are these. I will put up the model again:

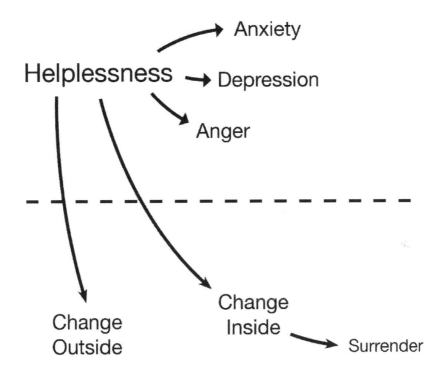

These are your options, folks: Choose to be responsible for being the one to make a change on the outside of you (this may include soliciting help from others), work to change something inside of you so you are no longer steeped in helplessness (this may also include soliciting help from others), or authentically surrender to the way things actually are.

Chapter 5 Questions:

With this chapter, I am beginning to lay the framework for you to think about answers for some of the later questions I laid out in the intro of the book. What do you know so far about your personal answers to the following questions as seen through the lens of surrendering to the things you can not change?

- In the face of all of my flaws how do I become the person I want to be?

- How do I get that other person over there to be who I want him/her to be, and do what I want her/him to do?

- Why does Life/God/The Universe either a) seem so crazy that the way the world works makes no sense, or b) hate me personally so much that I am punished again and again no matter how hard I try?

- Why bother to ever do anything? What is the point?

In addition

1) Where in your life do you already know that you want or need to make something happen?

2) What fear(s) are standing in the way of you reaching forward to grasp the most promising probability from your grid?

3) Are there any areas in your life where you may have been resisting the truth that there is nothing you can do to change an intolerable situation?

4) What does fear tell you will happen if you surrender?

Chapter 6: Addictive Behavior

At one point in human history, everyone knew they mattered. There were simply too few in the tribe for any person not to live in awareness of how important his or her contribution was to the group. Every pair of hands fed and clothed the tribe. Every member worked to keep the tribe warm. Every womb kept the fragile tribe from dying out. Every pair of eyes guarded the children. There was neither time nor space for existential wondering, "Do I matter enough?" Everyone did.

The abundance of the developing world brought with it many gifts, but it also made room for the demon of Comparison to slither in to our awareness, along with his consort, Judgment. Now we have the leisure time for wondering:

- "Do I matter enough?"
- "Do I matter as much as my brother?"
- "If he has more than me, is it because he is better (matters more)?"
- "If he isn't better, but has more, is it fair that I should have less?"
- "If I have less does it mean he took what was mine?"
- "Or does it mean that I matter less?"
- "If I matter less, is it my fault?"
- "If I collect more stuff that matters, will I matter more?"
- "How do I make sure I matter more?"

Out of Comparison and Judgment, the **Marble Game** was born. The Marble Game itself is an addiction. It is the first addiction, the one that primes us to search for outside ways of filling our bowl when the marble-gathering strategies we have developed are not up to the task. Addiction promises an end to struggle, an end to suffering. Addiction promises that if we just keep drinking more, taking more, watching more, buying more, collecting more, seducing more, we will stop feeling as if we don't matter. It's a nasty trick.

Section 1: The Monster in the Bowl

Obviously when chemical dependence becomes involved, there is an added layer of complication to this picture, but susceptibility to addictive behavior is deeply steeped in Marble Game fatigue. I.e. Addiction gets a foothold for emotional reasons. If you have ever wrestled with a dependence upon anything, this is your story:

Once upon a time, in their quest to devour the soul of humanity, Comparison and Judgment produced a beautiful honey-voiced demon-baby named Addiction. Oh, what a talented offshoot it was, with all the flexible shape-changing talents of Dad, and all of Mom's gift for knowing immediately where an individual's vulnerability lies. Born fully grown, Addiction was ready to join the family business immediately. Comparison and Judgment had been softening up humanity with the Marble Game for a few thousand years before Addiction came along, so the souls of many exhausted mortal players were ripe for the picking. One by one, Addiction patiently began making house calls on every human's bowl. Eventually it got around to you.

On a day when you were feeling particularly empty and exhausted from losing the Marble Game despite all your best strategies, when your depression or your anxiety or your rage felt so overwhelming that you feared you could die of it, something new sidled up to your bowl. Or maybe it wasn't entirely new. Perhaps you had seen it hanging around the edges of your awareness, and felt repelled by the energy of the thing, so you had ignored it until now. But on this particular day, perhaps you were feeling so alienated from the world, or like you were such a piece of worthless nothing, that all at once a little spark of curiosity arose in you about the smoky wraith hovering around the edges of your awareness. The second that thought was out, the eyes of Addiction were on you with the laser focus of a shark that smells blood in the water, and a creature of terrific magnetism slowly came into clearer focus. The more solid it appeared, the more you began to wonder why you had thought the spirit seemed so creepy before, because right then it appeared so friendly.

Addiction sidled up to you looking like the most delicious knight-princess-cowboy-sex-God(dess) you could ever have imagined. It leaned in, in a most intimate and familiar manner, it's warm breath tickling gently as it whispered in your ear, "Not only can you have all this, but you can **be** all this... All you have to do is let me in your bowl." Whoa. You were a bit taken aback despite the lovely smell wafting towards you on the creature's breath. Addiction went on talking.

"Oh the Game is such a racket. You know there's no way to win by yourself. It just isn't fair. But I can fix all that for you. I can help you win. If you let me help you, I'll slip right into your bowl. I'll fill it for you and plug the hole, and you will never be hungry for marbles again!" Oh that sounded good. You were feeling so tired and unappreciated and hurt. But you remembered that you had a friend once who had gotten mixed up with a creature that looked like this, and it hadn't turned out so well. So you hesitated. Addiction sensed the resistance and made itself look a bit smaller and more vulnerable. "Look, I can just get in for a minute. If you don't end up liking it, I'll just get right out again. I swear. It's no big deal. You won't even notice I'm there. I'll just take over plugging the hole for a minute so your marbles stay in, just to give you a break. And I'll get right out when you want me to."

You were sorely tempted. Addiction looked so good and smelled so good. How could it be bad just to try it for a minute? Sensing your resolve weakening, Addiction threw one foot over the lip of your bowl. "You know how all those hippie-types are trying to get you to meditate on the present moment, like doing all that work is going to help you win the Marble Game? What a drag! **I'll** bring you in to the present moment! How good does **this** feel?!" That was it. You caved.

As you watched, Addiction hooked its other leg over the lip of the bowl and began losing all of the skeletal structure in it's body, softening and elongating, as it slid bonelessly down in to the bottom; doubling back to curl around it's own serpentine body until it filled the bottom entirely. While the transformation may have been seriously creepy to watch, Addiction was right! The hole was plugged! The relief was incredible!

If that story didn't exactly fit you, perhaps this one does: Perhaps Addiction slipped up to you in a moment when you were making a major score in the Marble Game. At the time, you were so high on how good it felt to have your bowl so full, that when Addiction sidled up to offer you some more validation you didn't even notice the creepy undertone. "You are so good! You are so solid! Nothing can touch you now!" said Addiction. "People say you should be wary of me?! Ha! You're so unassailable you don't need to fear anything, let alone something that feels as good as me. And since you're so strong and everything, why don't you let me in for just a second and I can make you feel even just a tiny bit better! If you like it, I'll plug your hole for you so all these shiny new marbles stay in the bowl!" Feeling as unassailable as you did, it seemed like no big deal to scoot out of the way and let Addiction slip over the lip and down into your bowl.

However it seduces its way in, what you don't know, as it is getting all cozy in its new home, is that the underbelly of Addiction secretes a caustic numbing acid that slowly begins to dissolve the bowl of your identity from the inside out. You can't even feel it. For a long time all you see when you look in the bowl are the loving, liquid eyes of the demon gazing back at you <blink, blink>, and all you feel is relief. You think, "This really works! At last I can relax! I feel like I matter!"

For some period of time after that, you have a new best friend/lover/mother whispering lovely things about you in your ear, and it is as if all your prayers have been answered. The more connected you get to Addiction, the safer you feel. Meanwhile Addiction is down there secretly digesting not only the bowl itself, but every marble that is tossed into it. You don't even notice or mind, because your bowl is feeling fuller and fuller all the time.

After a bit, Addiction does start to ask for little things here and there if you want it to stay in the bowl: a little money, a little time. But its needs are so small compared to the resources you used to have to expend on your Marble Game-strategies that you give happily. In fact, you don't even

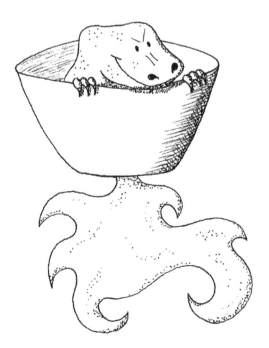

feel the need to give out marbles in your other relationships anymore. Your relationship with Addiction is so satisfying, that you are starting to feel as if you don't need anyone else for much of anything. "Those freaking blood-suckers, squeezing me for marbles, they never really cared about me. All I need to do is make sure Addiction has everything it needs and I am set." All your other relationships start to suffer, and you don't care, at least not enough to do anything about it.

This goes on for some time until the bowl of your identity begins to get so worn-away that you start to feel a little wobbly and confused, and you wander over to the bowl to find out what the problem is. For the first time Addiction doesn't seem so friendly. It begins to complain, "I'm not the problem! You aren't feeding me enough time, money or attention. I'm in here doing all the work keeping the hole plugged and you are neglecting me! I need more!" So you give more. It seems to work for a while. But it is a losing game for you. If you do finally wake up to the fact that Addiction is dissolving your bowl, and you are losing everything that ever made you you, and you manage to squeak out a protest, "Hey! You're dissolving my bowl!!" the response you get might sound something like, "Oh, this old thing? You don't need a bowl. I will hold you. I will take care of you."

The bigger Addiction gets, and the more space it takes up, the more efficient it gets at dissolving your bowl, and the more frail, confused, and out-of-sorts you feel. Addiction always requires more time, and more money, and more attention, more, more, more: a bottomless hunger that can never really be satisfied until finally in the end there is nothing left at all. You have given over your whole identity and been absorbed. There is no you. There is only hunger and Addiction, which are of course the same thing. A starving, single-minded wraith inhabits your body. The end.

Ok. That's the bad news. The good news is while it may be true that an addiction to marbles is unavoidable until you grow a bowling ball, the demon-Addiction that offers salvation from the Game can only come in to you if invited! I often think about the old human myth about vampires when I consider this angle. A vampire is a hungry spirit of the walking dead that sucks you dry and remakes you in its own image, just like Addiction. But vampires can only get in to your house if invited! Did our ancestors come up with allegorical stories to illustrate truths about the only outside force that exists with the **actual** capacity to steal our souls? Think of all of the stories about Satan offering mortals whatever they desire if they will only betray their own integrity. (Thus making it forever impossible to actually win The Game for themselves.) The mortal is untouchable until s/he agrees to a bargain with the demon. "Sign on the dotted line, and your soul is mine."

What might you be selling your soul to?

I just had the thought that it seems likely that 82% of you reading this chapter have been picturing a poor soul struggling with an addiction to alcohol or drugs. However, substance dependency makes up only a fraction, albeit a persistent fraction, of common addictive patterns and behaviors that have become the norm in our culture. I may be about to singe your nose hairs with this one, folks, but I put habitual television watching, habitual surfing the net, compulsive shopping, compulsive gambling, compulsive texting, compulsive exercise, compulsive sexual activity, substituting Facebook-culture for real community, substituting internet porn for intimacy with a real person, collecting "valuable" stuff, and compulsive hoarding in the same basket of addictive behaviors that can steal away your consciousness and possess your soul. I am not, of course, saying that any of those activities are "bad" in and of themselves, at least in moderation, when used for fun. They all, however, tend to distract you from the real world of the present moment. They all temporarily soothe the pain of anxiety, depression, and anger by providing an attractive escape from the present moment. They all provide the opportunity for Addiction to get a foothold into a vulnerable psyche.

If you or someone who loves you suspects that you might be sliding into dependence on an unconsciousness-engendering behavior or substance, I suggest you take it out of your life for a week or two, watch your response and see what happens. Are you resistant to my suggestion? Very suspicious… Ask yourself, am I engaging in this activity for the pure enjoyment of it? Or am I doing it because I am trying to escape the feeling that I have when I don't do it? If I decide to go without this activity for a week, are my thoughts preoccupied with the activity that is missing, or do I fall happily into other pursuits? If I decide to take a break from the activity, does my mind try to come up reasons why the break is stupid, not needed, or a waste of time? If I commit to taking a break, do I notice a spike in my irritability, anxiety, or depression?

Even if you find that none of the risky behaviors you engage in are at addictive levels yet, conscious-intentional-you might decide that spending less time fostering unconscious escape and more time fostering mindfulness is in the best interest of your happiness and your authorship. It is entirely up to you.

On the subject of substance use, I don't have enough personal experience regarding either the use of drugs, or working with clients with chemical-dependency issues, to feel as if I have a right to make blanket-statements like "drug use is a sure path to addiction." Even if I did have more experience, I don't predict that I would end up making a statement like that. Both in my practice and in my greater community, I have witnessed that a fair percentage of the population is able to use substances in moderation just for fun, in the same way some people can gamble without worry, or enjoy the occasional guilt-free shopping spree. Taking this line of thought farther, I know a small number of perfectly functional and self-actualized people who report that the use of present-moment-amplification chemicals like THC and psychedelics have assisted them in achieving altered states that got them off the hamster wheel permanently.

I don't have enough data to comment responsibly on the efficacy that particular "doing, to shift my sense of being" strategy. All I know is that all recreational drugs can and have been used as a way to temporarily deaden one's awareness of emotional suffering, and for some users they become a crutch that causes deeper injury. The less successful your marble-gathering strategies, and the bigger the hole in the bottom of your bowl, the less likely it is that you will be part of the segment of the population that can use drugs recreationally, or spiritually, at least until you have grown a fat, stable bowling ball for your bowl. There is also some portion of humanity that has been found to have a genetic or chemical predisposition to an addictive vulnerability to substances. (26) That segment of the population will never be able to use substances without risk of great harm to themselves and others.

Psyches that are the most hungry for validation (usually the ones who suffered the breaches of attachment in their early years that I outlined in Chapter 1) are far more vulnerable to the whole list of addictive behaviors at the top of this section. If I am describing you, going cold-turkey on all of them until you have achieved a stable and reliable bowling ball might not be a bad idea.

Finally, I have a deep resistance to telling other adults that I think I know what they 'should' do ("Should." Bleh!). But if you are struggling to manage your anger I am going to step out here and say **do not drink alcohol**. Alcohol and anger are a millenias-long, dangerous, toxic, and sometimes lethal combination.

Section 2: The Fourth Coping Tactic

In Chapter 2, I illustrated what happens when the best marble-gathering strategies that you have been able to devise aren't keeping your bowl full of marbles, and despite your best efforts there appears to be no way to win The Game. The Big Three coping tactics humans have developed to avoid experiencing the helplessness that results from losing The Game, are Anxiety, Depression and Anger. If you haven't guessed it by now, I must finally confess that there are actually four top reasons -- four coping-tactics, and Addiction is #4. Thus the **Bypass Your Tactic** model should by all rights look like this:

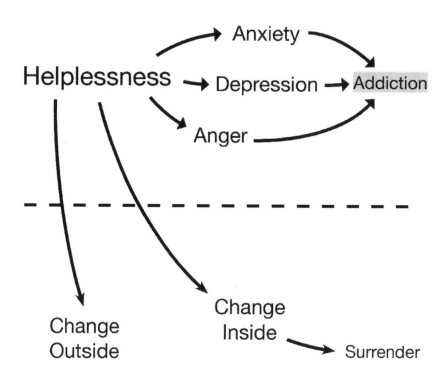

You will note, that I don't put Addiction on the same level with the other Big Three. I don't because it is most often the case that Addiction slips in as a coping tactic when you have been suffering from the "help" of one of the other three for awhile first. Addiction promises salvation from the suffering inflicted by all of the rest of them. And while Anxiety, Depression, and Anger go hand in hand with sinking consciousness (you getting lost in the thought-loops inside your mind), addictive coping-tactics engender an even deeper level of unconsciousness.

Another way of saying this is that the Hamster, the Bear, and the Bull are all manifestations of the unconscious thought loops that arise in your mind, to try to rescue you from helplessness. They try to be the champions that distract you from the most intolerable emotional experience you can have (helplessness). Yet, in taking you away from connection to the real world where you might address helplessness directly, they end up hurting more than they help. Addiction seduces even these three champions of unconsciousness, though only temporarily, taking the whole psyche deeper into nightmare, and further away from authorship. This is a self-reinforcing feedback loop one level deeper than the Big Three.

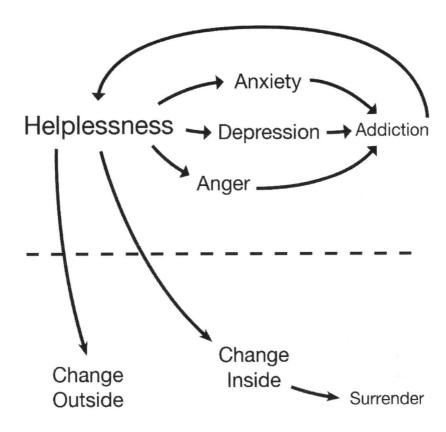

What is the way out of the multi-layered labyrinth of addiction?

Stand up and face your own grid of probability. Start choosing actions. You can start by **changing things outside of you**, like pouring all the pills in your house down the drain, getting a new cell number, moving to a new city, not hanging out with your partners-in-addiction, replacing an addiction to alcohol with a less-harmful attachment to AA, or getting support from someone who is not interested in judging you. There are countless cherries you could pick from the grid to assist you in kicking your primary addiction out of the bowl. (Go to chapter 3 for a review of "changing things outside of you" options.)

Then you could begin to change things inside of you, like coming up with word-vaccines to say in response to the voice of addiction, or cutting the string of your "I'm worthless and weak" beads in favor of working towards a string of "I am worth the shiny future I am creating" beads. You could drop old paradigms about how unfair and unfriendly life is to you, in favor of new, flexible views on reality, or choose from countless other possibilities that kick your primary addiction out of the bowl. (Go to chapter 4 for a review of "changing things on the inside of you" options.)

Finally, there may be some things that require your unequivocal surrender, if you are to tip Addiction out of your bowl and be free for good. These may be the hardest choices from the grid, albeit the most powerful. You may need to give up a fantasy that there exists an easy road to freedom-from-suffering. You may need to give up the fantasy that you can save the one you love from suffering if you just stay in Addiction's boat with him/her. You may have to give up the fantasy that you can save any person with your love at all. You may even need to let absolutely everything else go, at least for a while, in order to save yourself. And if addiction has taken over your life and you don't save yourself, don't think you can hold on to the illusion that you are of real use to anyone else. The lessons of the Marble Game are clear about that.

If you have had Addiction in your bowl for a long time, I pray that there is enough of you left to author your recovery. If you have it together enough to be reading this book, I believe in you. My bet is on you.

Section 3: The Trap of Acquisition

The hoarding of valuable stuff is humanity's most societally-acceptable addictive behavior. It is Addiction wearing Security's clothing, Addiction in the guise of entertainment. Money, cars, shoes, girlfriends, airline miles, fabulous entertainment systems, Facebook friends, pets -- whatever an individual has deemed to be special and valuable, the ownership of which validates that person's worth. Through the lens of the **Marble Game**, the hope is that "If I amass enough of this fabulous valuable stuff, I will finally feel like I matter!" Of course it doesn't work. The marbles that come with the acquisition of every new item just slip rapidly out the bottom of the bowl. To the collector though, the fantasy of the value of the stuff has so much weight that the meaning made of their continued hunger is, "Well, I just must not have enough to be satisfied yet!", so they go on collecting. Even cash loses value over time via inflation. We don't even get to hold on to the one thing in life that is supposed to be the most reliable. Inflation is built into the monetary system - inherent in the way the whole world economy must work for the current system to keep ticking (27). And perhaps the most monumental example of a sanctified post-modern practice of addiction exists in the Corporation, an entity protected as an "individual", with all the rights of a "citizen" under the United States Bill-of Rights, yet which exists not to reproduce or create, like a living person, but by law exists only to grow as big as possible, devour all competitors, and control as much as it possibly can (28).

If you will remember, I have asserted that:

- At the very core of human existential suffering is the delusion that "I don't matter".
- As a result, our core drive is to try to gather and maintain enough marbles to prove to ourselves and others that we do matter.

- But, salvation from suffering lies only in surrendering to the realization that the core of you has always been enough. You don't have to prove a thing.
- "I am enough" is what allows for the consciousness of free will, authentic connection, creativity, and authorship to rise in you.

There is a reason why so many spiritual traditions down through the ages have required a vow of poverty. The hope was that seekers of the Divine could side-step the acquisition trap. Addiction, the very embodiment of never-enoughness, is a bottomless void of insatiable hunger that tricks sufferers into thinking that there is a way to stay safe in life if you are just willing to hand your authorship over to something outside of you. "I will handle that internal black pit of emptiness for you if you give yourself to me." As such, Addiction is the anti-bowling ball, the Anti-authorship, and the closest thing to a real Satan that I can imagine in this existence. It will take the hole in your bowl, stretch it and force it around, until the gaping void bends around to eat the bowl itself.

Chapter 6 - Section 3 Questions

Are there patterns of behavior or thought in my life that I think might put me at risk for allowing Addiction into my bowl? Hold each risk factor up in the light of the following questions:

1) Am I engaging in this activity for the pure enjoyment of it? Or am I doing it because I am trying to escape the feeling that I have when I don't do it?
2) If I decide to go without this activity for a week, are my thoughts preoccupied with the activity that is missing, or do I fall happily into other pursuits?
3) If I decide to take a break from the activity does my mind try to come up with reasons why the break is stupid, not needed, or a waste of time?
4) If I commit to taking a break do I notice a spike in my anxiety, depression, or feelings of anger?

Is Addiction firmly in ensconced in my bowl already? Am I ready to address it? If so:

1) What are my best bets for getting the most bang for my buck in the arena of making the changes I need to make **outside** of myself to tip Addiction out of my bowl? (Go to chapter 3 for a review of "changing things outside of you" options.)
2) What are my best bets for getting the most bang for my buck in the arena of making the changes I need to make **inside** of myself to tip Addiction out of my bowl? (Go to chapter 4 for a review of "changing things outside of you" options.)
3) What do I suspect I may need to just let go of? And what are the things I won't even let myself think about letting go of, that I probably am going to have to let go of if I am to be successful?

Chapter 6 Questions

This chapter has hopefully offered you new ways of generating answers to some of the questions I posed in the Introduction. When you look through the lens of seeing your life and the lives of people around you through the lens of addictive behaviors and drives, what new answers are arising in you regarding the following questions:

1) Who am I and why am I so crazy?

2) Who is s/he and why is s/he driving me so crazy?

3) Why do I keep doing the crazy stuff I do… and then do it again and again?!

4) In the face of all of my flaws how do I become the person I want to be?

6) Why does Life/God/The Universe either a) seem so crazy that the way the world works makes no sense, or b) hate me personally so much that I am punished again and again no matter how hard I try?

7) Why bother to ever do anything? What is the point?

Chapter 7: Let Go So You Can Grow

"Suffering is not holding you. You are holding suffering.
When you become good at the art of letting sufferings go,
Then you'll come to realize how unnecessary it was
for you to drag those burdens around with you.
You'll see that no one else other than you was responsible.
The truth is that existence wants your life to become a festival."

-Osho

Section 1: On the Magic of Flexibility

Time is the element in the universe that is the most inexorable, and impossible to influence. Thus the temporariness inherent to a temporal existence creates the experiences that engender the greatest feelings of helplessness in our lives. These are the greatest existential horrors (i.e. the most engendering of utter helplessness) humankind contemplates:

- The inexorability of death and aging
- The eventual decay of every thing we will ever write or build
- The fact that every relationship we ever have will end
- Everyone we will ever love will eventually leave us (or we will leave them)
- And, in the end, after enough time has passed, it will be as if every one of us were never here.

For many philosophers down through the ages, the ultimate conclusion reached when staring into this frightening void has been that we don't matter. No one matters! (The Marble Game is born.)

Perhaps it is true that when measured against the scale of time itself every single human endeavor is nothing more than whistling in the dark. Yet, in the great yawning maw of the nothingness of everything, perhaps whistling in the dark is the most magnificent, beautiful, precious thing imaginable. Perhaps it is the only thing **that** matters.

Still, humans try to live forever, writing legends and tracking mythical objects to keep the hope alive that winning against time could be possible: the Fountain of Youth, the Philosopher's Stone, the Holy Grail. The very oldest recorded human story that we have discovered is the Epic of Gilgamesh, an ancient Babylonian king who went on a quest for eternal life. In the quest, he fails to fulfill the command to stay awake for seven days and seven nights, and the secret of immortality is taken from him.

I ended the last chapter exploring the psyche's practice of "acquiring" - collecting "valuable" stuff as a strategy for trying to keep mattering even after death. If I leave enough behind, I will have mattered enough so that no one will forget me. The colossal tombs of the Pharaohs of ancient Egypt are an example of an acquisition helplessness-coping-tactic designed to prolong a powerful existence, or at least leave a monumental stamp on the earth.

Holding on in the face of the inexorable pull of time, conserving everything we can, trying to keep things from changing (read "leaving"), as if we can keep time from passing is a ubiquitous human occupation. We cling to youth, our children, our sweethearts, our identities, our belongings, and our habits long after it is time to let go.

Two of the most common reasons people come to see me are that they lack, as they see it, either the drive or the impulse control to follow through with a change. I.e., they think their problem is about character flaws. But character flaws are not the reason people don't change. **People don't change because they want what they have now more than they want the desired future because of what they fear they will have to give up to get it.** That is, if I fear that the stuff/habits I will have to let go of in order to have the life I want is more valuable to me than that future may be, change will not happen. The truth is, no matter how much we protest that this is not true, we all make space to cultivate and safeguard the things that matter most to us.

If avoiding cold, tiredness, and being out of breath is more valuable to you than having the fitness you have always said you wanted, it doesn't matter how much you say you want to run in the morning, it isn't going to happen. If making sure you don't elevate your heart rate, trigger negative self-talk, and risk potential rejection is of higher value to you than opening the possibility that the girl you want will go out with you, it doesn't matter how much you want to date her, you won't ask her out. If hedging against possible future need for the stuff that is piled on every surface of your house is of higher value to you than having a home that is easy to navigate, no matter how much the mess bothers you, you will never get rid of it.

There is no personal judgment attached to these statements, by the way. This is just the way things actually work. That we cultivate what we are most unwilling to lose is a basic law of human behavior as inexorable as the gravity that keeps pulling us down. And, if you are not able to learn to allow time to take the things you have loved away from you when it is time for them to go, you will not welcome new ways of being.

Ok, I have to admit now there is another factor that comes into play in the quest for change. In the equation that illustrates what leads to stuckness, there is another factor on the side of "resistance to loss". Sometimes it is just challenging to keep in the front of your mind that you have committed to a shift in direction. Unconscious habit keeps taking over. If you can't stay awake to the fact that your priorities have changed, it is really hard to keep making choices that support the change. Thus: Resistance to loss + unconsciousness = Stuckness.

I am not going to say a whole lot here about unconsciousness. Both chapter 3 and chapter 4 have sections designed to assist you in your quest for rising consciousness. But I **am** going to talk a bit about learning to let go, and learning to manage the inevitable discomfort that comes with surrendering to time, and allowing loss to happen.

Section 2: Letting Go of The Past

Almost everyone I know is deeply attached to the stories they tell themselves about their lives, and the meaning they make of the stories. Identities tend to be created even more out of the **meaning we make** of the things that happen to us than the events themselves. "I am a shy person because when I was in the second grade, my teacher made us read in front of the class."

"I am bad with money because my parents never taught me how to manage it." "I treat my partner like a child because my Mom was an alcoholic and I had to be the parent in that relationship." "I have problems with arousal because I was molested as a child."

While it is true that the bad things that have happened to you in life can have a negative impact on you now, there are plenty of people who were laughed at as children who didn't end up with social anxiety, and plenty who are good with money but had to figure that out on their own. There are adult children of alcoholics who don't treat their spouses like children, and many people who were sexually abused as kids who go on to have very satisfying and wonderful physical relationships in their adult lives. In my experience, the most telling factor in a person's ability to heal the self of a troubled past, is the capacity to let go of the identity s/he has made from it and create a new strength-based one. The trouble is, most people are more attached to their identities than their desire to be free of them.

Letting go of the past as a reason for current unhappiness feels to many like a betrayal of the self -- "If I let go of my attachment to my story and stop reliving my victimization, I will have suffered for nothing!" "Who would I be if I stopped clinging to the fact that I was wounded?!" Having the opportunity to fall back on the past, as a reason for being unhappy now, is also difficult to let go of. Having been victimized is the perfect retreat to fall back on when it feels too risky to try to get what you want **now**. It is also the perfect reason not to risk trying again when you don't get what you want the first time you try. But blaming the past for your unhappiness keeps you trapped back there as you replay the script of your victimization over and over again in the present, through the negative way in which you interpret what happens to you now, the unconscious way in which you respond to people, and the manner in which you always expect to be victimized in the future because you were in the past.

This is not me saying "Your screwed-up life is your fault." (!)

Your life simply is what it is. What I am an advocate of is your acceptance of the idea that though in the past you created your experience of life unconsciously, in reaction to all the things that happened to you, you can let that go, and begin to change the life you have now by experiencing it and directing it more consciously.

What if it is true that you are born new in every moment and that every moment you have an opportunity to be with yourself and the world in a new way? Are you dragging the heavy bag of your past behind you on a choking cord around your neck? Are you fixated on the injustice you once suffered? Does your attachment to your own victimization punish the perpetrator, or make it any more likely that you will receive justice?

Are you weighed down with shame and self-recrimination for past wrongs you yourself perpetrated on other people? If you have hurt someone, apologize, make amends, and then let it go. What would it be like to set all of that baggage down and be who you are **right now**? If you really want to be the author of your own life, you must be willing to face your future without wearing the identity of a person who has been so abused and wronged that you are permanently and irrevocably damaged. Cut the cord.

"We would rather be ruined than changed; we would rather die in our dread than climb the cross of the moment and let our illusions die."

- W.H. Auden

Section 3: Letting Go in the Present

Releasing your own self-critical judgment

Letting go of negative judgment about the way things actually are right now can allow you to direct energy to more productive uses and even make space for something new to happen. You don't have to hate your life, run yourself down, get in shape, clean out the garage, burn your stash, or get help from a person like me. You don't have to hate your spouse to make a stand for change, or leave a situation that is sucking the life out of you. You don't have to resent your kids before you ask them to put their cell phones away at the dinner table. You can just want a different kind of life than the one you have now, and start advocating for it.

In the struggle to define their identities, a common practice of teenagers and twenty-somethings (though by no means restricted to them), is the practice of dramatically rejecting things in order to stress with the strength of the judgment, that the distained things represent the opposite of what an individual stands for. Gathering together in groups that share the desire for a common definition makes judgmental self-defining feel all that much more potent. We have virtually all engaged in this behavior at one time or another, enjoying the game of "us vs. them". Yet even the quasi-entertaining judging you have done with your friends is likely to drain your creative energy. It is easy to get into a habit of hanging out with people with whom you foster a connection based largely in shared criticism, gossiping about "**those** people over there" or "**that** kind of thing that we would never do." The more time you spend in life cultivating the unconsciousness that is fertilized by judgment, the less authorship you will have.

Try substituting "love" a few times in the place where "hate" usually goes in your vocabulary. Seriously. Just try it. Out loud! The worst real thing that will happen is you might feel silly, but it might make you laugh. It might even help you slip the chains of a paradigm that says "There is nothing I can do about how the way I feel about things." Or it might help you slip the chains of your paradigm that says, "If I don't keeping remembering to hate what I am against, I might lose track of who I **am**." Try it! Throw back your head and exclaim:

- "I LOVE eggplant!"
- "I LOVE getting up at 6:00 in the morning!"
- "I LOVE my husband's snoring!"
- "I LOVE having a negative balance in my checking account!"
- "I LOVE my thighs!" and
- "I LOVE MY MOTHER-IN-LAW!!"

I love this game! I love coming up with all things I can choose not get bugged about, and catching myself, and laughing when I do get myself all twisted up about things I can't change, or the silly stuff that is sure to be different tomorrow.

Releasing the tyranny of outside judgment

Are you organized around the need to be approved of by others? Moving towards a greater sense of freedom in the present generally requires that you release your attachment to the judgment the outside world has of you, and the fantasy that you have any control over that. Are you still trying to prove to a father who is impossible to please that you "have what it takes"? Are you mired in the legacy of your partner's cheating ex, trying to convince your partner that **you** are trustworthy? Are you trying to prove to your mother that you **do** love her while she is dragging a story around from her childhood that she is not lovable, and can not a absorb a word you say about it until she is willing to set that story down? Not only do you have limited power to impact the way that people see you, but they have their own unconscious reasons for needing to view you the way they do. Perhaps your mother (Dad, partner) has an unconscious vested interest in refusing to absorb your expressions of caring, because 1) her stance validates the meaning she makes of her own victimized past, and/or 2) if she never lets your love in, she can't be hurt if you snatch it away, and/or 3) as long as you have to keep trying to convince her, she will feel as if you won't abandon her.

Your father will never allow himself to notice that you "have what it takes" until he is able to set down his own story that he himself does not. Your partner will never believe you are trustworthy until s/he is trustworthy, or perhaps until s/he feels worthy of you, or realizes s/he would not die without you, etc.

What do you **know** about your self? Who are you really? Where are you censoring your true expression of self in order to gain outside approval, or avoid conflict, or keep from hurting peoples' feelings. The people around you are highly effective when it comes to unconsciously getting you to behave the way **they** want or expect you to. Where are you playing a role in someone else's script? What script would you would write if you could let go of your own self-judgment and your need for outside validation in favor of being sourced from within, manifesting your true self, and creating the life you actually want.

Releasing stuff and commitments

I'm going to go put my magic finger-tips to my psychic temples here for a moment… and predict that you are a person who is complaining on a regular basis that, "I don't have enough (time, money, energy, storage space)." Impressed by my psychic powers?

Not-enoughness is at the center of the Game, people! And everybody is playing it. One of the ways we combat the creeping helpless feeling is by filling up every spare minute in our schedules and every empty space in our closets with things, things, **things**!

Well then. The inverse of "I don't have enough time" is "I need to let go of some commitments." And the inverse of "I don't have enough money" is "I need to let go of some credit cards." (Or a house that is too big, or that little shoe addiction, or the illusion that if I don't send my kid to an Ivy League school s/he will never be successful, etc.)

I will take my psychic powers even further and predict that more than half of you reading this paragraph could have a stranger come into your closet when you were at work, steal 50% of your clothes, and you wouldn't even know what was missing when you got home. You might even think that somehow your closet had grown while you were gone! And, I **know** your kids would not notice if this happened to their toys. We have too much stuff to do, and we have too much stuff. We think we need it. We define our value by it. We try to stave off future scarcity with it. We try to camouflage our love-handles with it. We distract from self-judgment with it. We bribe our kids and spouses for marbles with it. Meanwhile, it makes us exhausted, ungrateful, and irritable. There is barely any room for us in our houses, or on our calendars. If you are feeling a little short of breath right now, it's time to let some stuff go! ☺

Releasing the people who need to go

For many of you, releasing the people who need to go will be the hardest thing there is. No matter how much they have taken from you without giving back, how many times they have broken their agreements with you, how little is their awareness of the impact of their behavior, or how much money they have stolen, how many times they left you stranded, got drunk and ruined your birthday, lied, cheated, even abused you, every fiber of your being will resist walking away.

Why do we stay in relationship with people who cost more energy than they give? Further, why do we stay in relationship with people who take all that we have to give and then extort more? It's the Marble Game, folks.

- Even if s/he is unreliable, we fear that if we let this marble-producer go, there won't be another one to take his/her place.
- The marbles this one gave me at one time were exactly the potent variety I always most wanted. If I let go, I might never find that again.
- If I let this one go, s/he might turn all the other marble-producers against me, and I'll end up having no one to prove to me that I matter.
- I don't believe I can take care of myself in the world without this person, even if I am the one always doing the 'taking care of' stuff. (My bowl is too empty, or the hole is too big.)
- "I can't be mean to anyone!" If I let this person go, I will no longer be eligible for the variety of marbles that my best strategies are designed to elicit. (i.e. "nice", "kind", "giving")
- If I let that person go, I will be responsible for his/her unhappiness, (and thus will no longer be eligible for the variety of marbles that my best strategies are designed to elicit, i.e. "responsible", "generous", "good guy").

Producing "you're so lovable that I still want you as my friend even though our relationship is not fair to me" marbles, is not your job. Just about **everyone** is lovable, if you get to know them well enough. Just about everyone **means** well! You don't have to hate people or even be mad at them to not have it be worth it to you to maintain a relationship with them. I want you to take a minute and remember that the Marble Game itself IS an addiction. It is a set-up that no one wins, unless they can figure out how to not need to play and be ok. Remember what real kindness looks like?

I outlined the concept called "Weed Your Friendship Garden" earlier in the book, but I am going to repeat what I said here, because you might need to hear it twice.

Who contributes to your life? Who gives you as much energy back as you need to give out to maintain the relationship? Who sees and supports your best self? Who manages their own anxiety in the face of your choices rather than blaming you for not staying the way they want you to be? Who gently calls you on your most self-damaging anti-anxiety strategies? These are your **friends**.

Who uses you and gives back nothing but more marble-solicitation marbles? When you usually feel irritable or bone-tired after getting off the phone, who was the person you were talking to? Whose conversation is a constant stream of complaints, criticism, and judgment regarding you, or other people in their lives? These are the addicts who are squeezing you for marbles, dragging down your consciousness, and sucking up your energy.

"Each time a door closes, the rest of the world opens up."

- Parker Palmer

Section 4: Letting Go of Fantasies About the Future

Next in your path is the release of any comforting fantasy you are guarding that says you have the power to avoid future pain or discomfort as long as you have enough foresight and the right kind of planning. Western culture is steeped in this paradigm. We, as a culture, believe that not only is it possible to achieve a pain-free existence, but we have the right to it. And, if we are experiencing discomfort, there must be something wrong. (Oh, and if you get enough exercise and eat enough bioflavonoids, you can live forever too.)

The reality is that pain is an integral part of life. It is an integral part of existing in a temporal universe. Loss hurts. And no matter how hard you try, no matter how much of your precious life-energy you spend trying to avoid it, pain will find you now and again.

Most pain can be fairly well managed unless you are clinging to a story from your past that you can't handle it, or a story that says you, personally, are a target for more than your share. Attachment to the belief that it is possible to avoid pain, as long as you make the "right" choice, is the direct cause of much of the resistance to change that I am addressing in this chapter. The belief that the right choice will allow the avoidance of discomfort while the wrong one will hurt you, leads to the very fear of making choices that keeps people stuck. Many of my clients are so fearful of making mistakes that they tend to put choices off or let other people make their choices for them. And some are so fixated on potential disastrous results that anxiety traps them within the prisons of their own minds, causing painful choice-paralysis most of the time.

All choices carry with them the loss of something. With every alternative comes negative consequence as well as positive. The same is true in reverse. This is true even of making no choices at all, which is of course its own choice. What if you were to make decisions about your future based on what interests and excites you rather than what frightens you? What if you were to accept as part of your identity that you are a person who can handle the unexpected collateral effects that life presents in response to your choices without being swayed from your chosen course -- unless you want to be? What if you were to give yourself permission to choose, change your mind if you want to, try new paths, and change your mind again?

Life is not safe. Time will always get you in the end. What I see happen in my practice and in my own life, again and again, is that decisions based on fear tend to produce unpleasant collateral effects. And if you won't choose -- if you let life happen to you, or you play very conservatively with your efforts to avoid the guiding information that pain offers, chaos of the least pleasant variety will seek you out and find **you**. I am not sure why, but I have some ideas about it that I am collecting for a future book. In any case, change will come, no matter what you do or do not do. You can choose to influence it, or be the passive recipient of it.

Where are you willing to embrace your own chaos so chaos does not embrace you? Given that everyone is destined to eventually lose, use your integrity as a compass and choose.

Section 5: Letting Go of Suffering

Pain is inevitable. Suffering is not. What is the difference between pain and suffering? The pattern of replaying memories of past hurts instead of being in the present moment, plus the pattern of anticipating the pain that may be coming down the pipeline in the future, is what puffs pain up to the level of suffering. Another way of saying this is: *Pain + avoidance of the present moment = Suffering.*

Suffering is the hoarding of pain! I learned this lesson with the birth of my second child. As many a mother can testify, natural childbirth is entirely doable if, and only if, one stays stringently in the present moment, letting the last contraction go as soon as it is over, and not allowing the anticipation of the next one anywhere near one's consciousness. Childbirth, as a mindfulness practice, was a revelation for me!

After a long time of working with a client, peeling back the layers of his or her defense against helplessness, we often eventually get to one of the oldest existential complaints in human history. My client will cry out: "But why must there be pain at all?! Why is life set up this way?!" (And let me just call your attention to the fact that the question is almost synonymous with "Why must there be loss?") Beyond the illustration I have laid out in this chapter regarding how loss is integral to a temporal existence, suffering is integral to our own evolution, and perhaps evolution in general. Why did giraffes evolve long necks? The adaptation only happened after thousands of years of the short-necked giraffes dying of starvation because they couldn't reach the higher leaves.

We need our pain. I will show you what I mean:

You and your puppy go on a hike: Part 2

Once upon a time you bought new hiking boots to go on a hike with your puppy. The two of you were in the hiking swing by this point in the relationship, happily climbing mountains together, enjoying the experience of following your authentic in-the-moment curiosity. On this particular day, you were wearing your brand new pair of hiking boots because your old cross-trainers were no longer up to the task of keeping up with your long exploration into new territories. This turned out to be a mistake, however, because unbeknownst to you it is a really good idea to break in hiking boots before you take them on a long hike for the first time. After a couple of miles, you began to feel some pain at the back of your heel.

"Hmmm, puppy. This is no good. This looming pain situation is threatening to ruin our hike!" But then you remembered! Eureka! You happened to have some forgotten ampoules of anesthetic in your backpack left over from that time you were called in to perform emergency dental surgery for underserved populations in northern Alaska! The day was saved!

Pulling out one of the syringes, you leaned down and pierced the needle straight through the boot into the back of your foot. It stung for a second, but in about five minutes, or so, you were good to go. Back to the trail you went, feeling great!

You and your companion walked all day, stopping at a stream for a few minutes of lunch in the middle, but making good time and reaching a campsite at the top of the mountain well before dark. There was plenty of time to build a fire, which you did, before sitting down to pull off your boots so you could change out of the sweaty socks you had been wearing. And what do you suppose you found when you pulled off your boot?

Perhaps your boot was full of blood. Perhaps the skin on the back was rubbed down to the bone. In any case, it is a fair bet that the next day there was going to be no chance that you would even be able to get the boot back on over the swelling, let alone get back down the mountain. Somebody would have to fly in and medivac you out. Not only was the solution to the situation likely to be extremely expensive, but you might even end up with permanent scarring or nerve damage!

I have created this elaborate illustration in order to point out a few things about pain and suffering that seem obvious in the context of the story, but likely less so in the context of the pain of your own life. Pain is life's arrow that points directly towards the spot where a change needs to happen. Always. Every time. The specific change is up to you. You have an entire grid of probabilities to choose from, and your life belongs to you. It would be within your province to just shoot your foot full of two ampoules the next day, wedge it inside that boot, and get down the mountain as best you can. That **is** the kind of thing that most people choose. If you are a dentist, you likely have a steady supply of anesthetic you could just keep using for the rest of your life.

However, the other lesson of the story is that if you ignore the pain's arrow, or drug yourself so you can't feel it, or distract yourself from the pain with addictive behaviors, you are guaranteed to foster more loss over time, thus engendering more suffering. Suffering is the LOUD voice of life trying to get your attention. It is your teacher. It is your guest. The only escape from it is waking up to the present moment to address the source of your pain directly, and choose a change.

You will remember that for a few people, "suffering" is their primary marble-gathering strategy. "The Greatest Sufferer wins!!" Just in case you were confused about this, s/he doesn't. Letting go of that one is recommended.

Section 6: Just Because Something Feels Bad Doesn't Mean Anything Permanently Bad is Actually Happening

You know the maxim "Stuck between a rock and a hard place?" That phrase gets at one of the most emotionally painful, yet most common of unpleasant human experiences: the double bind. Rather than occurring because something truly intransigent is happening, double binds simply demonstrate that a difficult loss is needed and a change has not yet been made. Just because something will feel bad doesn't mean anything permanently bad is actually happening. In fact, often something good could happen if you were willing to go through the pain of loss, and come out the other side. Many indigenous cultures have known this core human truth for thousands of years. We must let go of the things that no longer serve us to make space for something new to come in. Here are some examples:

Double binds of the self

1) To be satisfied and happy in my life, I need to feel thankful for my abundance. But if I don't keep living in the pain of scarcity, then I won't get the support I need from other people.
2) I need to be seen as broken and needy to get support. But I can't simultaneously be seen as needy and broken, and be seen as superior and "right".
3) I need human connection, in some form, for virtually all of the things that make life matter (creative endeavor, collaboration, celebration, shared present moments, etc.), **yet** there is no way to will or force another person to care about the things I care about, or to care about me.
4) I need human connection, in some form, for virtually all of the things that make life matter, yet humans inevitably let me down. Even the most conscious creative partners change their identities, change their minds, rewrite history, disappear sometimes, or go unconscious, often when I most need them to hold up their end.

Double binds of relationship

1) I want you to feel responsible for my feelings and cut me lots of slack because I have been so wounded by my crappy upbringing. **But** don't you dare intimate that I **need** any care from you, or that I am anything but tough.
2) Be vulnerable with me so I can feel close you. **But** if you do share your feelings, I will use them later as ammunition to judge you.
3) If I am vulnerable with you, I will give you ammunition to use against me later. **But** if I protect myself by not sharing, I will be accused of not caring about the relationship (or not having feelings, or being made of ice).
4) I need you to keep being broken so I can keep feeling useful by fixing you. **But** if you keep being broken I can't tolerate it because it means I am not doing a good job with my fixing.

5) Read my mind to know what I want because people who really love each other have magical mind-reading ability (and get it wrong on a regular basis), **or** stop trying to read my mind and get accused of not loving me anymore.

6) And here is the Big Daddy of relationship double binds, the **Self Versus Other Paradox**: How do I be true to myself and my life while at the same time being close and intimate with you, when your integrity and my integrity don't always agree on what life is supposed to look like?

Double binds of family life

Parents want their kids to succeed, but also want their kids not to abandon them, or mess with the marble-gathering strategies they have in place.

1) "Be successful so I can take credit and feel validated by my parenting job. **But** don't get so successful that you stop needing me."

2) "Prove to me that I did a great job parenting by being happy and successful. **But** continue to validate my paradigm that my unhappiness is not my fault because life is so unfair it isn't even **possible** to be happy, by you being unhappy too.

3) "Stop drinking and get a handle on your explosive anger so the kids and I feel safe in our own home, **but** don't stop playing the role of the bad guy in the family because I need you to stay in that position so I can feel like the good guy."

Double binds of some larger systems

1) The world keeps changing and new information keeps coming in that necessitates changes in perspective. In our culture, politicians are not allowed to be wrong. But they also are not allowed to change their minds. It is not possible in this life to be both right and never change your mind when you learn new things.

2) Military elite forces are indoctrinated with the double bind that they are superior to civilians as the guardian-angels of society, so they should be embraced by their grateful communities. **Yet** due to the terrible things they must both endure and do in the course of their work, they believe they are forever set apart, monsters who can never really return to community because no one can understand them but their angel/monster brothers.

3) Creative capacity is what makes humans human. Entrepreneurs and researchers who explore strange new worlds and come up with creative solutions to time's persistent problems are deserving of as much financial return as they can generate for their wonderful work. **Yet** in every system, including our own, the best innovations eventually get institutionalized within a dominant model that stifles competition, making it harder and harder for creative ideas to come to fruition.

Section 7: Giveaway

"Surrender – Truth is in paradox: Surrender and you get everything. Bend and be strong. When you reach your limit and are exhausted, new energy rises in you. When you release others, they come to you. The wise know this: Let go in order to preserve. Be empty and fulfilled." (McClure, Vimala, 1991)

Camille's story

In 2005 a touring musician I know well was offered $50,000 by a wealthy investor to leave her primary source of income (teaching high school English) to pursue music full time. After six months of talks, Camille (said musician) applied for a one-year leave from her school district, which was granted, and she and the investor hired an entertainment attorney to draw up the contract. The day they were to due to meet and sign, however, the investor did not show up at the appointed spot, at the agreed upon time. Camille was stood up. Then the investor did not return phone calls – eleven phone calls – made by a frantic Camille wondering what had happened!!!

She had disappeared.

Camille had no job to return to that fall. Someone else was being hired. Furthermore, if she wanted to get her job back the following year, under the terms of her "leave" she could pursue no endeavor but music. Camille was in a double bind. Her choices were to pursue music and starve, or get a different job and sink her teaching career. Starve she did, or rather, the more common American equivalent of starving: running up $25,000 of credit card debt.

In the space of her very first year of touring, Camille experienced a series of additional "disasters" one after another, all adding up to foster in her the conclusion that "the universe is trying to tell me that I am on the wrong path!" She had her car broken into and her entire $5,000 sound system stolen out of the back. She rolled her ankle and fell hard while carrying her $2,000 primary guitar. It was smashed irreparably. She was in a car accident that totaled her primary touring vehicle. "Suffering" was Camille's middle name. At one point she was ready for the whole failed experiment to be over so she could just "learn her lesson" and go back to teaching. Then magical things started to happen.

- Because Camille could no longer bring her own sound system to a gig, she was now forced to eschew lower-end venues that don't have their own systems, in favor of trying for bookings at higher end venues. These were not venues she would have attempted to get booked in before, as someone just starting out. But, out of necessity now, she pursued the kinds of bookings that pay better, are more prestigious, and get better press.
- Because she had smashed her guitar, she was out at a Seattle music store looking at new guitars one day and got into a random conversation with a rep from Gibson Guitar. They exchanged cards, he ended up really liking her music and suggested that she pursue an endorsement deal with Gibson. This is never something she would have thought to do on her own, a new musician just starting out, but she did it on the rep's suggestion. Gibson liked her, and voila! She now owned a new, even fancier guitar, and had landed a prestigious endorsement.

- Even the traumatic loss of her sturdy, reliable tour vehicle made way for her to use a couple thousand dollars from the eventual settlement she received from the at-fault party's insurance company to buy a temporary cheap replacement vehicle AND pay off most of her hefty credit card debt.

Due to all of the experiences that had felt so "bad" while they were happening, by the end of one year, Camille found herself at a point in her career she never could have imagined reaching in such a short time, a point she would not have achieved without the tremendous good fortune of losing all the things she thought she needed to succeed. Today, Camille makes a fine living doing what she most loves in the world, and she never did go back to teaching high school. In the end, even the original traumatic loss of the investor was a blessing in disguise. Camille reaps all of the benefits of her hard work herself and owes nothing to anyone else, let alone the kind of person who would set an artist up and then betray her like that.

Back to vampyric-wisdom!

In the last chapter, I noted that many demons from mythological stories require only that a mortal surrender personal integrity (soul) to receive anything they want in exchange. Many mortals choose eternal life. The joke of course is that no one ends up wanting the life they end up being forced to live. A life untouched by time ends up being no life at all.

Vampires give up their souls and the ability to decay in exchange for an eternal life plagued by insatiable hunger not unlike addiction. In some stories, core lessons about human existence are played out by vampires who are portrayed as bored, listless creatures who envy human attachment to life and are plagued by a lack of purpose and meaning. At worst they are wandering creatures in constant torment, searching for something to fill the void.

When you are in a double bind, reflect that our human lives are precious and intense in large part because they can't last. Time marches on. Pain is inevitable. There is no living without enduring loss. So, given that you cannot avoid loss, use your integrity instead of your fear as a compass, step up, pick a path, and choose what to lose.

Chapter 7 Questions

Can you use the following questions to guide you in the practice of letting go:

1) What do you suspect you need to let go of, but resist considering?

2) Look at each coping strategy, hoarded identity, paradigm, habit, item, or person that needs to go, and ask yourself if you were willing to make the change, what do you fear you would lose that you cannot bear to let go of?

3) If you become able to make the change, what benefits might come your way?

4) What do you habitually judge without even thinking about it?

5) Outline the double binds in your life. What would you need to release to be able to escape the double bind?

6) Where are you willing to embrace your own chaos so chaos does not embrace you?

This chapter contained new ways of considering all of the questions I posed at the beginning of this book. Take some time and think about them again through the lens of resisting a temporal existence by judging time, and judging the pain that time inherently brings.

1) Who am I and why am I so crazy?

2) Who is s/he and why is s/he driving me so crazy?

3) Why do I keep doing the crazy stuff I do... and then do it again and again?!

4) In the face of all of my flaws how do I become the person I want to be?

5) How do I get that other person over there to be who I want him/her to be, and do what I want her/him to do?

6) Why does Life/God/The Universe either a) seem so crazy that the way the world works makes no sense, or b) hate me personally so much that I am punished again and again no matter how hard I try?

7) Why bother to ever do anything? What is the point?

Chapter 8: Envisioning the You, You Are Becoming

'Time' gets a bad rap in the previous chapter, as the source of all pain in the universe. In the interest of even-handedness, I think it is only fair to note now that time is also the source of all growth and change as well. Life itself is not possible without time. And time is the thing that is going to facilitate making the space to create the life and self you want, whenever you are ready to start.

Section 1: Creating a Vision

"You never change anything by fighting something that is already existing.
To change something, build a new model and make the existing thing obsolete."

- Buckminster Fuller

As I intimated at the end of the last chapter, only half of the reason for letting go of the things that need to go, is so life doesn't hurt so much. **The lesson of Giveaway** illustrates that the other half of the reason for releasing what needs to go is that the empty space created is a prerequisite for anything new to come in.

Who are you becoming? What will you be calling in to the space you are creating?

On the first day of therapy I send every one of my clients home to consider the same question. I write it on a sticky:

"At the end of this course of therapy, what will have changed, either within you or within your life, so we both know our work was successful?"

When I hand the sticky over and ask them to consider their answer for the next session, I read the question aloud. Then I give a little speech, the same speech I am going to give to you right now:

> "I want you to find a quite space where no one is going to bother you for twenty minutes or so, and close your eyes. Then I want you to really try to put yourself out there at the end of our work together, as if you are looking back at this moment. All the work has been already been done, that needed doing, to get you to where you are now. Really feel what it is like to be there. How does it feel to be you living inside your body now? What is different on the inside of you? What has changed in your life so that now you know it is time for us to celebrate your changes and be done with our work together?"

The next session, we go over the answers together and use them as a starting point for creating a vision for therapy.

My process for creating a vision is closely related to, but not quite the same as the common practice of "making goals" for therapy. For me, the word "goal" conjures up societal pressure, and I worry that it may push forward the cultural value that "the best path to success is a straight line." (I.e. the most effective way to get from "A to B" is to formulate a plan ahead of time and stick to the plan.) I don't think that that is the most effective, or even necessarily the most efficient way to get to point "B" a lot of the time. In fact, if a determination to stick to the path you decided on at the beginning of the journey, based on the information you had at that time, governs your entire trip, there is a really good chance you will be unconscious to short cuts or help that might be offered along the way.

On the road to a successful outcome, the most potent visions are worded in such a way as to leave room for both new perspectives to enter in to the equation and for success to be achieved by both changes on the inside and the outside of the client. For example, in goal-oriented language a client might say "At the end of this course of therapy, I will have achieved a mid-management level position at one of the following three Fortune 500 companies." That same idea, when translated into visioning language, sounds like this: "At the end of this course of therapy I will have achieved satisfaction and abundance in my work life." Another example of goal-oriented language would be, "At the end of our course of therapy I will be free of my mother!" That same idea in visioning- language would sound something like, "At the end of our course of therapy, I will have come to peace with regard to my connection, or lack thereof, with my mother."

Moving towards, as opposed to moving away

Successful change comes about when the vision you want to embody becomes more attractive than the things you are leaving behind. It happens when your attachment to what you are trying to let go of is extinguished in the face of something even more desirable, a future that is calling out to be realized. One simple way to say this is "It is easy to change when your old identity just does not fit you any more." Some examples:

Want to lose weight and keep is off?

- No more negative self-talk or complaining about the way things are now.
- Create a clear mental vision of what paradigms and behaviors support the desired identity, and fall in love with them!
- In your mind, imagine that it is the future and feel your changed physical form all around you as vividly as possible.
- Fall in love with the experience of walking. Love it while you are doing it, the feeling of moving your body, the way you feel afterwards - all loose and warm. The way the wind feels going past your face as you pelt down the trail, the friendly faces of your fellow walkers as they receive you in to the camaraderie of the walking community (or the running, climbing, biking, or rowing community).
- Stay conscious to loving the way your body feels after a week or two weeks -- stronger and more flexible -- how good it is to live inside of a moving-you. Get to know the delicious pain/pleasure of stretching out tired muscles.

- Notice how physically sick you feel when you park your body in front of the television for hours on end, or when you eat more than you need. Focus on the bloated, lethargic feeling and then notice how different your entire life feels to you when you have been walking every day for a week.
- Don't talk about how much you hate to exercise ever again. Let that story go. It is not your story any more.

Want to quit smoking?

- Fall in love with the identity of "smoke-free guy".
- Flesh it out for yourself. Get to a place inside of you where you know that the identity of "ex-smoker" is sexier, cooler, and more desirable than "smoker".
- How does smoke-free guy look different? What does he wear?
- What does that guy do in place of smoking? Where does that guy hang out now? Who does that guy hang out with?
- Feel, inside and out, how smoking-you is so much lamer and smellier when compared with the clean-lunged, white-toothed you, who is coming down the pipeline.
- Glory in your returning sense of smell, and the fact that you can once again taste foods that haven't had any flavor for years.
- Revel in your sense of freedom from domination by those little wads of burning leaves. They'll never force you outside the building into the cold again!

You get the idea.

Barriers to achievement: when success itself is a threat

It is common for a new client to come to me and say on the first day. "I am a self-sabotager. I know that I have the potential to be successful, but I self-sabotage!" A lot of the time, with further exploration, it turns out that what is really going on is that the individual can't maintain the level of consciousness required to effectively follow through with a course of action. However, on occasion, I **do** run into a client who has an authentic fear of success, i.e. success might bring with it the loss of something else that person values more than winning. Here are some examples of some of those types of fears:

- "If I make a vision for myself, I will be setting myself up for future self-judgment and maybe even judgment by others, because I'll never end up achieving it.
- "I am scared to conceptualize what I really want because thinking about what I don't believe I will ever have, hurts."
- "I am scared of conceptualizing what I really want because if I don't end up getting it, I will be devastated by the disappointment."
- "If I am to get what I want, I will have to change, which is sure to upset the people who depend on me to stay the way I am now."
- "If I ever let myself get what I want, then I am setting myself up for the devastation I will feel when I lose it."

If you don't remember what to say to the internal hamster who whispers fears like these in your ear, review chapter 7. You'll be ok.

Section 2: In Celebration of a Curly Road

As I intimated earlier in the chapter, maintaining the flexibility to be influenced by new information is a desirable practice on the road to having a life you love. Having a vision doesn't mean you are married to it, nor that you are a failure if you get part way there and change course. It is engaging in forward motion that is key. One day, when you look back to reflect, you may see that the best reason for choosing the direction you went at the beginning of the journey, is that if you hadn't been on that path, you wouldn't have found the information you needed to direct you to the better road where you are now. Here is a story illustrating what I mean:

A young man starts on a journey towards a castle where he hopes to be taken on as a squire. Along the path to the castle, he comes to a crossroads. Looking down a road he didn't know existed, he sees a dragon attacking a different castle, and runs to join the fray. Coming from a different direction allowed him to surprise the dragon, so it is his blow that is victorious, and the king of that castle offers him an immediate knighthood! But when he joins the court of that castle, he hears of another castle further north with a Queen who rules alone, and sets off on his new horse, determined to win her hand.

A linear life is not automatically better. A vision that is achieved faster is not automatically better. Breadth and depth are often richer and more interesting. For self-reinforcing internal motivation, follow your questions and follow your interest. There is no such thing as wasted time. Every experience is part of your life-school. Every person you meet on your path might have information that is useful to you, as long as you are awake in present moment to notice what is being offered to you.

"The path of vision is an organic construction, driven by curiosity and directed by listening to the self sing." – me

Chapter 8 Question

This chapter helps answer the question from the intro:

- In the face of all of my flaws, how do I become the person I want to be?

Now it is time to make your Vision for Change:

Find a quiet space where no one is going to bother you for twenty minutes or so, and close your eyes. Then I want you to really try to put yourself out there at the end of your work, as if you are looking back at this moment. Imagine that all of the work has been done that needed doing to get you to where you are now. Really feel what it is like to be there. How does it feel to be you living inside your body now that the changes are behind you? What is different on the inside of you? What has changed in your life so that you now know it is time for you to celebrate your changes and take a break from personal work?

In Conclusion

Now you are acquainted with **The Marble Game**, and many of its offshoots and extrapolations. The Marble Game is not a game at all, of course. It is more like a maze. The longer and harder you play, and the more attached you are to your strategies for winning, the deeper and more lost you become. The only way to beat the Game, is to wake up to the realization that **the Game was playing you** all the time. Wake up and figure out how to stay conscious, so you can keep yourself from playing. This is not easy, particularly when the vast majority of the rest of humanity is unconsciously playing every minute, and if you **do** figure out how to quit, they will think you are crazy, selfish, and/or just plain mean.

However, it is worth it. It is my belief that virtually all of the human behavior on the planet that we would judge as "most negative" (i.e. all the conflict, the violence, the lying the sneaking, the affairs, the rape, and the child abuse, all the oppression of minority groups, the poisoning and destruction of our biosphere, **all of it)** stems from only two sources, either:

1) Competition for natural resources (water, food, fuel, shelter). The competition that we see everywhere in the natural world, which I view it as sort of "normal" competition, or

2) An incomprehensibly insane competition for a thing that everybody already has: <u>YOU MATTER</u>. I matter. We all matter. People who are addicted to the Game are walking dreamers in a hellish, self-perpetuating nightmare wherein they think we all must compete with each other in the constant competition of "I matter more than you", and that only the top few get to win.

Balancing Paradoxes

"Carrying such a tension of the opposite is like a crucifixion. We must be as one suspended between the opposites, a painful state to bear. But in such a state of suspension the grace of God is able to operate within us." - Zweig & Abrams

- We matter so much, and yet we will ultimately come to nothing.
- We are powerful, masterful creators of reality, the gods of our own universes, yet we are fragile and insignificant.
- We have little control over the chaos of existence, yet hold tremendous influence over our own experience.

Also, according to the ancient philosophical text, the Tao Te Ching, a human being exists **to** balance paradox. We have our heads in heaven and our feet in the dirty decay of the physical world, yet somehow within the fragile husk of a human being, an unlikely, magical alchemy can take place; when we somehow manage to balance within our beings the two strongest opposing forces of the universe: sprit and body -- energy and matter. The text goes on to say that not only are we the bridge between these two planes of existence, but that it is through the balancing of the paradox that we ourselves evolve, if we are not destroyed.

This is true. I see it in my clients. I see it in myself.

You may notice that this book is full of paradox and contradiction. That is intentional on my part. A life of authorship does not arise from finding the capitol "T" truth about existence **so we can finally keep ourselves safe from Chaos**. We are small creatures on the scale of all that exists, so pretending we can ever know unshakeable truth is both hubris and fatal to the creative energy of the human spirit. The kind of life I want, and the kind that I want for you, comes from asking questions and playing with possible answers, answers that just lead you to ask even more fascinating questions! If we are not here to play and build and seek and learn and **keep** learning, then I do not know what we are here for.

The ocean of infinite chaotic universes is always there for you to dip the toes of your mind into if you can stop suffering on behalf of your false identities, surrender to the present moment, and be here, now, for it.

Post-script

I began this book with a list of questions -- the most common questions people who walk into my office are asking -- not coincidentally, also the most common questions humans have been asking themselves for thousands of years:

1) Who am I and why am I so crazy?

2) Who is that person I thought I knew, and why is s/he driving me so crazy?

3) Why do I keep doing the crazy stuff I do even though I want to change?!

4) In the face of all of my flaws how do I become the person I want to be?

5) How do I get that other person over there to be and do what I want?

6) Why does Life/God/the universe either a) seem so crazy that the way the world works makes no sense, or b) hate me personally so much that I am punished again and again no matter how hard I try?

7) Why bother to ever do anything? What is the point?

I realized half way through the writing of it, that while I have addressed all of the questions to some extent, were I to address them as fully as I wanted to, this book would have ended up weighing more than my cat. So, while I never intended to write more than one book, I suspect that I am not done.

With this book, I ended up addressing one's relationship with the Self; answering questions 1-4 in the process. Much of the material I created addressing relationships between people (in answer to question #5), I moved over to a file on my computer, currently entitled "Marble Game II". And yes, there is even a third folder entitled "Marble Game III" where I have been storing material and ideas that address questions 5 and 6 more fully than I was able to do here. Wish me luck! Just the thought of committing to another book makes me feel like hiding in my bathtub right now -- though that might just be because I have been editing for twenty-nine out of the last forty-eight hours.

I think I can get there, barring unforeseen chaos, if you are patient.

Gaelen Billingsley
1/19/2015

Citations

1. Brazelton, T. Berry & Greenspan, Stanley I. (2000) Cambridge, MA: Da Capo Press

2. Henry, JP & Wang, S, (Nov. 1998) Effects of Early Stress on Adult Affiliative Behavior, Psychoneuroendocrinology, 863-75.

3. American Psychiatric Association (2000). *DSM-IV-TR.* Arlington, Virginia.

4. Seigel, Daniel (2003). *Parenting From the Inside Out,* New York NY: Penguin Putman Inc.

5. Johnson, Sue. (2008) *Hold Me Tight.* New York, NY: Little, Brown and Company.

6. Schnarch, David. (2009). *Passionate Marriage,* New York, NY: W.W. Norton and Company.

7. United States Census Bureau - quickfacts.census.gov

8. Seigel, Ronald D. (2010). *The Mindfulness Solution: Everyday Practices for Everyday Problems.* New York, NY: The Guilford Press.

9. Kohn, Alfie. (1999). *Punished by Reward.* Boston, NY: Houghton Mifflin Company.

10. Progoff, Ira. (1992). *At a Journal Workshop: Writing to Access the Power of the Unconscious and Evoke Creative Ability,* J.P. Tarcher.

11. Cameron, Julia & Bryan, Mark. (1992). *The Artist's Way.* Westminster, London: Penguin Group.

12. Mutrie, N. (1988). Exercise as a treatment for moderate depression in the UK National Health Service. In *Sport, Health, Psychology and Exercise Symposium Proceedings,* pp. 96-105. London: The Sports Council and Health Education Authority.

13. Cacioppo, John T. & Patrick, William. (2009). *Loneliness: Human Nature and the Need for Social Connection.* New York, NY: W. W. Norton & Company.

14. Hanh, Thich Nhat. (2010). *Peace is Every Step.* London, England: Ebury Publishing.

15. Tolle, Eckhart. (2004), *The Power of Now.* San Francisco, CA: New World Library.

16. Tolle, Eckhart. (2009). *A New Earth.* Westminster, London: Penguin Group.

17. Bridges, William. (2000). *Way of Transition.* New York, NY: Perseus Books Group.

18. Chödrön, Pema. (2000). *When Things Fall Apart.* Boston, MA: Shambhala Publications.

19. Mindell, Arnold. (1995). *Sitting in The Fire.* Lao Tse Press.

20. Hanh, Thich Nhat . (2003). *Anger: Wisdom for Cooling the Flames.* New York, NY: Riverhead Books.

21. Frankle, Victor. (2006). *Man's Search for Meaning.* Boston, MA: Beacon Press

22. Marano, Hara E. (2008). Pitfalls of Perfectionism in *Psychology Today,* March Issue.

23. Coens, Tom and Jenkins, Mary. (2002) *Abolishing Performance Appraisals: Why they Backfire and What To Do Instead.* San Francisco, CA: Barrett-Koehler Publishing.

24. Southern, Russell D. (1995, December 31). Hamartia, cHata, and Related Concepts [Weblog post]. Retrieved from http://www.ibiblio.org/bgreek/test-archives/html4/1995-12/11891.html

25. Lewin K. (1943). Defining the "Field at a Given Time." *Psychological Review.* 50: 292-310. Republished in Resolving Social Conflicts & Field Theory in *Social Science*, Washington, D.C., American Psychological Association, 1997.

26. Thacker, S.B. (1984). Genetic and Biochemical Factors Relevant to Alcoholism. Alcoholism: *Clinical and Experimental Research.* Jul-Aug: 8(4) 375-83

27. Achbar, Mark & Abott, Jennifer (Directors). (2003). *The Corporation* [Motion picture]. Canada: Zeitgeist Films.
Joseph, Peter (Director). (2007). *Zeitgeist* [Motion picture].

Additional Resources

1. Fisch, Richard, Weakland, John H., Segal, Lynn. (1982) *The Tactics of Change: Doing therapy briefly.* San Francisco: Jossey-Bass, 36.

2. *McClure, Vimala. (1991). The Tao of Motherhood.* Willow Springs, MO: Nucleus Publications, *43.*

3. Miller, Peter. (2013) *Principles of Addiction: Comprehensive Addictive Behaviors and Disorders Vol. 1,* Academic Press.

4. *Muller, Wayne. (Spring 1998)* Stories of Courage and Grace, *Noetic ScienceSciences Review, 16-18.*

5. Palmer, Parker. (2000) *Let Your Life Speak: Listening For the Voice of Vocation,* Jossey-Bass.

6. Seigel, Ronald D. (2010). *The Mindfulness Solution: Everyday Practices for Everyday Problems.* New York, NY: The Guilford Press.

7. Schore, A.N. (1997). Early organization of the nonlinear right brain and development of a predisposition to psychiatric disorders. *Development and Psychopathology, 9,* 595-631.

8. Schore, A.N. (2000). Attachment and the regulation of the right brain. *Attachment & Human Development, 2,* 23-47.

9. Schore, A.N. (2001). The effects of early relational trauma on right brain development, affect regulation, and infant mental health. *Infant Mental Health Journal, 22,* 201-269.

10. Spangler, David. (1996). *Everyday Miracles: The inner art of manifestation.* Bantam Books, 45.

11. Zweig, Connie, and Abrams, Jeremiah. (Eds.) (1991). *Meeting the Shadow: The hidden power of the dark side of human nature.* New York: Norton, 89.

Made in the USA
San Bernardino, CA
10 February 2016